AYURVEDIC ASTROLOGY

AYURVEDIC ASTROLOGY

Self-Healing Through the Stars

BY DAVID FRAWLEY

SINCE 1903

MOTILAL BANARSIDASS
PUBLISHING HOUSE • DELHI
Email: mlbd@mlbd.in • Website: www.mlbd.in

2nd Reprint : Delhi, **2022**
First Indian Edition : Delhi, 1988
(First Edition Published in 2005 by ***Lotus Press,*** *P.O. Box 325, Twin Lakes, Wisconsin 53181, USA)*

Cover & Page Design/Layout : Paul Bond, Art & Soul Design
Illustrations : Hinduism Today Magazine
Copy Editing : Betheyla Anuradha

ISBN: 978-93-91024-73-4 (Cloth)
ISBN: 978-93-91024-74-1 (Paper)

Printed & Published by
Rajendra P Jain *for*
Motilal Banarsidass Publishing House
A-44, Naraina Industrial Area, Phase I,
New Delhi–110 028 (INDIA)
Email: mlbd@mlbd.in
Website: www.mlbd.in

VAMADEVA SHASTRI in his latest book, "Ayurvedic Astrology," unlocks ancient astrological understandings of the human body's inherent weaknesses based on positions of the planets and stars at birth. In so doing, he guides us to avert sickness by applying detailed traditional Vedic remedial measures and then helps us understand the karma behind illnesses when they do manifest.

Our Gurudeva, Sivaya Subramuniyaswami, founder of Hinduism Today magazine and Kauai's Hindu Monastery, always stressed that wellness is balance, and if the imbalance called illness occurs, those on the spiritual path first apply self-healing. Gurudeva said, "Vedic Astrology explores the stars and planets as they move in the heavens and their subtle effects on our physical, mental and emotional condition, mapping the ebb and flow of our karma...congested, unresolved, seeking-to-be-dissolved karma manifests as knots in the nerve system which can be seen as darkness or redness in the aura. You can carefully work with them through hatha yoga, ayurveda, massage, chiropractic and acupuncture. With this union of approaches, results will be obtained that will be very satisfactory."

Here, for the first time in a single book, two of India's remarkable gifts to mankind—Vedic knowledge of healing and Jyotish—are interwoven in a tapestry of wellness, providing invaluable tools for professional astrologers, ayurvedic practitioners and novices of both sciences.

Acharya Ceyonswami, Hinduism Today

Table of Contents

Foreword

By Chakrapani Ullal

VEDIC Astrology is an ancient science which is both universal and timeless. This vast body of knowledge encompasses all earthly phenomena past, present and future. Vedic Astrology is based on the laws of nature which express the unity within the diversity of life, and support the idea of an underlying intelligence governing all things with great precision and compassion. Vedic Astrology seeks to impart to mankind a tool with which to understand and live in greater harmony with nature, to maximize opportunities for growth and minimize suffering.

Vedic Astrology is the study of the subtle energies emanating from the sky upon people, plants, animals and the Earth itself. These energies influence the human body and mind on all levels. The astrological chart has the capacity to indicate good or ill health, strong or weak vitality, proneness to disease or accident, emotional stability or instability, intellectual soundness or mental insanity. One should not underestimate the role of the planets in causing or indicating disease and suffering in life as well as indicating happiness and well-being.

The ancient seers of India understood the close relationship between the laws of nature and mankind, and as a result of this natural connection developed a system of health called Ayurveda, the medicine of life itself. Although Western thinking has come to embrace these profound and essential truths to some degree with the discovery of Quantum Physics, this understanding of the nature of existence has been the basis of Vedic knowledge for thousands of years.

The Vedas are, in contemporary terms, "holistic" in their approach to all knowledge. Human ailments can be linked to the outcome of the gravitational pulls exerted by the planets through rotation and revolution, which is why Astrology has such a close relationship with Ayurveda. Astrology is used as a diagnostic tool for Ayurvedic practitioners in the treatment of disease – it provides the understanding of a person's karma which can help the healer optimize their efforts. Furthermore, the dasha system of Vedic astrology – its unique set of planetary periods – is particularly important for the timing of both disease and treatment, indicating the patient's likelihood of full and lasting recovery or further disease.

Astrology indicates and Ayurveda analyzes the bodily patterns which consist of three health tendencies called Doshas or biological humors. These are Vata, Pitta and Kapha, which equate to wind, bile and phlegm as bodily substances. Vata means motion, Pitta is connected with heat and light, and Kapha indicates inactivity and conservation. The great Ayurvedic teacher Sushruta says that "just as the Sun, the Moon and Wind are necessary for the regular functioning of this world outwardly, so are Vata, Pitta and Kapha necessary for the regulation of health in the human body". When the planets are in disharmony in the sky, the balance in the human body between Vata, Pitta and Kapha becomes disturbed, thus creating ill health.

Vedic astrology is famous for its remedial measures of gems, mantras and yajnas (rituals). It shows us how to bring the benefic energies of the cosmos into our human lives in order to create powerful forces of change and transformation. These methods can help reduce our negative karmas and provide us with the spiritual attitude to deal with those difficulties that we cannot change. Such remedial measures can also help with health concerns and the treatment of disease when applied with regard to Ayurveda. Ayurveda teaches the proper lifestyle, diet, herbs, exercise and behavioral patterns to implement the wisdom that astrology teaches us and to complement these astrological remedial measures.

Western medicine has developed a system which treats one part of the body without regard for the body as a whole. This approach to healing has become infamous for treating the symptom rather than dealing with the underlying and primary causes. More importantly, in the process, it has often resulted in creating greater problems than it has attempted to solve, creating side-effects often more dangerous than the disease. Different from this, Ayurveda is a holistic form of treatment which is meant to harmonize the body, mind and spirit. As long as our culture ignores astrological influences and tries to treat disease without their consideration, it will miss much information which can help alleviate many unnecessary and avoidable difficulties.

Dr. David Frawley is not only a prolific writer, thinker and researcher – he is considered to be a true scholar of Vedic culture. His profound understanding of Vedic culture is not only the result of his academic research but is backed by his intimate knowledge of India through his connections to its people in its villages, towns and cities. He has contributed to the spread of Vedic knowledge in the West as well as its preservation in India, which has earned him the title of Pandit Vamadeva Shastri.

Dr. Frawley has written numerous books on Astrology, Ayurveda, Yoga, Mantra and Meditation all of which are significantly relevant to those wanting to learn and practice these ancient Vedic sciences. His current volume "Ayurvedic Astrology" shows how these two sciences of life and light fit together and can be used in harmony to provide a greater understanding and deeper application of each. The book addresses both the predictive and treatment sides of both systems with clarity and precision.

This is probably the first book available that jointly examines both Ayurveda and Vedic astrology in detail for the modern reader. Even in the traditional literature on these subjects, there are few works that cross reference both so directly and completely. It is likely to be the standard work in the field for serious students for years to come.

Chakrapani Ullal
Vedic Astrologer
www.chakrapani.com

Author's Preface

OVER the past few decades, interest in Ayurvedic medicine has grown rapidly worldwide, with many new books on the subject coming out on a regular basis. Ayurveda is now recognized as one of the foremost systems of traditional and natural medicine, with deep spiritual and yogic insights, including an important usage of astrology.

Following in the footsteps of Ayurveda, interest in Vedic astrology has also grown exponentially. It is now honored as one of the most accurate and profound systems of astrology available. It has also been the subject of a number of new books, including several that refer to its connection with Ayurveda. The following book –Ayurvedic Astrology – focuses on the interface between these two fascinating systems. It shows how to use them together in a practical manner in order to optimize your karma in life, unlocking the healing potential of the stars.

Ayurveda (Vedic medicine) and Vedic astrology are closely related branches of Vedic science designed to harmonize ourselves with the greater universe of consciousness. The two have been used together throughout the centuries in India to promote balance and well-being in all aspects of our nature. This book explores the astrological aspect of Ayurvedic medicine, which is also the medical and healing aspect of Vedic astrology. For the spiritual connections between the two systems, it brings in the role of Yoga, the Vedic science of Self-realization.

Ayurvedic Astrology presents the main astrological factors behind health, both physical and mental, according to the Vedic vision of the unity of the human being and the cosmos. It emphasizes the special typologies of both Vedic systems, combining the doshic (mind-body) constitutions of Ayurveda with the planetary types of Vedic astrology. This correlation shows how psycho-physical and planetary forces reflect one another in our makeup and in our expression, including noting their disease-causing potential.

In addition to this 'diagnostic side', the book presents the corresponding Vedic 'treatment measures' for promoting healing and for improving awareness. It shows how Ayurvedic therapies, like diet and herbs, can be used to help balance planetary influences; and how astrological remedial measures, like gem therapy, can help improve our overall health and well-being. The book also brings in yogic methods, especially the use of ritual, mantra and meditation, showing us how to propitiate the deities or cosmic forces working through the planets.

While the first two sections of the book are oriented toward the general reader, the third section contains about thirty sample charts for those interested in a more technical application of astrological principles. To understand this section requires some background in Vedic astrology such as explained in introductory books on the subject.

Ayurvedic Astrology is not meant to fully explain either Ayurveda or astrology to someone who knows nothing about the subjects. The first two sections of the book are less technical, but can still benefit by supplementary reading. The third section contains about thirty sample charts for those interested in a more technical level of applying astrological principles. It requires some understanding of the calculations used in Vedic astrology to entirely appreciate.

Ayurvedic Astrology is meant to complement my other books, including Astrology of the Seers and Yoga and Ayurveda. A reader with little background in either subject can benefit from examining these books as well. In this regard, I have already presented some important material on the astrology of healing in Astrology of the Seers which I have not repeated in the present work. Even so, there is much information on this profound subject that I could not cover. Most notably, I have not addressed the role of the Nakshatras or lunar constellations, though this is very important, because it will be the subject of a separate volume.

I hope that this book will encourage further research in the field of medical astrology and its related psychological and spiritual branches. I would not regard it as the last word on this study but merely as an initial and introductory examination to a vast system of knowledge with unlimited benefits for humanity. I would also like to express my appreciation to my teachers Dr. B.L. Vashta and Dr. B.V. Raman for their inspiration and a special thanks to Hinduism Today for the illustrations.

May this union of the Vedic sciences of light and life transform your approach to both healing and to astrology for the well-being of both yourself and the entire planet!

Dr. David Frawley
June 2005

Organization of the Book

Part I explains the basic principles of Jyotish (Vedic astrology) and Ayurveda (Vedic medicine). It emphasizes the correlation between astrological factors of planets, signs and houses and Ayurvedic factors of doshas (biological humors) and tissues of the body. Central to it is the relationship between Ayurvedic constitutional types and astrological planetary types. It covers physical health, psychological well-being and spiritual development from a joint Ayurvedic/Vedic astrology perspective.

Part II explains the main treatment or remedial measures of Vedic astrology, with reference to Ayurveda. It begins with outer methods like foods, herbs, and aromas, and extends to inner methods like gems, mantras and planetary deities, which are dealt with in great detail.

Part III contains thirty-three sample charts demonstrating the correlation between the constitutional types of Ayurveda and the astrological types of Vedic astrology. This section is more technical but can be appreciated even by a beginner in Vedic astrology.

The Appendix provides glossary, bibliography, footnotes, additional information and resources.

PART ONE

The Vedic Astrology of Healing

The Vedic Vision

1

ALL great ancient civilizations centered their cultures on profound systems of astrology, connecting conditions and events on the Earth with cosmic influences deriving from the stars. Whether it is India or China, Egypt or Babylonia, or the Mayas and Incans of America, we find in each case an astrological foundation for their spiritual cultures. Astrology and its measure of sacred time formed the basis of their calendars, which sought to organize human life according to celestial forces more certain than our merely personal desires and calculations. Even the ancient cultures of Europe like the Greeks, Romans, Celts and Germans, had detailed systems of astrology, as have all communities that recognize the sacred nature of the universe.

Similarly, all systems of traditional medicine East and West possess corresponding forms of astrology, which are essential to both their theory and their practice. Notably, Traditional Chinese Medicine (TCM) has the I Ching and Chinese astrology, while the Ayurvedic medicine of India has Vedic astrology. Traditional European medicine going back to the Greeks included western astrological traditions, which were part of pagan traditions in general.

Connecting healing and astrology — or the practice of medical astrology – is one of the deepest and most lasting investigations of our species. It is as old as all such great ancient cultures and their astrologically based rituals to keep human life in harmony with the cosmos. We have long looked to the stars and the heavens for guidance, grace and healing energy, for understanding human existence in a deeper perspective in which we can touch the eternal and the infinite. Today we are entering into a new planetary age, in which ancient, native and traditional systems of healing and spirituality are once more being honored. In this context an examination of the astrology of healing is relevant, if not crucial for reclaiming that older and perhaps wiser heritage of our species.

Vedic Astrology and Ayurvedic Medicine

Vedic astrology is India's traditional system of reading the stars, the planets and the entire movement of time. It was originally called Vedanga Jyotish, meaning the study of light (Jyoti) which is a limb of the Veda (Vedanga). It was also called Jyotirveda, the 'light Veda' or 'science of light'. Ayurveda, which means the 'science of life', is the corresponding Vedic system of natural healing for both body and mind. Both are living branches of an ancient sacred science that arose in an older era in which humanity had a greater intuitive connection with the sacred universe. Unlike corresponding western traditions, their continuity, though shaken by hostile forces, has remained unbroken. These systems are undergoing a renaissance today as we once more learn to look within.

Vedic astrology is an extraordinary predictive and counseling tool. There are many wonderful stories of how Vedic astrologers can pinpoint specific events in a person's life with uncanny accuracy. Yet Vedic astrologers are not only good at prediction, they can relate deep wisdom about a person's life purpose, karma and spiritual path. I myself have visited several Vedic astrologers in India who could relate the main events of my life, my future development, and past and future life implications with extraordinary precision and with notable wisdom. Some Vedic astrologers are thought to be psychics for this reason, though they may be only describing what the Vedic birth chart can reveal to one trained and experienced in astrological insight.

Similarly, Ayurveda is a precise and comprehensive tool for healing physical and psychological well-being, promoting optimal health, energy and vitality. There are many instances of Ayurvedic doctors introducing changes in a person's life, from simple dietary or life-style modifications, to special herbs or internal cleansings that can literally rejuvenate us, curing long standing and intractable health problems of various types. Because of such occurrences, some Ayurvedic doctors are regarded as magical healers, though they may only be employing practices based upon understanding the laws of nature and the movement of the life-force, such as Ayurveda has taught them.

These two Vedic systems and their magic come together in the 'Vedic astrology of healing' or 'Ayurvedic astrology'. Ayurvedic astrology shows us how to optimize both factors of our health and our destiny, our vitality and our karma, so that we can realize our highest potential in life, with our earthly life following the model of heavenly forces and their consciousness-promoting outcomes. Ayurvedic astrology shows how we can heal ourselves through the stars, bringing the energies of the cosmos into our lives so that we can once more touch the universal light.

The Cosmic Person of Light

We live in an ecological age in which we must recognize that the Earth is a single organism, a 'planetary being' endowed with its own life and intelligence. The planet on which we live is not just a material formation but an organic field possessing a self-regulating awareness that we must adapt to if we are to survive as a species.

According to Vedic astrology, each planet has its own being and consciousness. It is a God or Goddess, a cosmic entity worthy of honor, not a mere physical or chemical globe. On this foundation, Vedic astrology is not simply a mechanical or predictive science but an art of interacting with these higher cosmic powers and bringing their beneficial forces into our more limited world.

The entire universe forms a greater organism or universal being which encompasses all the worlds. This is the Purusha or Cosmic Person of Vedic thought, who is said to be made of light and to dwell in the Sun and the stars.[1] In addition to all the individual living creatures, there are greater cosmic beings and powers ruling over the different layers of existence from subatomic to supragalactic realms, and all of these beings are integral aspects of the Purusha, the higher Universal Being. The planets of our solar system are the main cosmic beings or powers that govern our life and expression on Earth.

One of the key laws for understanding this greater 'conscious universe' is that what happens on one level of existence is reflected on all other levels. Several important dictums arise from this like as above, so below, and as without, so within. The Cosmic Being upholds within itself various interdependent dimensions or planes of existence; material, biological and spiritual.

Life and the Stars

All life on Earth derives from the stars, primarily through the light of the Sun. Biological life arises from the sunlight digested by plants through the process of photosynthesis, which creates the food that sustains all creatures. However, the lights of the planets also consist of reflected sunlight. One could say that the planets, like plants, are light receptacles designed to transmit light in various ways.

The effects of sunlight and moonlight on organic life are well known relative to the life-cycles and reproductive habits of plants and animals. That the light of the other planets may affect life on Earth may seem less likely, given how dim their light appears to our earthly vision, but considering the extent of their electro-magnetic fields, and the fact that the entire solar system is a single organism, we must recognize this probability as well. In addition, we must consider that the light of the stars and their electro-magnetic fields also influences life in our solar system. The web of life is a web of light interconnected to the stars and planets.

All entities in the universe are involved in the creation of light in one form or another, whether it is the light produced by the stars or that developed internally by living creatures as part of their metabolisms. We are all plants, planets or light production mechanisms.

Not only is life a transformation of light, but so is the mind whose function is to illumine and perceive through an internal light. This light is ultimately One and universal. It is not simply a physical force but a power of consciousness, which is the highest and most subtle form of light. The connection between physics, biology and spirituality, which is the basis of Vedic astrology, is not an overextension of the imagination but a natural progression that parallels the unfoldment of the universe. It explains how the mind of God works building up the worlds in various layers and textures of light, animate and inanimate.

Vedic Science

Vedic astrology or Jyotish is the foremost of the six Vedangas or 'limbs of the Veda'.[2] It is said to be the 'eye of the Veda' through which all Vedic knowledge can be properly applied. Ayurveda is the foremost of the four Upavedas or 'secondary Vedas'[3] through which a true Vedic life can be properly lived. Ayurveda and Vedic astrology are closely intertwined not only with each other but with all other Vedic sciences, including the great wisdom traditions of Yoga and Vedanta and their profound paths of Self-realization and God-realization.

The Vedas themselves are ancient mantric texts of great profundity and mystery, deriving from the meditative insights of the great Himalayan seers or rishis over five thousand years ago. The Rig Veda, the most fundamental of the four Vedas, is perhaps the oldest book in the world, looking back to the dawn of history. It carries the collected wisdom of our ancient spiritual ancestors, connecting us to previous humanities and so-called lost civilizations before what we call history began.[4]

The Vedas derive from a yogic approach to reality. They were said to have been directly perceived from the Cosmic Mind in the state of Samadhi or inner unity between the seer and the seen. This affords them an insight and an authority that goes beyond our ordinary knowledge sources born of the mere brain, senses and human mind.[5] The central message of the Vedas is that the universe dwells within our own consciousness, which extends beyond all time and space. We are the entire universe, which is the expression of our own deeper Self.

The Vedic mantra, which is the basis of all Vedic texts, is a special code of vibratory or sound-based knowledge, inherent in cosmic space. It contains the keys to cosmic law or dharma, the underlying truth principles that sustain the cosmic order. These dharmas are not just physical laws but ethical and spiritual principles, the most notable of which is the law of karma. Through these Vedic mantras we can understand our individual dharma, our social dharma and, ultimately, all the dharmas in the universe.

Vedic knowledge is perhaps the ultimate science because it can unlock all the secrets of nature, bridging the internal to the external, and unraveling the parallel processes of cosmogenesis and the development of individual life. Vedic mantras show how the forces of nature from the elements to the stars work within us as physical and psychological forces. Through this special insight taught by the Vedas, we can reintegrate ourselves into the conscious universe, realizing our existence as a single organic being of love, light and bliss.

A Vedic Parable

One of the greatest Vedic sages was Atharva, after whom the Atharva Veda, one of the four main Vedic texts, was named. In the older Rig Veda, to which this story goes back, he was already a legendary figure.

Atharva had a son named Dadhyak, who is the central figure in the story that follows.

Dadhyak by his profound austerities had received the highest knowledge of immortality, called the 'knowledge of honey' (Madhu Vidya) because it carried the supreme bliss. Dadhyak gained this knowledge as a special gift from Indra, the greatest of the Vedic Gods, and like his Greek counterpart Zeus, the lord of heaven who wielded an irresistible lightning bolt against his enemies. Naturally this precious wisdom had to be protected. Indra forbade Dadhyak from teaching it, even to the other Gods. Indra placed a special curse on Dadhyak, saying that if Dadhyak tried to teach it, Indra would come and immediately cut his head off.

Of course, all the Gods wanted to learn this knowledge, which would fulfill their greatest wishes. Among these many Gods, the most curious and precocious were the Ashvins, the twin youths or horsemen, who were also the doctors or physicians of the Gods. The Ashwins already possessed all other magical powers except this special teaching, without which all their healing powers would be defective. So their desire to gain it was immense and they would use all the skill and cunning necessary to acquire it.

The Ashvins approached the sage Dadhyak and requested that he teach them this secret knowledge. Dadhyak predictably replied, "I cannot teach you or Lord Indra, before whom even you must bow, will cut my head off." The Ashvins, not being put off even by the fear of Indra replied, "That is no problem. We can receive the knowledge and you can protect your head as well. First with our magic powers we will give you the head of a horse. Then you can safely teach us through the horse's mouth. When Indra comes and cuts off your head, which has become that of a horse, we will replace it with your original human head."

And that is exactly what they did. The Ashvins, who themselves had horse's heads, gave Dadhyak the head of a horse. He taught them the secret knowledge through it. Indra then came and cut off the horse's head and the Ashvins gave Dadhyak back his original human head.

This story has many deep meanings. In terms of Vedic astrology, the horse's head became the constellation Ashvini that marks the beginning of the zodiac in the sign Aries. The horse's head is also the Sun, which is exalted in Aries, a sign that represents the head. The twin Ashvins represent both the duality behind time with its alterations of days and nights, and the state of balance through which we can go beyond time. The horse's head is a key to the deeper meaning of Vedic astrology, the knowledge of which the Ashwins are the teachers.

Relative to Ayurveda or Vedic medicine, the horse is a symbol of Prana, the life energy that derives from the Sun and which is the source of all healing powers. The Ashwins as the great doctors of the Gods were famous for their powers of rejuvenation and were even capable of resurrecting the dead. As twins they represent the ability to balance our energies and create wholeness, and were important early teachers of Ayurveda.

Relative to the practice of Yoga, the horse's head is a symbol of the soul that sacrifices its bodily identity to unite with the higher Self. The horse's head is the soul that transcends the limitations of time and space and becomes free to travel at will through the entire universe, like the Sun, as a being of light. More specifically, the cut off head is the opened crown chakra through which the honey bliss or Soma flows. The Madhu Vidya or honey knowledge is that of the supreme Bliss of the Self. It is an important Vedantic teaching, starting with the oldest Upanishads.[6]

To discover our true nature we must first offer up our false nature, our ego and all of its attachments. To speak the higher truth we must sacrifice our personal opinions and preconceptions. To gain our head, we must first lose it. The Ashwins represent this transformation from duality to unity. The higher knowledge is paradoxical, transcending our ordinary sensory means of cognizance and connecting all forms of knowledge together in the light of consciousness.

The Sun and Prana

Behind all light sources in the universe is the supreme light of consciousness, the Light of lights or inner Sun, which is the original form or face of God. This spiritual Sun exists within our own minds and hearts as the power of illumination at the core of our being, our own true inner Self. Returning to it is the ultimate goal of life.

The Vedic mantras are said to arise from the breath of the Godhead (Brahman) or the universal Prana. The power of these mantras resides in the rays of the Sun and through them function as doorways to the stars. Through Vedic practices one can gain an energetic access to the worlds of our Sun and Moon, or the worlds of the Nakshatras, the stars beyond our Sun, extending to the timeless realms beyond all creation to the ultimate realm of unchangeable light.

The Vedas tell us that the inner Sun is Prana and that the movements of the inner Sun or our life-force are measured or metered by the movements of the outer Sun.[7] This unity of the Sun, the power of time, and Prana, the force of life, reflects the unity of the external universe or macrocosm and the internal universe or microcosm. This correspondence of time (Kala) measured by the stars and life (Prana) measured by the breath is an important concept in both Vedic astrology and Ayurvedic medicine and the basis of their connection. Through it, Vedic astrology and Ayurveda mirror each other as external and internal images of light and life. These factors figure importantly in Yoga practice as well, especially in the science of Svara Yoga, though which we judge the influences of the planets based upon our breath alone.[8]

Ayurveda and Vedic Astrology

Ayurveda is called "the mother of all healing" because it embraces all forms of healing including diet, herbs, bodywork, surgery, psychology and Yoga. It accepts anything internally or externally that promotes health, well-being and happiness. Ayurveda explores the qualities and effects not only of foods, medicines and behavior but also of climates, the weather and the stars (astrology).

Ayurveda provides an integral mind-body system of both diagnosis and treatment. First it shows us our individual constitution according to the three doshas or biological humors of Vata (air), Pitta (fire) and Kapha (water), as well as how this constitution is affected by everything from genetics to environment and emotions. Then it outlines various treatment measures to enable us to achieve optimal health and vitality. These treatments range from simple dietary measures to complex herbs and special purification procedures. Ayurveda aims not only at the cure and prevention of disease but also at rejuvenation and longevity. Beyond ordinary health care measures it has special methods to allow us to achieve a higher level of vitality and awareness — a spiritual Ayurveda that is part of the practice of Yoga.

Possessing a similar scope to Ayurveda, Vedic astrology contains all aspects of astrology, including the reading of birth charts (natal astrology), mundane astrology (the effects of astrological influences on society), astrological timing and forecasting (muhurta), and answering questions (prashna). In addition to these usual astrological considerations, Vedic astrology encompasses all forms of divination, including palmistry and numerology, of which several Vedic forms exist. It also includes astronomy and meteorology, which reflect karmic as well as physical forces.

In the form of natal astrology or the reading of birth charts, the Vedic system helps us understand our personal lives in all areas, including health, wealth, relationship, career and spirituality. Like Ayurveda, it has a broad range of treatment measures including the use of colors, gems, mantras and the worship of deities to aid in our greater well-being and life unfoldment. These are called Jyotish-Chikitsa, the therapies of light or astrology.

Ayurvedic Astrology

Yet, though they have their specializations in many areas, both Vedic astrology and Ayurveda have a significant overlap as well. Vedic astrology contains a medical system based upon Ayurveda, while Ayurveda contains a system for the timing of disease and its treatment based upon Vedic astrology. We can designate this combined usage of Ayurveda and Vedic astrology more simply as 'Ayurvedic Astrology'.

Ayurvedic astrology is the medical branch of Vedic astrology, adding to it the Ayurvedic view of health and healing. It uses the language of Ayurveda to understand the effects of the planets on the body and mind relative to health, disease and longevity. Ayurvedic astrology also uses Vedic astrology as an aid to Ayurvedic analysis, diagnosis and treatment, showing how planetary factors cause disease and how balancing planetary factors can be an important aid in any cure.

Ayurvedic astrology combines these two great disciplines, using Vedic astrology to plot the influences of time and karma and Ayurveda to show how these relate to our state of Prana or vital energy. Combining these two great disciplines together, there is nothing that we cannot treat or cannot understand.

Vedic astrology considers that the determination of physical and mental health is the foundation of all astrological analysis. Whatever other indications may occur in a chart — whether for career, wealth, relationship or spirituality — these cannot bear fruit if a person has significant physical or mental impairments. Traditionally, the ascertainment of longevity was the first factor to be examined by a good astrologer. This was not a simple matter of determining how long a person was likely to live, but part of a general determination of the vitality of a person, showing the energy available to activate the opportunities afforded them by the chart. In this regard, medical or Ayurvedic astrology is usually the first step of all astrological examination.

However, Ayurvedic astrology is not simply a physically-based medical astrology. It reflects the psychological and spiritual dimensions of Ayurveda as well. It is concerned with all levels of our well-being, which depend entirely upon our connection to the Soul, the real person or Atman within. In this regard, Ayurvedic astrology is concerned with healing body, mind and spirit, using the tools of the entire universe, the foremost of which is the light of the stars and planets. It expands the field of Ayurveda to its broadest possible range.

Astrology, Ayurveda and Yoga

2

BOTH Vedic astrology and Ayurvedic medicine are part of the greater system of Yoga, a system which aims at Self-realization, our union with the Divine Being within us as the ultimate goal of life. For this reason we can call Ayurveda 'yogic medicine' and Vedic astrology 'yogic astrology'. Ayurveda is concerned with our connection to the Divine Self as the source of all life within us, and Jyotish (Vedic astrology) with our union with the Divine Self as the source of all light and therefore all activity and manifestation in the external world.

In this chapter we will examine how these three systems — Yoga, Ayurveda and Vedic astrology — interrelate to provide us with an effective and comprehensive methodology to deal with our karma in life, which is manifold on many levels, without and within. All Vedic disciplines aim at helping us understand, adjust to and, to the extent that it is possible, transform our karma.

Medical astrology has always been one of the most popular aspects of astrology. Among the first questions people ask astrologers are "How long will I live?" or "How healthy will I be?" Even wealth and fame are no guarantee of long life or freedom from disease. We are all concerned about our health and vitality, which is the foundation of everything else that we attempt in life.

Medical astrology also has a great scope for practical application and everyday usage as our health and energy fluctuate with the rhythms of time, from days, months, years and stages of life to special astrological periods like the dasha systems of Vedic astrology. Medical astrology provides a good angle from which to learn astrology and to verify its complex workings.

If we add the psychological component to medical astrology, it becomes a yet more interesting and valuable study. We are all curious about how our psyche has developed both in this life and in previous lives, and how it is likely to evolve and change in the future. An important question people routinely come to astrologers with is "Will I be happy?," as our psychological state is often more important for us than our physical condition.

Adding a spiritual or yogic side to medical and psychological astrology, we can create a complete system of well-being for body, mind and spirit. This can help us answer the ultimate questions like "What is the meaning of life?" or "Who am I?" or "What in us, if anything, survives death?" Answering such questions, after all, is the real purpose of why we are born.

Our Three Bodies

As human beings, we are not mere lumps of flesh, but a composite of three bodies or encasements for the soul — the physical, the astral and the causal.[9] The physical body is the sphere of the gross elements of earth, water, fire, air and ether, the visible body born of our parents and sustained by the food that we eat. This is the body that we all know and experience in our outer life on Earth and in the waking state of consciousness.

Within this gross organism resides a more refined vesture that works behind our physical functioning — the astral or subtle body made up of the vital force, the senses, and the outer aspect of the mind. It is composed of the subtle elements or sensory potentials of sound (ether), touch (air), sight (fire), taste (water) and smell (earth). Normally we experience the astral body indirectly through the physical body by means of the mind and emotions. But in dreams, visions and inspiration or after death we can experience it directly.

The causal body is the deeper mind or sphere of the soul that holds the inmost desires, impulses and tendencies (samskaras) that propel us along the cycle of rebirth. It is comprised of the gunas (qualities of nature) of sattva (harmony), rajas (agitation) or tamas (inertia). On a higher level, the causal body is the abode of our life wisdom, heart feelings and soul urges that continue with us from birth to birth.

Normally we are not directly aware of the causal body except when we are in contact with our deepest aspirations. We touch in with it in the state of deep sleep and only enter into it directly when we enter into a state of superconsciousness beyond the ordinary mind and ego. Awakening it is one of the main purposes of Yoga. The causal body is the vehicle of the soul or reincarnating entity and persists throughout all our incarnations, with the astral body arising out of it.

Ayurveda and the Three Bodies

Ayurveda has as its primary concern the right functioning of the physical body, showing how to correct the various imbalances that can arise within it. However, as the physical body is energized by the vital force and connected to the mind and to the soul, which is the ultimate source of life, Ayurveda considers impacts of the astral and causal bodies as well.

In general, we could say that the physical body relates more to Kapha, the biological water humor of Ayurveda, because it is composed mainly of this element. The astral body relates more to Pitta, the biological fire humor, owing to its connection with our perceptual faculties. The causal body relates more to Vata, the biological air humor, owing to its power to energize the other two bodies with life and consciousness.[10]

The astral body is the subtle form or model, the life imprint, out of which the physical body arises. By changing its internal energies we can alter our outer physical functioning as well. Such 'working on the subtle body' is the basis of pranic or energetic healing that Ayurveda also employs.

The causal body holds the underlying will and motivation in our hearts. By changing our deepest thoughts and intentions we can alter both our physical body and its vital energies. This is the basis of spiritual healing in Ayurveda, which targets the causal body.

Vedic Astrology and the Three Bodies

Vedic astrology similarly considers the role of all three bodies. It starts out with an examination of our physical health concerns, but then extends to all the main factors of our well-being — career, relationship, creativity and spirituality — bringing in the roles of the astral and causal bodies as well. Each of these different concerns is denoted by specific houses in the birth chart. These houses along with their planetary significators are examined with precise rules of delineation and interpretation for determining their results.[11]

Our overall birth chart relates primarily to the subtle or astral body, which is the greater sphere of our life energies. It reflects the entire range of our activities, of which our physical health is just one factor. The birth chart is like the blueprint of the astral body, which forms the matrix or energy pattern for the physical. Astrology, as its name suggests, is primarily an astral science, having as its main concern the subtle or astral body, our body of the stars. As the astral body mediates between the physical and the causal, it can help us understand the other two bodies as well.

- Astrologically speaking, the physical body is indicated primarily by the Ascendant or rising sign and its ruler, and the nature of the influences upon them. It is also connected to the planet Mars, the planet of work in the material world.
- The astral body, which indicates our emotional or feeling nature is reflected primarily by the Moon — its position and influences in the chart, its sign and Nakshatra (lunar constellation). It also is reflected in the fourth house, the house of the mind and its planetary ruler.
- The causal body or soul works mainly through the Sun, which indicates character, will and individuality. For the causal body, we look to the Sun's placement in the chart, as well as the fifth and ninth houses, the houses of dharma, and the Navamsha or ninth divisional chart.
- The Ascendant, Moon and Sun are each closely examined in Vedic astrology to help us understand how our three bodies are functioning in this life. When all three are harmoniously placed, our lives are likely to unfold in the best possible manner on all levels.

Yoga and the Three Bodies

Yoga in the Vedic system is a science of meditation aimed at Self-realization or union with the Divine as its ultimate goal.[12] Yoga or spiritual practice of any genuine type is the main concern of the soul or the causal body, the immortal part of our nature, whose intentions go beyond physical or psychological well-being to our eternal welfare.

Yoga begins with the balancing and clearing of the physical body through various asanas or yoga postures in order to provide the foundation of health necessary to support its deeper practices. In this regard Yoga interfaces with Ayurveda and its healing approaches.

On this physical foundation, Yoga uses pranayama (breath control), pratyahara (control of the senses), and dharana (concentration of the mind) for working on the subtle or astral body. Through developing more prana and through focusing the mind as in the practice of mantra, Yoga can help us change the energy pattern of the subtle body. Such yogic approaches are important remedial measures in Vedic astrology because they help to bring harmonious planetary energies into our minds.

Dhyana (meditation) and samadhi (absorption) are the main yogic tools for developing the causal body and are the most important aspects of traditional Yoga. Yoga leads us from the physical to the subtle and then to the causal in order to discover our true Self and the higher Being behind all three bodies. In this regard the ultimate concern of Yoga is to take us to a condition of consciousness beyond all three bodies.

Integral Use of Ayurveda, Vedic Astrology and Yoga

Through using all three disciplines together — Ayurveda, Vedic astrology and Yoga — we gain access to all the main tools and techniques for working with the physical, astral and causal bodies, thereby addressing all aspects of our being. Ayurveda provides the foundation of right living through the proper care of the physical body. Vedic astrology shows how to optimize our karmic potentials, which are the main concerns of the subtle body, through a proper understanding of our birth chart and its planetary influences. Yoga shows us how to awaken to our soul or causal potential and develop it scientifically through the use of various Yoga techniques.

Ayurveda provides the basis for a harmonious life in the material world. Astrology provides a good map of the territory to be covered in our life activities in order to achieve our goals. Yoga shows us a way to realize the supreme goal that each successive birth is leading us towards.

For an effective treatment of our entire being, we must consider not just the physical body but also the astral and the causal bodies. This is the importance of applying Ayurveda, Vedic astrology and Yoga together. In fact, we must consider all three bodies regarding the achievement of any important goal of life, which all rest on proper vitality (supported by Ayurveda), right karmic actions (supported by Astrology) and spiritual intent (supported by Yoga). Even for the practice of Yoga, which is meant to take us beyond time and space, we must first consider where we come from in terms of time (astrology) and space (the body or Ayurveda). If we pursue our spiritual practices without a proper Ayurvedic life-style, we may create physical or psychological imbalances that eventually block our inner journey. If we pursue them without understanding our birth chart through Vedic astrology, the timing or manner of our practices may not be appropriate or effective.

Astrology and Healing

Through its ability to help us understand our physical constitution or body type, Vedic astrology shows our overall disease propensity, indicating the types of health problems that we are most likely to be vulnerable to. In addition to this, it can indicate the timing of disease, so that we can know when we are likely to get sick and can guard ourselves against it. Once we have come down with a disease, Vedic astrology can be an important aid in its prognosis, showing our ability to get well, so that we can know how easily we are likely to recover.

Vedic astrology is not only helpful for ordinary disease conditions; it has a special relevance for helping us understand conditions, both physical and psychological, which may not be curable by the usual medical methods. It provides us a precise methodology for dealing with diseases that derive from internal and karmic causes, whose roots reside not so much in the physical body but in our mental state or the condition of our will, the factors of the astral and causal bodies.

Vedic astrology is not only concerned with the diagnosis and timing of diseases, it also offers us various methods to either treat disease or increase our resistance to it. The treatment methods or remedial measures of Vedic astrology primarily aim at the astral body. Diseases reflect negative planetary influences, which are disruptive forces in our astral environment. Gems, mantras (words of power), yantras (power diagrams), special rituals (pujas and yajnas) and other yogic methods can help counter these influences and replace them with those that are positive.

Such subtle methods are particularly effective for dealing with mental and psychological disorders, which are primarily imbalances in the subtle body. They help strengthen the aura and immune system, and can remove negative karmic influences, negative thoughts and subtle environmental pollutants, like low level radiation.

The planets project the basic energies operating in the solar system. As such, our entire lives can be arranged to improve our planetary influences. The right diet, the right herbs, the right location to live, the right livelihood, right relationships, and the right spiritual practices can all be used to balance planetary forces.

For example, Mars is a hot planet and can cause fiery or Pitta disorders like fever, inflammation, infection, as well as traumas and injury if afflicted in the chart. Its influence can be countered by cooling foods, cooling herbs, a cool climate, and cool colors, as well as by special gems and mantras for the planet, adjusted according to the planetary periods and transits operative in the individual chart.

However, treating the physical body is more complex than what may be revealed in the birth chart and should not be attempted through astrology alone. Medical astrology should support but not substitute for a full medical treatment. But astrology can be helpful for medical problems, even if we cannot see the full scope of a person's condition in the chart. It can show us the probable development of a disease, even when its specific nature and symptoms may not be clear. It can tell us when we are likely to fall ill and for how long, even when it cannot pin point the exact illness or its treatment. In the hands of a good astrologer, however, it can tell us these additional factors as well.

Vedic Astrology and our Karmic Code

The soul can be defined as our 'karmic being' as opposed to our merely human personality, which is its mask. It carries our karmic propensities called samskaras from one body to another. Our karma, we could say, is the DNA of our soul. Just as the body has its particular genetic code, the soul has its particular 'karmic code'.

The soul's karmic code is based upon the life patterns it has created — the habits, tendencies, influences and desires it has set in motion over its many births. These karmic tendencies or samskaras ripen like seeds in the soil of our lives, taking root and sprouting according to favorable circumstances. Our soul's energy is filtered through our karmic potentials, which create the pattern of our lives down to subconscious and instinctual levels.

For the evolution of our species as well as for our own spiritual growth, we must consider both the genetic and karmic codes. We cannot understand ourselves through genetics alone, which is only the code of the body; we must also consider the karmic code, the code of the mind and heart. Note how two children in the same family can share the same genetic pattern, education and environment and yet have very different lives, characters and spiritual interests. This is because of their differing karmic codes.[13]

Fortunately, there is a way that we can discover our karmic code as clearly as our genetic code — which is through Vedic astrology. The Vedic astrological birth chart is probably the best indicator we can have of the karmic code of the soul. The pattern of the birth chart is like the 'DNA of the soul' behind the current physical incarnation. The positions of the planets in the birth chart provide a wealth of knowledge through which we can read our karmic code in great detail.

In this regard, the Vedic astrological chart is probably the most important document that we have in life and is much more important than our genetic code. Yet like our DNA it is a code written in the language of nature that needs to be deciphered by a trained researcher in order to make sense of its indications.

In addition to showing our karmic code at birth, Vedic astrology can plot its unfoldment through the changing course of our lives. Vedic astrology has elaborate methods of timing through its system of planetary periods (dashas), annual charts (bhuktis) and transits (gochara). That is why Vedic astrologers can be so amazingly accurate both in their delineations of character and in determining the outer events of our lives.

Through the astrological remedial measures of planetary gems, mantras, yantras and meditation on planetary deities, Vedic astrology also provides us with methods to optimize our karma and take us beyond the limitations of our karmic code. This is an equally important component, the therapeutic aspect of the Vedic astrology or what we can call 'Ayurvedic astrology'.

Therapeutically it is imperative for individual growth that each one of us not only becomes aware of our karmic code but also learns the means to improve it. The Vedic system provides us with some of the finest tools in this regard, through its many and varied disciplines including the sciences of Yoga, Ayurveda and Vedic Astrology.

This does not mean that a proper examination of our birth chart will answer all our questions in life; we will still have to act. The chart however, will show us how to act in the best and wisest possible manner. In this regard, the birth chart is our karmic guide to life, and the tools of Vedic science are probably the most important tools of karmic improvement.

To change ourselves it is not enough to alter our genetic code; we must alter our karmic code as well. However, to change our karmic code is no easier a matter than altering our genetics! It requires a great deal of motivation, concentration and expertise — and the efforts must be done completely within ourselves rather than in an external laboratory. Changing our karma codes requires that we dynamically change the way we live, breathe, see and think, altering our very ego or sense of self.

The Science of Karma

Our soul is a 'karmic being', a doer or actor in a universe shaped by its own actions. Astrology as a science of time is also a science of karma. Time is not merely a blank continuum, but reflects a karmic flow, a giving of the fruit of action to all beings. In this regard astrology is the most important of all sciences because through comprehending time and karma, it can unlock the energy and motivation behind everything that occurs in the universe. There is nothing in our birth chart that does not have karmic implications on one level of our life or nature or another.

All true healing must occur first of all at a karmic level. It must be capable of removing the negative effect of our actions and promoting those which are positive. As karma and time are interrelated not only with each other but with the entire universe, all true healing should consider astrology as well.

A good astrologer can perhaps be best defined as a 'karmic counselor', guiding clients on how to better optimize their karmic potential in life and helping them to understand their unique karmic code and how to best implement it. In the same way, a good healer is also a 'karmic healer'. This healer helps clients remove the karmic causes, including the wrong attitudes and inappropriate life-styles behind their diseases, not simply just alleviate their symptoms.

Both Ayurveda and Vedic astrology are important means of karmic rectification. Ayurveda helps us rectify our karma relative to our physical and mental habits and the impulses that may be out of harmony with our mind-body type. Vedic astrology helps us rectify our karma relative to the deeper samskaras that may be out of harmony with our planetary type and our soul's level of manifestation. They both lead us to Yoga, which can help us go beyond all the influences of karma. We should not forget this karmic orientation as we examine the scope of Ayurvedic astrology.

Doshas and Planets: Prime Factors of Astrology & Ayurveda

3

BOTH Ayurveda and Vedic astrology share an energetic view of the universe, recognizing certain harmonic keys to our existence on all levels. They hold that the order of life on Earth and the structure of the universe, specifically the solar system, are intrinsically related and follow the same laws and development of forces.

In this chapter, we will examine the prime factors of the biological humors or doshas of Ayurveda and the planets or grahas of Vedic astrology and show how they are related. This information will provide us the basic language through which we can examine the two systems and their interrelationship in more detail.

The Three Doshas or Biological Humors

Ayurveda classifies our life energies into three primary biological forces called doshas, meaning 'factors of decay', owing to the problems they cause when out of balance. The doshas are a similar concept to the biological humors of ancient Greek thought (which also had astrological equivalents).

First and foremost is a principle of energy, movement or change connected to the wind and the air element called Vata dosha, which means the 'life-wind'. Second is a principle of light, heat or combustion connected to the Sun and the fire element called Pitta dosha, which means 'that which cooks things'. Third is a principle of matter, inertia or preservation connected to the Moon and the water element called Kapha dosha, meaning 'what holds things together'.

To complete the astrological paradigm, the main planet ruling over Vata dosha is Saturn, which represents the negative side of our vital energy as entropy, time and decay. Yet Vata also relates to Mercury on its positive side as a force of movement, communication and expression.

In terms of physics, we could say that Vata is the principle of energy in the universe, Pitta is the principle of light, and Kapha is the principle of matter. Matter, light and energy are the three main factors in the world that can be converted into one another. The three doshas of Vata, Pitta and Kapha are their biological counterparts.

The three doshas are modifications of the five great elements of earth, water, fire, air and ether, which represent the five levels of matter as solid, liquid, radiant, gaseous and etheric. Each dosha projects the qualities of its respective element through the biological process. This is its basic force or "force element."

VATA is cold, dry, light, mobile in qualities, just as wind or air is cooling, drying, has no weight and is continually active and changing directions.
PITTA is hot, light and penetrating just like fire which is burning, luminous and spreading.
KAPHA is cold, damp, heavy, opaque and immobile, just like water, particularly water in a lake or enclosed area.

In addition to their primary elements as air, fire and water, each dosha relates to a secondary element that serves as its container or medium of expression. This is the field of operation in which the dosha operates or its "field element." In astrological parlance, the force-elements of the Doshas are like the planets and the field-elements of the Doshas are like the signs ruled by the planet.

VATA is air that is held in the ether or the spaces in the body, the bones, joints, the sensory orifices and the mind. It has etheric qualities of lightness, pervasiveness and ungroundedness.

PITTA is fire that is held in water or oil which serves as its fuel, the blood, enzymes and acid secretions. It has watery qualities of oiliness and liquid movement (just like warm water moves quickly).
KAPHA is water that is held in the confines of the earth, the bodily fluids that are held within the linings of the skin and mucus membranes. It has earthy qualities of heaviness, density and obstruction.

Each Dosha creates a certain aspect of the physical body:

VATA creates the nervous system and is responsible for all forms of movement, homeostasis and discharge of impulses. Such factors relate mainly to Mercury in astrology.
PITTA creates the digestive system and is responsible for the conversion of nutrients on all levels. These factors usually relate to the Sun in astrology.
KAPHA makes up the bulk of the bodily tissues, which are mainly composed of earth (muscle, skin, bone, teeth, hair and nails) and water (blood, plasma, fat). These mainly relate to the Moon.

The doshas are not simply physical but also emotional factors:

VATA as an emotional force, on the negative side, creates fear and anxiety, which are airy or destabilizing emotions. On the positive side, it gives creativity, comprehension and adaptability, like the wind moving freely and harmoniously. These are mainly the respective qualities of Saturn and Mercury in astrological thought.
PITTA as an emotional force, on the negative side, creates anger and animosity, which are fiery or aggressive emotions. On the positive side, it gives insight, courage and daring, as well as personal warmth, fire as a creative and protective force. These are the qualities of Mars and the Sun.

KAPHA as an emotional force, on the negative side, creates attachment, greed and clinging, which are stagnating watery emotions. On the positive side, it creates love, faith and loyalty, watery emotions of endurance and support. Astrologically, such emotions relate to the Moon and Venus.

Each Dosha creates an aspect of the mind or intellect:

VATA creates the mental sphere as a whole, which like Vata, is composed of air and ether elements. The mind is space in substance and faster than the wind in motion. This relates mainly to Mercury in terms of astrology.

PITTA creates the mind's power of reason and perception, which brings about mental judgment and the digestion of experiences. These relate mainly to the Sun and Mars.

KAPHA creates our emotional sensitivity, love, caring and nurturing qualities, the factors of the Moon and Venus.

The doshas relate to the seasons and stages of life and like the planets govern over time cycles:

VATA governs decline, decay and death, as in the time periods of old age, sunset or the fall and winter seasons. These factors relate mainly to Saturn in astrology.

PITTA governs the mature or midlife phase as in adult life, noon or the summer season. These relate mainly to the Sun and Mars.

KAPHA governs birth and growth, the initial or formative stage of development, as in childhood, morning or the spring time. These relate mainly to the Moon. Yet also governs fertility and reproduction governed by Venus.

There are also higher forms of the doshas that govern positive health, rejuvenation, vital energy and emotional and mental well-being. The higher form of Vata is called Prana, which is responsible for the creative and transformative powers of the air element. The higher form of Pitta is called Tejas, which is responsible for the creative and transformative powers of the fire element. The higher form of Kapha is called Ojas, which is responsible for the creative and transformative powers of the water element.[14] It is the transformation made possible through these subtle energies of the doshas that is targeted for the purposes of astrological healing.

Doshas and Planets

Vedic astrology uses the seven classical planets visible to the naked eye—the Sun, Moon, Mercury, Venus, Mars, Jupiter and Saturn. To these it adds the two lunar nodes, the north node or Dragon's head called Rahu, and the south node or Dragon's tail called Ketu. These points in the Moon's elliptical orbit at which eclipses occur are very important in the Vedic system. Some Vedic astrologers also use Uranus, Neptune and Pluto, but few afford them the importance of the other planets.

The term for planet is Vedic astrology is graha, meaning something that holds or seizes us. The planets are carriers and transmitters of cosmic influences. They reflect karmic and pranic energies on both individual and collective levels. They can be described as doshas because like the biological humors they not only sustain us through their proper function but cause decay and death when in excess or out of balance.

The main correlation between Vedic medicine and Vedic astrology is that between the doshas and the planets, with three planets corresponding to each of the three doshas.

- Vata Dosha — Saturn, Mercury, Rahu
- Pitta Dosha — Sun, Mars, Ketu
- Kapha Dosha — Moon, Venus, Jupiter

Saturn like Vata dosha is a cold, dry and nervous planet that brings about completion or decline. Saturn indicates Ayus or the term of life in the birth chart and so is a key to the Ayurvedic interpretation of the chart. The Sun like Pitta dosha is a hot and penetrating planet governing digestion, combustion and transformation. The Moon like Kapha dosha is a cold and damp planet that allows for the consistency and cohesion of our bodily tissues.

Vata Planets: Saturn, Rahu and Mercury

Saturn governs over both disease in general and longevity, which is the result of how we handle disease. It rules over all Vata systems as a whole, and specifically over elimination, including the colon, which is the main site of Vata's accumulation behind the disease process. Saturn causes most Vata disorders from arthritis to nervous system disorders and all manner of chronic diseases and conditions of debility. Saturn is the general significator of disease and bad health, which in Ayurveda result mainly from Vata dosha, said to cause the most numerous and severe diseases of all three doshas. An inimical Saturn in the chart must be carefully examined for its health implications.

Rahu, the north node of the Moon, is said to be like Saturn in energy, only having a subtler action. Rahu causes mental and nervous system disorders as well as mysterious and degenerative diseases, often with a rapid onset or quick development. It strikes us down in an unpredictable manner that is hard to prevent or reverse. Combined Saturn and Rahu influences appear behind severe Vata conditions and major health disorders from cancer to nervous breakdowns or severe mental disorders. These two planetary influences must be watched very closely in medical astrology.

Mercury is a mutable and impressionable planet that takes upon itself the influence of the other planets it is associated with. This is why often in Vedic astrology it is related to all three Doshas. However, Mercury in and of itself is more of a Vata or airy planet, with its correspondence to the nervous system, the mind, communication and rapid motion. We might say that Mercury represents the youthful and healthier form of Vata, while Saturn is the older and generally unhealthier form of Vata. Owing to its connections with the mind, afflictions to Mercury are crucial factors for psychological Ayurveda. As representing the state of childhood, Mercury is an important indicator for the health of children as well.

Pitta Planets: Sun, Mars and Ketu

The Sun governs the fire element in the body, providing light, heat and color on all levels. It rules over all Pitta systems as a whole from the digestive system to the eyes and the perceptive aspect of the mind. The Sun is the general indicator of our physical vitality and the positive reflector of our Prana or vital energy, which comes from the Sun as the bestower of all life. A well-placed and strong Sun in the birth chart indicates good health and strong resistance to disease, while a weak or afflicted Sun causes health and vitality problems, generally of a chronic or persistent nature starting with weak digestion and poor metabolism.

Mars governs Pitta more specifically, particularly through male energy, which is fiery and aggressive in nature. Mars, being a more malefic planet, is more likely to cause Pitta type diseases than the Sun, and indicates fever, inflammation, infection and acute conditions. It also causes reckless action and accidents, including those that require surgery, causing health problems for people who are otherwise constitutionally strong. Mars is the main planet to examine for Pitta disorders and second only to Saturn as the most disease-promoting of the planets.

Ketu is said to resemble Mars in its influence, but just as Rahu with Saturn, in a more subtle way. It governs diseases of a nervous and mental nature like Rahu, but with Ketu involves coordination or strength of the muscular system, including the onset of neuro-muscular problems. Like Mars it is connected to fevers and infections, particularly of a deep-seated or chronic nature, including those that are hard to cure. It can also indicate accidents, injuries or wounds, particularly those owing to collective factors like wars or catastrophes. When Mars and Ketu combine their influences in the chart, severe Pitta problems or violence are likely.

Kapha Planets: The Moon, Jupiter and Venus

The Moon governs the water element, the bodily fluids in general and all Kapha systems as a whole. It rules over our emotions or feeling nature which is mainly a Kapha activity[15], as water allows us to be receptive and to nurture. A strong Moon contributes to good Kapha in the body and to a Kapha constitution. However, the Moon has some airy or Vata qualities by its changeable nature, particularly when it is close to the Sun and lacking in brilliance, as a new Moon. Afflictions to the Moon impact health in infancy as well as can disturb the psychology (even more so than in the case of Mercury).

Venus governs Kapha in a more specific way, just as Mars does Pitta, particularly through female energy, which is watery in nature, and through the reproductive system with which it has a special connection. Like the Moon it also has some Vata or airy qualities, including changeability. Venus endows us with a Kapha or watery type of beauty and grace. It causes diseases mainly through luxury, dissipation or self-indulgence, even when the basic constitution may not be weak.

Jupiter is a planet that creates bulk in the body and so is a Kapha planet, although it represents more the active side of Kapha energy. Opposite Saturn as the planet of disease, Jupiter is also the planet of positive health, which in Ayurveda occurs owing to good or healthy Kapha in the body. Jupiter indicates the benefic influence of the soul and its healing energy. Jupiter also governs the mental aspect of Kapha, giving a steady and profound intelligence along with emotional sensitivity, calm and faith. Like Venus, however, it can cause disease through self-indulgence or complacency.

Uranus, Neptune and Pluto

We can correspond the distant planets of Uranus, Neptune and Pluto to Vata, Pitta and Kapha at a deeper or more collective level. Uranus has an electrical energy and erratic action like Vata. Neptune has a watery and imaginative energy like Kapha. Pluto has a Mars or fiery energy like Pitta. This is an area for further research.

Doshas, Planets and Elements

Both doshas and planets correspond to the five elements, which form their main common ground of correlation. There are however some differences and variations that should be borne in mind.

Mercury is often related to the earth element because of its ability to facilitate clear communication and action in the outer world through the concrete or information oriented mind that it rules. However, it does not necessarily make a person heavy or Kapha physically. It is usually more Vata in this regard.

Jupiter is often related to the ether element because it creates expansion and aids in the development of the abstract mind, philosophy and religion. It does not, however, make a person Vata, light or etheric, but, on the contrary, creates bulk and weight. Otherwise the correspondences of elements and doshas are the same.

The Fivefold Universe

Element	**Earth**	**Water**	**Fire**	**Air**	**Ether**
Sense Quality	Smell	Taste	Sight	Touch	Sound

Element	Earth	Water	Fire	Air	Ether
Sense Organ	Nose	Tongue	Eyes	Skin	Ears
Motor Organ	Anus	Urinogenital	Feet	Hands	Voice
Dosha	Kapha	Kapha	Pitta	Vata	Vata
Planet	Mercury	Venus, Moon	Mars, Sun, Ketu	Saturn, Rahu	Jupiter

The Signs and the Doshas

Vedic like Western astrology uses the twelve signs of the zodiac. However, in the Vedic system, the signs are a twelvefold division of the fixed stars, what is called a 'sidereal zodiac', not tropically based as is the case with the signs of western astrology based upon the equinoxes.[16] The difference between the two systems, which coincided nearly two thousand years ago, is now around 24 degrees, with the point of the vernal equinox around 6 degrees of Pisces sidereally, moving backward toward the sign Aquarius.[17] While those trained in western astrology may find this reorientation of signs to be confusing, it is not only more accurate astronomically, but is arguably the original form of astrology, which began with the observation of the fixed stars.[18]

The twelve signs of the zodiac from Aries to Pisces represent the fields in which the nine planets operate. They are an extension of the qualities of their ruling planets, for example, with Mars-ruled Aries having a strong Mars energy in its qualities. Like the planets, the signs also correspond to the elements.

- Air Signs – Gemini, Libra, Aquarius
- Fire Signs – Aries, Leo, Sagittarius
- Water Signs – Cancer, Scorpio, Pisces
- Earth Signs – Taurus, Virgo, Capricorn

Fire signs usually endow a person with a good vitality, strong digestion, good circulation and excellent resistance to disease, owing to the ability of the fire element to both nourish the body and burn up pathogens.

Air signs afford a good development of the mind and nervous system along with a good creative and expressive energy, but do not give good endurance and so the person can suffer from overwork or overexertion. They are also more prone to psychological problems.

Water signs provide a good development of the bodily tissues, which consist primarily of water, but have a tendency towards disease through excess water or weight, so their resistance to disease can be limited. They can be emotionally sensitive when afflicted.

Earth signs have the weakest potential in terms of health because they keep ones energy on a physical level and can increase entropy or the forces of decay, but they can also give athletic, healing or creative powers. Their range for both health and disease is the greatest of all the signs.

Air signs in general correspond with Vata dosha, relating to the mind, nervous system, communication and other Vata fields of activity. Fire signs correspond to Pitta, relating to the digestive system, circulatory system, perception and other Pitta fields. Water signs correspond with Kapha, relating to the bodily fluids, emotions and other Kapha fields. Earth signs represent the body and its structure, mainly Kapha fields, but more as a field in which the other three elemental forces can operate.

Some Vedic astrology texts relate Earth signs to Vata or the air humor. This is because earth signs relate to the physical body and keep our energy more at a physical level. They make disease more likely and disease is mainly caused by Vata, particularly the earth sign Virgo, the main sign relating to poor health. Earth signs are also more likely to cause depression in a person, which keeps our energy at a physical level and causes Vata to increase. In this regard, we could say that air signs represent the healthy side of Vata, while earth signs have a propensity towards the unhealthy side of Vata. Yet we must also remember that earth signs afford the greatest capacity for accomplishment in the physical realm as well and are commonly found among athletes, artists and performers, not just those suffering from health problems!

In addition to their correspondence to the elements, the signs relate to three qualities as moveable (cardinal in Western astrology), fixed, and dual or ambivalent (mutable in Western astrology). These qualities have doshic implications, though of a less consequential manner. Pitta dosha is usually moveable, cardinal (colorful), direct or determined, like fire which burns in a specific manner depending upon its fuel. Kapha is fixed or steady, like water that does not move unless acted upon by an external force. Vata as air is mutable or ambivalent. Sometimes it blows (moves quickly), sometimes it doesn't blow at all.[19]

The doshic impact of earth signs can be interpreted relative to these three qualities. Fixed earth, Taurus, has a more Kapha quality with the Moon, a watery planet exalted in Taurus. Mutable earth, Virgo, is related to Vata with Mercury, a Vata planet exalted in Virgo. Cardinal earth, Capricorn, though not as strongly, has some relationship to Pitta with Mars, a Pitta planet exalted in Capricorn.

Yet regardless of the qualities of the signs themselves, we must remember the general rule that the nature of the planets is more important than that of the signs. The planets represent the force, while the signs represent the field in which these forces operate. The force always tends to dominate its field of activity.

While the doshas of the planets and signs should be looked at together, greater weight should be given to the nature of the planets. Another important method is to look at the qualities of the sign according to those of its ruling planet.

- Aries, Leo and Scorpio are ruled by fiery planets Mars and the Sun and partake of the fiery (Pitta) nature of these planets.
- Taurus, Cancer, Libra, Sagittarius and Pisces are ruled by watery planets Venus, the Moon and Jupiter and partake of the watery (Kapha) nature of these planets.
- Gemini, Virgo, Capricorn and Aquarius are ruled by airy planets Mercury and Saturn and partake of the airy (Vata) nature of these planets.

Divisional Charts

Along with the usual birth chart, called the rashi chart, Vedic astrology employs a number of subtle, harmonic or divisional charts, which are mathematical subdivisions of the birth chart.[20] Planetary positions in several divisional charts are considered important for health. Most notable of these are the positions in the drekkana (harmonic third) for Prana and general vitality, navamsha (harmonic ninth) for the connection with the soul and for longevity, in the dvadashamsha (harmonic twelfth) for ancestry and congenital influences, and in the trimshamsha (harmonic thirtieth) for specific diseases and injuries. The navamsha is the most important of these and should be examined in the same way as the basic birth (rashi) chart.

In determining health, a good Vedic astrologer will examine several of these divisional charts with the rashi (birth) and Moon charts. In addition to these, another specific factor often examined for determining the Ayurvedic constitution is the navamsha sign of the Moon.[21]

Planets and the Tissues of the Body

The influence of the planets extends to the tissues (dhatus) of the body as described in Ayurveda. As with the doshas, there is not a final one-to-one correlation to the planets but a number of important correlations.

1. PLASMA (Rasa dhatu) – The Moon's rulership over the water element in the body and Kapha dosha brings its influence to the plasma or basic bodily fluid as well. A strong Moon provides good hydration to the body, which is the main function of the plasma. Classical Vedic astrology also considers Mercury because of its association with the skin, with which the plasma is connected. An afflicted Mercury can cause skin diseases, which often arise from a sensitive mind and nervous system.

2. BLOOD (Rakta dhatu) – In Ayurveda, Pitta or the fire-humor is a waste-material or by product of the blood. This connects it to Pitta planets like the Sun that governs the heart which drives the blood. In classical Vedic astrology, the role of the Moon as governing bodily fluids, of which the blood is the most important, is also considered. Mars as the planet causing most Pitta and blood disorders must not be forgotten either.

3. MUSCLE (Mamsa dhatu) – Mars is a planet of work and action, which in the physical body occurs mainly through the muscles, so its role relative to the muscles is important. Classical Vedic astrology also considers Saturn, which is responsible for the structure of the body. The muscles are the main tissue that forms the body.

4. FAT (Meda dhatu) – Jupiter is the main planet responsible for bulk, weight or largeness in the body, so its role relative the fat tissue is central. Yet the Moon's role to allow us to hold water and weight must also be considered.

5. BONE (Asthi dhatu) – The bone is the main Vata tissue in the body and is intimately connected to the absorption of Prana in the large intestine, both of which factors relate to Saturn. Classical Vedic astrology also considers the role of the Sun because only if the Sun is strong and digestion good can the bones be properly built up.

6. NERVE OR MARROW (Majja dhatu) – Mercury's connection to the nerves (gray marrow) is well known in both western and Vedic astrology. The role of Mars relative to the red marrow of the bones is another aspect of Majja Dhatu in Vedic thought. Saturn and Rahu as causing nervous system disorders, largely by depleting the nerve tissue, should not be overlooked either.

7. REPRODUCTIVE (Shukra dhatu) – The Sanskrit name for Venus as Shukra also refers to the reproductive fluid. The strength or weakness of the reproductive system is closely connected to the placement of Venus in the chart. Yet the Moon's general role in fertility is another significant factor.

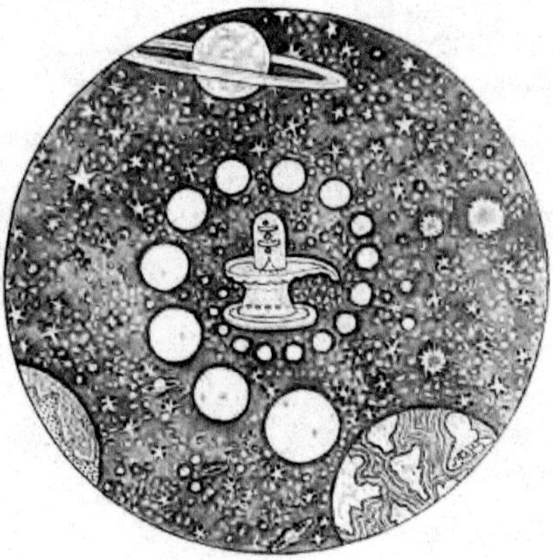

Ayurvedic & Astrology Types

4

DETERMINATION of individual constitution is perhaps the most important factor behind correct physical and psychological treatment. We cannot simply look at all people, with their varying shapes and sizes, temperaments and inclinations, as the same. The same recommendations of food, exercise or even of meditation cannot be equally valid for everyone. One of the great values of traditional systems of medicine and astrology is that they provide individual typologies, which take these natural differences into account.

Ayurvedic medicine determines individual mind-body types according to its view of the three doshas or biological humors. Vedic astrology classifies people into personality types according to the nine planets. In this chapter, we will show how these two systems of typology correlate. By interfacing Ayurvedic biological types with the Vedic astrological types, we have a precise classification that can help us understand the full range of our potentials in life.

Ayurvedic medicine categorizes individuals according to which of the three doshas of Vata, Pitta or Kapha predominates in their nature, in what proportion and to what degree. The doshas reflect the condition of our prana or vital energy and our resultant psycho-physical expression, so we could also call these 'pranic' or 'vital energy' types.

Vedic astrology classifies people in several ways but most important is according to the dominant planet in the birth chart, with individual types based upon the Sun, Moon, Mars, Mercury, Jupiter, Venus, Saturn and the two lunar nodes (Rahu and Ketu). These planetary types are 'karmic types', reflecting our overall life-movement and experience. They reflect not only bodily and mental traits, but also the full range of our life-experience, inwardly and outwardly.

The great majority of people are one type primarily, either doshic or astrological, which usually can be easily ascertained. Yet even among the same types are higher or lower (spiritual or materialistic), strong or weak, or healthy and unhealthy manifestations. Once the individual type is determined, such variations can then be examined.

While planetary types are more numerous than doshic types, the three main doshic types can be increased to seven, with the addition of dual (Vata-Pitta, Pitta-Kapha, Vata-Kapha) or triple types (Vata-Pitta-Kapha), and all nine planetary types have their doshic ramifications. As each one of us contains the influences of all the planets and all the doshas to some degree, such typologies remain relative – a good orientation toward our unique nature, but not the last word on who we are.

1. The Three Ayurvedic Doshic Types

You can determine your Ayurvedic mind-body or doshic type by taking an Ayurvedic constitutional test, such as are found in Ayurvedic texts. Consultation with an Ayurvedic doctor is another way. You can also examine descriptions of these types below and see where your characteristics most commonly fall. I have also added a few basic planetary correlations to the usual doshic traits.

Vata Types

Vata types are usually taller or shorter than average in height. They are thin-boned with thin builds, with muscles not well-developed and often with prominent veins. Their skin is dry, cracked, or rough, and lacking in luster. Their teeth are not always well formed and may be crooked or have spaces in between. Vatas often have the appearance of being undernourished and find it hard to gain weight. Their connection with Saturn, a drying, reducing and emaciating planet, is usually in evidence in their appearance.

Vatas have a variable or erratic digestion with a strong appetite at some times and very little at others. They easily suffer from constipation, abdominal distention and gas. Their urine is scanty and they seldom perspire very much. They are particularly sensitive to cold, wind and dryness. These factors also reflect the influence of Saturn that causes retention of waste materials, debility and poor resistance to disease. Vatas more commonly end up suffering from wasting or degenerative disorders, or nervous system problems (Saturn and Rahu problems).

Vata types are active and energetic often beyond the scope of their physical structure, following a kind of nervous energy from within. They enjoy speed and like running, flying and movement of all types, though their endurance is not strong. They suffer from overwork, over exercise and tend to overextend themselves. Their activity level reflects mainly the influence of Mercury, which allows them to move quickly, with their poor stamina reflecting Saturn and Rahu which reduce their vitality. Vatas are often Mercurial when young but Saturnian when old.

Vatas are light sleepers and suffer from insomnia or restless dreams. This is particularly true if Rahu dominates their chart, which creates a nervous hypersensitivity. Vatas are talkative and communicative and can be good conversationalists. They can be highly intellectual and grasp many different points of view. But sometimes they are superficial in their ideas and talk on mechanically. Their will is indecisive and they seldom stick with anything for long. While they may be knowledgeable of many different things, they often cannot determine which is right and waver in their views. These are largely Mercurial traits.

Vatas can be highly socially oriented and like to mix with others (particularly when Mercury is strong). Yet when Vata is too high (Saturn and Rahu), they often become loners, suffer from alienation and find themselves unable to relate to anyone.

Vata types suffer emotionally most commonly from fear and insecurity. They suffer from anxiety, depression or ungroundedness (generally Saturn and Rahu). They have quickly changing and often unstable emotions. They easily get spaced out and may be absent minded. Their memory is often short term or erratic. They are not entirely present in their bodies and may be a bit clumsy. Yet when well developed they possess the greatest agility of body and mind of all the Ayurvedic types.

Relative to career, Vatas make good teachers, consultants or computer programmers, and work well with the media. They are excellent at thinking, writing and organizing data, reflecting once again their connection to Mercury. They have a strong artistic side and can be poets, musicians or dancers. They like to be rebels, tend to be eccentric and are innovative in their ideas, which can lead them into a spiritual direction in life. This is usually due to a Saturn influence. Yet an afflicted Saturn can keep them in subservient roles in life, working for others, and not getting a lot of recognition for what they do.

Pitta Types

Pitta-types are usually of average height, build and frame and generally possess good health. They have well developed muscles and a ruddy or glowing complexion. Their skin is prone to acne, rashes and other inflammatory skin disorders, and is usually a bit oily. They bruise and bleed easily. Their eyes easily get red or light sensitive and they often have to wear glasses. Their hair is thin, often red or blond in color, and they tend towards early graying or balding. They are sensitive to heat and prefer all things that are cooling. The warming influence of the Sun and Mars is evident in all their traits.

Pittas possess an appetite and thirst that is good, sharp or excessive, though their weight usually remains moderate. Their discharges of feces, urine or mucus tend to be of yellow color and large in quantity, reflecting an excess of bile. They sweat easily and their sweat and other discharges may be malodorous. Their sleep is moderate in duration but not always good in quality. They have many dreams, which are often passionate, sometimes violent or disturbing.

The health of Pittas may suffer more from accidents than disease, which often occur from their own recklessness or aggression. When they do have diseases, these are usually of a febrile, infectious or toxic blood type often involving the liver, spleen or small intestine. These are usually Mars-caused problems, though Sun-caused heart diseases or Ketu-caused nervous system disorders also occur for them.

Pittas are prone to anger and are competitive, if not domineering. They have strong wills and can be impulsive and sudden in their actions (Sun and Mars influences). They like to be leaders and shine in what they do, but can be fanatic or insensitive. They like the use of force and are prone to argument or violence. They enjoy color, drama and passion and can be good orators and debaters.

Pittas are intelligent, perceptive and discriminating. With a good understanding of mechanics and mathematics, they make good scientists and technicians. They often like to work with tools, weapons or chemistry. They have probing minds and are good at research and invention. They can also excel as psychologists, doctors or surgeons. They can have the deep insight that goes with Ketu on spiritual matters and can be good astrologers.

Most military persons, policemen, lawyers and politicians are Pitta types and Mars is usually their strongest planet. They have a natural interest in law and punishment. Yet Pittas may lack compassion and have a hard time seeing a point of view that is different from their own.

Kapha Types

Kapha-types are usually short and stocky and heavy in build. Sometimes they are tall but they always possess a large frame with big bones. Their skin is thick and their flesh is well developed. They hold excess weight and water unless they work hard to keep it off. Their eyes are large and white, with large lashes. Their hair is abundant and thick. Their teeth are large, white and attractive. They sleep easily, often excessively and may be lazy. They suffer from cold and dampness but possess strong endurance. In short, Kapha physical factors reflect mainly the influences of the Moon and Jupiter. However, they often have attractive facial features, reflecting the influence of Venus.

Kaphas easily accumulate phlegm in their bodies and suffer most from bronchial and pulmonary disorders, including asthma. They easily get edema and can have weak kidneys as well. They are most prone to obesity and its consequent diseases like arthritis, heart disease and diabetes. Yet if they can control their weight they are the longest living and healthiest of all the types. Their diseases are also mainly of the Moon and Jupiter.

Kaphas are emotional types with much love, devotion and loyalty (Moon and Venus influence). Yet they also possess much desire and attachment and may be greedy or acquisitive (Venus and lower Jupiterian influences). Kapha women are often romantic and sentimental and cry easily.

Reflecting the influence of the Moon, Kaphas are generally conservative, traditional or conventional in their behavior and beliefs. They like to belong and seldom rebel, functioning best as part of a family or community rather than on their own. They are largely content, if not complacent in their disposition and accept things as they are. They are stable and consistent but sometimes stagnate. They do not like to change and find it difficult to even when they want to.

Kaphas are friendly, particularly with people they know, and create life long associations. Yet they can have difficulties relating to strangers or foreigners. While they do not like to hurt others, they can be insensitive to the needs of others if these are different than their own.

They do not take hints easily. Often they have to be confronted or criticized before they take action.

Mentally, Kaphas are slower than the other types in their ability to grasp new information, but what they learn is retained. They are not creative or inventive but do carry things out and make them practical. They are better at finishing projects than at producing new ideas. They like to bring things into form and create institutions and establishments. When their Jupiter is strong they can be highly intelligent, however, with much power of memory and concentration and great steadiness of mind. In this case they can even be good philosophers and yogis.

Kaphas are usually good parents and providers and like to care for others. Kapha women are good mothers and wives, excelling at cooking, baking and homemaking, again owing to the strong lunar influence. Kapha types may be cooks or work in restaurants. With their large chests, good lungs and good voices, Kaphas make good singers. They like to accumulate wealth and hold firmly to what they get. They do well at real estate and property management and make good bankers. They are able to accumulate things externally, just as they tend to hold weight or emotions internally.

2. The Nine Planetary Types

The nine planetary types are more specific than the three Ayurvedic types and can be used to expand them. Sun, Mars and Ketu types are usually Pitta in terms of Ayurveda, but in slightly different ways. Moon, Jupiter and Venus types are usually Kapha. Saturn, Mercury and Rahu types are usually Vata. But these doshic connections are only general and exceptions do exist. In some individuals, also, two or three planets may be relatively equal in strength, in which case their delineations should be modified accordingly.

For determining the planetary type, Vedic astrology emphasizes the dominant planet in the chart, particularly relative to the Ascendant which relates to the body and the overall personality. While this often is the ruler of the Ascendant, it is not always the case, particularly if another planet aspects both the Ascendant and its lord. Aspects to the Moon and its lord, final dispositorship and other factors also come into play.

The tenth house is also important because it marks the career and social projection of a person. Note the astrological factors discussed under each planetary type below and the sample charts in Part III for more information.

Sun Types

The Sun represents the positive or balanced side of fire energy, Agni and Pitta. Sun type individuals are usually the most healthy of all because their strong fire energy affords them good digestion, good circulation and the ability to burn away any toxins or pathogens that might cause disease. They have strong immune systems and seldom come down with anything severe.

The influence of the Sun is most evidence in their face and head, with their complexion bright, golden or reddish in tinge. Their eyes are lustrous, perceptive or full of light. Usually they are of moderate build with good muscles and they seldom become overweight or underweight. Sun types can have a secondary Vata dosha, however, as they run a bit on the dry side.

Sun types suffer from heat and so do better with cool foods and cool climates. Though they like sunshine, they can suffer from too much direct exposure to the Sun. Their main health danger is through overwork, overheating themselves, or through trying to take responsibility for everything. This can give them heart problems or stomach problems (ulcers), pushing the solar energy in their bodies beyond its healthy limits. Sun types like to have children but are not usually happy with them. Their standards are too high and their children tend to revolt against them or disappoint them.

Psychologically, Sun types are compelling, dominant and king-like or queen-like, characterized by a strong will and determined vital energy. They are independent, regal, proud, and sometimes vain. They have strong emotions, generally of a personal nature, but are seldom overcome by them. They like to be leaders and authorities, naturally gaining power over others and often excelling in politics. They prefer to be the bestower of light and may turn others into their satellites. They are highly perceptive, critical, and can probe deeply into things. They can make good scientists or psychologists and develop new insights.

Usually Sun types have a philosophical or religious disposition and are ethical in their actions. Their higher interests come out more strongly later in life, when they often become contemplative. In youth they are largely people of action rather than words and command a strong presence in the world. There is something noble or aristocratic about them and they like to associate with people and projects of principle and value.

Yet if defeated in life, Sun types can fall quickly just like the setting Sun. Their death is often sudden, most commonly by heart attack. Once their period of success is over and they are no longer in the limelight, they easily suffer from loneliness and regret, unless they learn to turn within, which is also within their capacity.

Astrological Factors

Sun types are created when the Sun is strongly placed in the chart. This can occur when the Sun is located in the Ascendant or in other angular houses (especially the tenth), particularly if it is also placed in its own sign (Leo) or sign of exaltation (Aries). Leo ascendants are usually solar types unless some other planet dominates both the Ascendant and its lord the Sun.

Other planets located along with the Sun or in the Leo, the Sun's sign, are contributing factors for creating solar types. The Sun's aspect on the Ascendant and its lord is another important consideration. Planets located with the Sun are generally overpowered by it and give it more strength with the exceptions of Ketu and Saturn, which can weaken it.

Moon Types

Moon type individuals are dominated by the water element and Kapha dosha in both their build and in their behavior. They have round attractive moonlike faces as well as round, well-developed bodies. Their complexion is usually fair or whitish in tinge, and the whites of their eyes are pronounced. They possess an abundance of vital fluids and tend to have thick, shiny oily hair. With age Moon types tend to become heavier and put on weight and water. This often happens after the birth of the first child in the case of women or after the age of forty.

Moon types run cold and damp and easily accumulate phlegm and mucus. They have strong lungs and good voices but easily suffer from congestion. They can develop water retention (edema), particularly in the thighs and feet. Usually they live long and are healthy overall, but often have some continual though fluctuating minor health problems. They may be prone to laziness or excessive sleep that weakens their health.

Moon types like to take a maternal role, functioning in a loving, caring, nurturing and helpful role for others. They are loyal, dependent and responsive, making good friends and marriage partners. They are often good cooks and frequently are domestically oriented. Their life is often centered in human interaction, though this may extend from the family to the nation as in the case of Moon type politicians.

Once they overcome their basic shyness and learn to relate on a public level, Moon types can succeed socially and become sensitive leaders who can influence the masses. This is particularly true if there is some Saturn influence on the Moon. For women, such a publicly oriented Moon can turn her into something of a matriarch.

Psychologically, Moon types are emotional, sensitive and changeable like the Moon itself. They are romantic and sentimental and can cry easily. Though easily hurt, they easily forgive and forget. Yet their emotional sensitivity is not always sensitivity to the emotions of others and they may be so caught in their own responses that they cannot really sense what others are feeling. Their emotional force may provide them artistic talent, particularly for public performances, but also good expression, including through poetry.

Higher Moon types have psychic and spiritual abilities, with spiritual devotion and contemplative powers. They can be healers, psychics and mystics owing to their power of empathy. However, if the Moon is disturbed in the chart (as under joint Saturn-Mars influence or with Rahu) emotional turbulence can be indicated, including psychological derangements.

Moon types have a secondary Vata dosha, which contributes to their emotional changeability. As the Moon is an important astrological factor in itself, second only to the Ascendant, there are also different Moon sign types relative to the signs in which the Moon is located, which we will discuss in the chapter on 'Vedic Astrology and Psychology'.

Astrological Factors

Moon types are created by a strong Moon in the chart, which most commonly occurs when the Moon is located in the Ascendant or in other angular houses, particularly if it is also placed in its own sign (Cancer) or sign of exaltation (Taurus). Cancer Ascendants are generally Moon types, unless another planet dominates the Moon, such as often occurs when the Sun is also in Cancer. The Moon's aspect on the Ascendant and its lord can make the person into a Moon type as well. The Moon in conjunction with Jupiter or in an angle from it also contributes strength to the Moon.

Note that the Moon should be a good distance from the Sun in order to have its full strength. The full Moon in particular is common in the charts of Moon types, particularly if it is also located in earth or water signs or in angles.

Mars Types

Mars represents the negative side of Pitta dosha and the fire element, which affords Mars types a predisposition for excesses and for diseases of a fiery nature. While Sun types run hot and dry and maintain a good digestive power, Mars types combine heat and dampness, which weakens their digestion and makes them prone to infectious diseases. They suffer from excess bile and acid. Their blood runs hot and they easily accumulate toxins. Owing to this dampness in their systems, Mars types have a secondary Kapha dosha or water element that can come out in some circumstances.

Mars types have moderate builds with good muscles. Often their features are angular or sharp (Martian, masculine or even militant). Their circulation is good and their complexion tends to be red with oily skin and they bruise or bleed easily. Their eyes are piercing but light sensitive and easily get inflamed. Their appetite and thirst are strong but they tend towards loose stool or diarrhea.

Mars types possess a strong energy and have periods of very good health. Their diseases, which are usually acute, arise more from bad living habits than from an inherently weak constitution. They suffer physically from alcohol, cigarettes, meat, hot spices, oily and fried foods, overdrinking and overeating. Usually their liver is their weakest organ and they tend towards hepatitis, cirrhosis and hypertension. Mars types are also the most prone to injuries, accidents and traumatic diseases, often from their own rashness or aggressive behavior. They may have surgeries or have organs removed (particularly if Mars combines with Saturn).

Psychologically, Mars types are perceptive, critical and argumentative. They are bold, daring and adventurous and make good debaters, speakers, and lawyers. Their sense of logic is strong but can follow their anger more than their real sense of justice. They love to win and hate to lose. Psychologically, they harm themselves with anger, jealousy and hatred.

Mars types, however, are very loyal to their friends and like to form alliances, though usually formed in response to some external threat or opposition. They work better in disciplined groups and like hierarchy and authority. They have strong passions and are very possessive. Their sexual energy is powerful but not always refined. They tend to overindulge and burn themselves out.

Mars types possess a good sense of mechanics and often make good scientists, researchers and workers with machines, tools and weapons. They do well in the legal, military and police fields. Medicine, like surgery, and psychology, can also be within their domains.

A higher Mars type also exists. This is the highly perceptive and self-disciplined yogi, the spiritual warrior. These higher Mars types can be highly austere. They know how to control their minds, and possess a strong will towards transformation.

Astrological Factors

Mars types are created by a strong Mars in the chart, like Mars located in the Ascendant or in other angular houses (Mars does well in the tenth house), particularly if it is also placed in its own sign (Aries or Scorpio) or sign of exaltation (Capricorn). Mars ruled Ascendants (Aries and Scorpio) usually create Mars types, unless another planet dominates both Mars and the Ascendant. Aries or Scorpio Moon or Sun signs are contributing factors, as is the aspect of Mars on the Ascendant and its lord.

Since Mars has special aspects on the signs fourth and eighth from it, these also must be carefully weighed. As the sixth house is the house of disease, Mars posited here has an effect by location on disease and by aspect on the body as a whole through the Ascendant. A combust Mars usually imparts a Mars energy and contributes to Pitta in the constitution but not always in a healthy manner.

Mercury Types

Mercury types are usually intellectual, or at least communicative, in their disposition with sensitive nervous and digestive systems. The influence of Mercury is more mental than physical but a Mercury physical type does exist. Mercury types tend to be taller or shorter than average, thin in build and generally attractive (a more harmonious Vata type). They are often youthful in looks and facial features, or have a changeable (Mercurial) appearance and expression.

Mercury types represent the healthier side of Vata dosha. Their skin and other bodily secretions are moister than other Vata types, which tend to be dry. They run on the cool side and have sensitive lungs.

They are susceptible to allergies, hay fever and bronchial disorders. Their heart is also sensitive and they are prone to palpitations.

Mercury types possess good prana or life-energy, live long, and have a certain glow about them. They are often athletic and make good runners or basketball players but their endurance is not always high. Commonly they are athletic when young but shift over to becoming more intellectual when older.

Psychologically, Mercury types possess quick minds, a good sense of information and fluent powers of speech. They are congenial and compassionate, with a good sense of relationship and interchange. They are usually friendly and talkative but can be introverted from an excess of thinking. Their emotions are similarly quick, changeable and easily affected by their environment, but overall they are happy, enthusiastic and driven by curiosity. They are witty and have a good sense of humor.

Relative to career proclivities, Mercury types excel at languages and at statistics, though they may get caught in trivia. They are helpful and service oriented and can be comfortable with background or dependent roles. They make good secretaries, teachers and writers. They work well in the mass media and make good moderators and interviewers. They often have special powers of acting and are good at imitation.

Mercury types are good at business, trade and commerce and like to keep their accounts in order. With their strong sense of consideration and their desire to create harmony, they can become excellent doctors and nurses. They love nature, particularly plants and are good at gardening. They have a refined sense of taste, which can be expressed through poetry, music or design. They are often interested in Yoga, mantra and other tools for improving their minds. While not specifically spiritual in orientation, they have an inquisitive nature that if directed toward the spiritual path can take them far.

Astrological Factors

As Mercury is a mutable planet it easily takes on the nature of the planets that it is associated with, making it hard at times to determine how strong Mercury actually is in the chart.

Generally, Mercury types are created by a strongly placed Mercury in the chart, such as occurs when Mercury is located in the Ascendant or in other angular houses, particularly if it is also placed in its own sign (Gemini or Virgo) or sign of exaltation (Virgo). Mercury ruled

Ascendants (Gemini and Virgo) usually create Mercury types, unless another planet dominates both Mercury and the Ascendant. Gemini or Virgo Moon or Sun signs are contributing factors. The aspect of Mercury upon both the Ascendant and its lord is most important as well.

Mercury is not as much influenced by proximity to the Sun as other planets because it is never far from it. Mercury with the Sun in a sign of Mercury or in other air and earth signs will usually make Mercury even stronger.

Jupiter Types

Jupiter represents the positive, active or healthy side of the water element and of Kapha dosha. Jupiter types usually possess strong Kapha constitutions, with a good development of muscle, flesh and sometimes fat. Their heads, hands and feet are large and they can get on the heavy side later in life. Their complexion is tinged yellow or golden and they usually run a little on the warm side, with steady and strong circulation and a good metabolism.

Jupiter types have great strength and enjoy physical work, exercise and like to be outdoors. They are more active and athletic than other Kapha types and this is essential to their well-being. Generally Jupiter people are healthy and live long, but they can suffer from self-indulgence or from attempting too much in life. Their weakest organs are their pancreas, spleen and liver. They suffer mainly from overeating sweet, rich and oily foods. Excessive sugar consumption can lead them to diabetes. Once they become sedentary, the benefits of their robust constitution are quickly lost.

Psychologically, Jupiterian types are joyful, jovial and content. They are gregarious and generous and enjoy being with people, accumulating friends and family around them. They are enthusiastic and expressive and like the display of energy and show. They have a strong sense of play and show, but seldom become vulgar. They seldom worry but tend towards over optimism. They may tend to overindulgence or even dissipation, often through unwise associations, if Jupiter is influenced by Venus or Rahu.

Jupiterian careers include expansive business ventures, banking and management. Jupiter types usually do well financially and accumulate property, friends and associates to help in their endeavors. They also gravitate towards law or the military, somewhat like Mars types, but more out of a sense of justice than one of any innate aggression. Relative to the arts, they are most attracted to music. They often have a good healing energy and one feels energized being around them. They frequently have interests in philosophy, religion and spirituality.

Jupiter types are balanced, kind and compassionate and they always try to be just. They are highly moral and ethical and can be devoutly religious. Yet their sentiments and ideals may be too grandiose or more than is fitting the circumstances. They tend towards conventionality in their beliefs, liking to be popular, and can get caught up in ceremony and hierarchy. Sometimes the outer aspect of religion becomes more important for them than the inner essence.

Jupiters have a strong sense of devotion, are calm minded and usually at peace within themselves. They often develop a contemplative bent later in life. They are interested in the bigger picture or broader principles, rather than details or mere information. Their spirit is positive, expansive and helpful. They like to contribute to the forward movement life and help bring about new developments in knowledge and understanding.

Astrological Factors

Jupiter types are created by a strong Jupiter in the chart, like Jupiter located in the Ascendant or in other angular houses, particularly if it is also placed in its own sign (Sagittarius or Pisces) or sign of exaltation (Cancer). Jupiter ruled Ascendants (Sagittarius or Pisces) usually create Jupiter types, unless another planet aspects both the Ascendant and Jupiter. Sagittarius or Pisces Moon or Sun signs are contributing factors. Jupiter with the Moon or in an angle from it is another strengthening factor (Gaja Kesari Yoga in Vedic astrological parlance).

Jupiter's aspect on the Ascendant and its lord contributes strength as well. In this regard remember to examine Jupiter's special trinal (fifth house and ninth house) aspects.

Venus Types

Venus types are the best looking of the planetary types, representing the more attractive side of Kapha dosha. They are usually moderate in build and average in height, seldom very tall or very short, very thin or very heavy. Their features are roundish and their tissues well-developed but they seldom get obese. As they are concerned about their appearance this helps them keep their Kapha from getting too high.

Venus types have attractive eyes, hair and skin, which glow. Their hands are well-formed, delicate and without deep lines. Their sexual vitality is strong and they have feminine features, even in men. Yet they have strength and endurance and a reserve of vital energy.

Venus types usually have good health and longevity and love life. They like to keep their bodies in good shape but may get more caught in outer beauty than in real physical fitness. They try to look young, even if it means resorting to makeup, surgery or other corrective measures. They suffer mainly from diseases of self-indulgence and from problems of the reproductive system.

Psychologically, Venus people are romantically inclined, though often with a degree of vanity. Relationship problems or losses affect them more deeply than the other types. They are strongly socially minded and prefer to do things with others, if not for public show. Yet they are usually receptive and can be quite vulnerable, particularly if the Moon in their charts is afflicted. They possess colorful imaginations and have vivid dreams, along with various creative capacities.

Venus types love comfort and elegance and like to adorn things, starting with their own bodies. They enjoy fine jewelry and beautiful homes and are often good at business and sales. They have a good sense of form and often become good artists or designers. Like other Kapha types, they can easily get into accumulating wealth and property, and particularly collecting objects of art. Yet Venus types accumulate things more for social value than for simple investment. Their lives often revolve around gaining and holding the positive opinions and feelings of others. They like to lead others, but more out of a desire to charm than a need to dominate.

Venus types are generally ethical and they often possess genuine love and devotion. However, they will bend the truth to suit their desires and like to project beauty, glamour or illusion as to what they want. Their spiritual inclinations are mainly toward the path of devotion and Divine love (Bhakti Yoga), as well as to Tantra. They incline to psychic pursuits as well and many astrologers have strong Venuses in their charts.

Astrological Factors

Venus types are created by a strong Venus in the chart, like Venus located in the Ascendant or in other angular houses, particularly if it is also placed in its own sign (Taurus or Libra) or sign of exaltation (Pisces). Venus ruled Ascendants (Taurus or Libra) usually create

Venus types, unless another planet aspects both the Ascendant and Venus. Taurus or Libra Moon or Sun signs are contributing factors.

The aspect of Venus on the Ascendant and its lord is most important. It is also best if Venus is not combust, which weakens it. Though Venus will not suffer if it is simply in the same sign as the Sun, it becomes weak if it is within ten degrees of the Sun, particularly if less than five degrees.

Saturn Types

Saturn types are usually the least attractive of the planetary types. They possess typical Vata frames, being overly tall or short, thin and bony. They may have large noses or large teeth. Their hands and feet tend to be large. Their skin is often dry, rough or cracked and tinged brown or black. Their hair is often brittle and their nails may be cracked. However, when Saturn's influence is modified by Venus, they can possess a certain beauty or mystery, though they generally remain on the lean and dry side.

Saturn types are the most disease prone of the planetary types. They often have low vitality and poor endurance. They run cold in terms of both temperature and temperament and have poor digestion and poor circulation. They tend towards constipation and to the accumulation of waste materials in the body. When Saturn is strongly afflicted, they are often chronically ill and may die young. They are prone to degenerative diseases like arthritis or nervous system disorders. However, a strong Saturn does give good longevity and the ability to survive disease and hardship.

Psychologically, Saturn types are serious minded. They are at best practical and realistic, at worst pessimistic and may suffer from depression. They are generally introverted and solitary and either selfish or detached. The many difficulties they have to face in life can make them insensitive to the needs of others. They may be miserly and over calculating. As what they gain in life only comes through much effort, they are generally unwilling to share it and do not like to give it up. They tend to worry, fear or anxiety, seldom smile and are rarely really happy or carefree. While they work hard, they often end up in servile roles and seldom get the recognition that they deserve.

However, a more expressive and sensitive Saturn type does exist, particularly if Saturn's influence is mollified by Venus or Mercury. They can become good doctors, artists or philosophers, with a strong work dedication and selflessness. Higher Saturn types are yogis, ascetics or monks who renounce the world, preferring solitude. They possess detachment and are free of their emotional nature. They are beyond the concerns of the world.

Lower Saturn types may be criminals, underworld figures or tyrants (particularly when the influence of Saturn combines with that of Mars). They are suspicious and paranoid, greedy and selfish. They are trapped within the narrow bounds of their own ego and bodily concerns and cannot get out of them by their own action.

Astrological Factors

Saturn types are created by a strong Saturn in the chart, like Saturn located in the Ascendant or in other angular houses, particularly if it is also placed in its own sign (Capricorn or Aquarius) or sign of exaltation (Libra). Saturn ruled Ascendants (Capricorn or Aquarius) usually create Saturn types, unless another planet dominates both Saturn and the Ascendant. Capricorn or Aquarius Moon or Sun signs are contributing factors.

Saturn's aspects to the Ascendant and its lord are most important. As Saturn aspects the signs third and tenth from it, these aspects must be weighed carefully. Saturn in the eleventh house is often strong, aspecting the Ascendant and being located in the best upachaya house (house of increase) where it usually does well. Yet Saturn in the fourth house can also be strong, aspecting both the house of the mind and the Ascendant. Saturn with the Sun or the Moon contributes to a Saturn influence on the person, through it is not always healthy.

Rahu Types

Rahu types have a certain mysteriousness or unpredictability around them, like shadowy Rahu itself that can eclipse the Sun or Moon, which makes them hard to understand. There is a kind of cloud around them, which can have its allure or attraction, or can function like a shadow having a disturbing affect upon us.

Rahu types are mainly Vata in their physical and mental traits, with a mixture of Saturn and Venus traits that can afford them a certain unusual or dark beauty. They are generally thin in build and quick in movement with sensitive nervous and digestive systems. They are not strongly present in their bodies and can seem to be spaced out. Their immune systems may be weak and they are more susceptible to contagious disease than other types, as well as to degenerative and nervous system disorders. They often suffer from insomnia and difficult dreams.

Relative to psychology, Rahu types are usually intelligent, intuitive and creative but in an unconventional manner. They are often scattered or wishful in their thinking.

While they are good at creating new ideas, they are not always successful at making them work. Emotionally they are also sensitive, moody and changeable. Their egos are inflated but weak. They often suffer from a certain vanity and have unrealistic desires. They are more prone to emotional imbalance than the other types.

Rahu types like to cast a spell or web around others and are good at art, music, performing, acting and designing. They do better in new circumstances and are often on the cutting edge of new changes and revolutions in society. They are particularly good at working with the mass media, which is a Rahu type business. They do better working with outsiders, with foreigners or in foreign countries and often live away from their family or place of origin.

Rahu individuals are ambitious and want to achieve great things, though they often fail at ordinary actions and easily overextend themselves. When they do achieve great success in the world, it is often unfulfilling to them personally and may cause them psychological problems. They tend to live beyond what they are able to accomplish.

On a psychic or spiritual level Rahu types are often possessed by something, whether it is another entity, curses, unfulfilled longings from past lives, or simply driven by their own imagination. While they incline towards psychic, occult and astral pursuits, these can be dangerous for them as they have a lot of vulnerability to subtle energies. They may become mediums, do channeling or practice Tantra but are easily caught in illusions about what they do. They often have good healing powers and a great deal of empathy and can be very devoted. While interested in astrology, they usually do better at an intuitive level as they are seldom good at calculation.

Astrological Factors

Rahu types are indicated by a strong Rahu in the chart. Most important is Rahu on the Ascendant or Rahu with the Ascendant lord. Rahu with the Moon or the Sun is also significant. Rahu located in angles (particularly the tenth house) or Rahu in upachaya houses (three, six, and eleven) are contributing factors.

A strong lord of Rahu (ruler of the sign in which Rahu is located) also can be important. Rahu located in an angular house with its ruler located in a trine house (or vice versa) is another factor of strength. Often Rahu, because of its shadowy nature is more of a secondary planetary type.

Ketu Types

Ketu types resemble Mars types, and are usually Pitta in their constitution, with moderate height and build, wiry, a little muscular, and running on the warm side. Yet they also have secondary Vata characteristics, being lean, nervous, dry, and having a fast metabolism.

Their eyes are particularly piercing and probing. Their circulation is strong but with a tendency to toxic blood conditions, skin diseases, ulcers and hypertension. They often suffer from neuromuscular disorders and may have a lack of coordination. They are prone to accidents, require surgery, or suffer from violence as in wars and other mass catastrophes.

Psychologically, Ketus are independent thinkers but with a fixation on some particular cause or project that can become an obsession. They are introverted and individualistic to the point of eccentricity. They go their own way and may rebel against the social order. They may debase themselves by following lower social influences. They are intolerant of criticism and react in a strongly defensive manner. They possess a lot of self-doubt and can be self-destructive. Yet emotionally they are often preoccupied, unresponsive, if not insensitive.

We find Ketu types in Mars ruled professions like the military, law or police but usually taking the more research-oriented or investigative roles. They are also good in science and mathematics and excel with computer work. They are fascinated with the past and may make good historians, archaeologists or geologists. Ketu types have sharp, perceptive and discriminating minds. They are good at concentration and deep examination to the point of forgetting all else. They are best at obscure studies and are able to find the light even in darkness.

Ketu is the indicator of astrologers, psychics and those with much occult knowledge, so many Ketu types can be found in these spiritual fields as well. Higher Ketu-types are yogis (Jnanis) and possess much spiritual knowledge and realization. They see the illusory and transient nature of all the things of the world and can go their own way regardless of outer circumstances. They are able to see through and go beyond the ego. They may not always be recognized or appreciated but they find happiness in their own studies and pursuits.

Astrological Factors

Ketu types are indicated by a strong Ketu in the chart, particularly by Ketu on the Ascendant or with the Ascendant lord. Ketu with the Sun or Moon is also significant. Ketu in the twelfth house, with which it has a special affinity, is another factor. Ketu like Rahu, as a shadowy planet, is often more of a secondary type in the chart.

More Complex Planetary and Doshic Types

While planets generally follow their dominant dosha, exceptions to this rule do exist, particularly for planets that reflect more than one dosha. The Moon and Venus, though primarily Kapha, have secondary Vata qualities. Ketu, though primarily Pitta, has secondary Vata qualities. Mars, though primarily Pitta, has secondary Kapha qualities. Jupiter, though primarily Kapha, has secondary Pitta characteristics. Mercury, though primarily Vata, has secondary Kapha characteristics. So it is not unusual, for example, to speak of a Vata Moon type or a Pitta Jupiter type.

Ultimately we can cross reference the three doshic and nine planetary types into twenty-seven total doshic and planetary types. For example, under Vata, the norm is Mercury, Saturn or Rahu Vata types, with Moon, Venus and Ketu sometimes occurring as Vata types. However, there are some instances in which we can speak of Vata-Sun, Vata-Mars or Vata-Jupiter types. Such additional types occur when the planetary energy is dominant at a karmic or life-experience level, but a different dosha prevails at a physical or health level. Yet as these variations are exceptional, we will not delineate them here.

In addition, our human interactions color how we interpret the types of other people. We react to others relative to how their planets affect our own, not the other person's dominant planet overall. For example, if another person's Mars is conjunct our Moon, we may find them to be martial or Pitta in energy, when it is simply a case of their Mars being unfavorably placed relative to our chart. For this reason, we should not judge planetary types by our personal assessments alone without duly examining the birth chart.

Disease Factors in Vedic Astrology

5

OUR state of health reflects our interaction with our environment, which on the level of subtle and cosmic forces includes the influences of the planets. Too much or too little of a planet's energy in a person's birth chart, like too much heat or cold externally, can cause disease. In this chapter we will examine the relationship between astrological imbalances and disease conditions.

BENEFIC AND MALEFIC PLANETS

For determining their overall results, planets are divided into two groups: benefic or expansive and malefic or restrictive. Benefic planets usually promote health and malefics cause disease. Yet this is only a general rule. Malefic planets cause disease owing to their destructive effects, but can increase resistance to disease if well-placed. Benefic planets work to create positive health if well placed in the chart but can cause disease when poorly placed. In this regard, the Sanskrit for malefic is krura, which means 'forceful in action'. The term for benefic is saumya, or 'gentle in action'. We need the right balance of aggressive and gentle energies, though the harsh energies more often cause us pain.

- Malefic (Krura) Planets—Saturn, Mars, Rahu, Ketu, Sun
- Benefic (Saumya) Planets—Jupiter, Venus, Moon, Mercury

Saturn is the greatest malefic influence over the long term, promoting the forces of decay, degeneration and death. Mars can be a great malefic as well but tends towards short term action, causing sudden accidents, injuries or infections. Rahu is like Saturn but acts on a subtle or psychological level, disturbing the mind and nervous system. Ketu is similar to Mars but like Rahu operates on a subtle or psychological level overheating the mind and nervous system. The Sun's influence on health is dual; as a general malefic it works to weaken or burn up the factors in the chart that it influences, but as the significator of the self and vitality it serves to benefit the health of a person.

Jupiter is the great and enduring prime benefic promoting long term health, wealth, wisdom and happiness. Venus is an important benefic as well but not as lasting in its results as Jupiter; it gives happiness, wealth, enjoyment and creative powers of a more short term nature. The Moon is generally benefic but can become malefic if located too close to the Sun, which weakens its brightness. As a rule, if the Moon is sixty degrees or more from the Sun it is benefic;[22] otherwise it is malefic. Mercury is benefic in itself, aiding in harmonious thought, action and expression, but easily takes on the influences of malefic planets if conjoined with them.[23]

Relative to Ayurveda, we must remember that Vata dosha, which generally indicates the forces of decay, causes the greatest number of diseases, particularly those of a degenerative nature or debilitating in long term effects. Pitta is second to Vata as a disease-causing dosha, producing febrile, infectious and bleeding disorders, which are generally acute. Kapha is third, providing physical strength and stamina, but causing diseases from excess indulgence, lack of activity or overweight, conditions that are usually chronic but mild in their results.

A good rule to remember is: Weak planets in the birth chart, both benefic and malefic, generally cause Vata disorders, even if the planets themselves are of Pitta or Kapha qualities. Planetary weakness as a whole translates more into Vata problems, which cover most conditions of physical weakness and degeneration.

Yet a strong Saturn and Rahu, which are both malefics and Vata in their influences, also mainly cause Vata problems if they afflict the factors of health in the chart like the Ascendant or its lord. Strong Pitta planets, like the Sun, Mars and Ketu, on the other hand, generally cause Pitta problems if so placed. Strong Kapha planets usually cause Kapha diseases only if the combinations are not harmonious, like Jupiter–Venus aspects or influences (Jupiter and Venus are enemies in Vedic astrology).

SATURN

Saturn is the general significator of disease, old age and death, representing the negative power of time. It produces chronic and wasting diseases, constitutional and congenital weaknesses, conditions of low vitality, weak digestion and poor resistance to disease.

Saturn causes overall depression of bodily and mental energy and hypofunction of all organs and systems. Diseases arising from the accumulation of waste-materials or the inability to discharge them properly are under the domain of Saturn, from constipation to the build up of all manner of toxins. Saturn's slowing and reducing effect causes numbness, stiffness, rigidity, spasms, tremors and pain. Afflictions of Saturn, particularly as combined with Mars, can result in surgery, causing our body to be disfigured or our organs to be removed.

Saturn-related diseases include arthritis, rheumatism, broken bones or osteoporosis, nervous disorders of various types, pain and paralysis, and hard to treat conditions like cancer. Saturn causes premature aging, deafness, failure of vision, emaciation, tremors, deformity and poor growth. It gives deficiency of vital fluids, infertility, impotence, dehydration, pain and itch.

Yet a well-placed Saturn provides good longevity, as well as resistance to disease or the ability to recover from disease. Psychologically, it grants coolness and calmness of mind and the strengths and virtues of discipline and self-control.

RAHU

Rahu indicates mysterious and difficult to treat diseases of various types. It shows collective health problems like epidemics and plagues, and can cause weakness of the immune system, a break down of the endocrine system and degenerative diseases like cancer. It indicates poisons, pollution, radiation and other environmental problems. It gives nervous indigestion, loss of appetite and parasites. It indicates the use of drugs, whether medicinal or recreational, and their side effects.

Rahu causes psychological and nervous disorders, including stress, insomnia, bad dreams, palpitations, tremors, insanity, and paralysis. It produces neurosis, hysteria, vertigo, fright and convulsions. When highly afflicted, it can make a person suicidal or manic-depressive.

Rahu's disease-causing effects are strongly feared in Vedic astrology and should be carefully examined in the chart. However, they are unlikely to manifest unless triggered by the influence of another malefic (like Mars or Saturn) by aspect or association, or if Rahu strongly influences the Ascendant or another benefic, particularly the Moon.

A well-placed Rahu, on the other hand, provides a strong immune system, psychological adaptability, and good karma, including access to good health care as needed.

Mars

Mars represents injury and accidents, particularly those that cause bleeding, including surgery. It indicates acute infectious diseases, with elevated temperature and the build up of toxins. It produces fever, inflammation and burning sensations of various types.

Mars causes liver and gall bladder disorders including hepatitis, jaundice and cancer of the liver. It produces toxic blood conditions including acne, boils and ulcerative sores, herpes and venereal diseases. It results in blood disorders like anemia and cancer of the blood or leukemia. It produces stress, hypertension, stroke and heart attack, covering most of the conditions of high Pitta.

A well-placed Mars, on the other hand, gives good physical and sexual vitality, athletic ability, work capacity and resistance to disease. It is an important indicator of positive health and vitality.

Ketu

Ketu like Rahu causes mysterious, collective or psychological imbalances. It indicates mass catastrophes, wars or accidents involving larger numbers of people. At a physical level, it causes neuromuscular disorders, cancer and febrile diseases, particularly those that damage the brain or nervous system. Like Mars it causes infection, bleeding or toxicity but often at a deeper level of the blood or nervous system. It makes a person prone to surgery, including wrong surgical practices.

A well-placed Ketu, on the other hand, gives resistance to disease, acuity of the mind and senses, and physical strength and agility. It can provide us the insight and intelligence to avoid disease-causing factors in life.

Sun

The Sun as the source of light and life is the general giver of health, vitality and energy. When strong it promotes overall physical and mental harmony and well-being. Yet, when afflicting other planets or houses of health, the Sun can cause fiery Pitta diseases, much like Mars. It makes us prone to circulatory system disorders, including heart attacks. It can give high fevers that exhaust the body fluids.

When weak or afflicted, on the other hand, the Sun gives chronic and wasting disorders, generally Vata or Pitta problems. These include weak heart, poor digestion, ulcers, degenerated metabolic functions (like hypotension or hypothyroid), arthritis, and poor vision or failure of the eyesight. Usually in these cases there is also pallor and anemia, and the resistance to disease is low.

Moon

The Moon causes diseases mainly when weak, which results mainly in airy diseases or Vata problems. The lungs may be weak, the vital fluids insufficient, and the mucous membranes easily dry or damaged. In the extreme, there may be asthma, pneumonia or other pulmonary disorders. Nervous or emotional imbalances are likely, with moodiness, depression or hysteria. There is often insomnia, bad dreams and lack of mental calm or peace.

When strong but badly placed the Moon gives Kapha disorders, with excessive mucous in the system, swollen lymph glands, or the formation of tumors (generally benign). It will give edema and other water retention, kidney or fluid problems, overweight and inertia. Afflictions to the Moon also negatively impact fertility and reproduction.

A well-placed Moon, however, provides a well-developed physique, good vital fluids, emotional balance and mental fortitude, reflecting a good genetic inheritance and access to positive health care.

Mercury

A weak Mercury, like a weak Moon, causes mainly airy or Vata diseases, with weak lungs and a sensitive nervous system. It results in cough, allergies (both skin and food allergies) and hay fever. There may be speech defects, hypersensitivity, lack of intelligence, growth difficulties (endocrine problems) or poor coordination. Such problems are more likely in childhood.

A strong Mercury, however, gives good health, healing powers, mind-body coordination and strong endocrine function, as well as the intelligence to handle disease. It is an important factor of positive physical and mental health and adaptability.

Venus

Venus, when weak, mainly causes airy or Vata disorders. The kidneys and reproductive systems are the main problem areas. For women there will be infertility, menstrual irregularity or menstrual pain and cramping, with a tendency to miscarriage. For men there will be impotence, prostate problems or other reproductive limitations. There may be chronic kidney or bladder infections or stones in the urinary tract. The complexion will be poor and the skin will lack in moisture or softness.

A strong Venus, however, gives good health and vitality through a strong reproductive system and overall good creative energy and love of life. It is an important factor for good longevity.

Jupiter

Jupiter is the planet of positive health, promoting vitality, healing and good living habits on all levels. A strong Jupiter can go far to mitigate any other disease-causing influences in the chart.

When poorly disposed, Jupiter mainly causes watery or Kapha diseases. As a planet of expansion, it produces overweight, edema and diabetes. This can lead to poor circulation, accumulation of cholesterol and weak liver function leading to heart attacks and other problems. Jupiter may cause tumors but generally these will be benign. It can give excessive growth of the tissues of all kinds.

When weak and afflicted by malefics, Jupiter more commonly causes airy or Vata diseases like emaciation, lack of strength, shortness of breath, nervous disorders and hormonal imbalance.

Signs and Houses and Disease

The houses are a twelvefold division of the sky based upon the point of the zodiac rising on the eastern horizon. Their meanings are similar in both Vedic and western astrology. However, in the Vedic system the house cusp marks the middle of the house, not its beginning as in the western system, which causes some differences in their calculation and placement.

The houses parallel the signs in terms of many of their indications, with some variations. The signs and houses as fields of activity correspond to certain parts of the body as follows:

1. ARIES governs the head, the brain and the eyes, specifically the front of the head down to the eyes and the back of the head to the

base of the skull. It reflects the Mars, fiery or Pitta energy in the head. The first house similarly rules the head and the brain.

2. TAURUS governs the face, the upper neck to the larynx and the back of the neck to the shoulders, including the cerebellum. It reflects the Venus, watery or Kapha energy in the face and neck. The second house governs the same regions, particularly the vocal cords and the faculty of speech.

3. GEMINI governs the shoulders, the upper arms and upper chest, including the lungs. It reflects the Mercury, airy or Vata energy of movement and expression in the upper region of the body. The third house governs the same regions, particularly the arms.

4. CANCER governs the front part of the chest to the border of the ribs and the elbows, including the stomach and the breasts. It reflects the lunar, Kapha or watery energy in the chest, heart, lungs and stomach. The stomach, which is like the mother, is the main site of Kapha in Ayurveda. The fourth house governs the same regions, particularly the emotional aspect of the heart.

5. LEO governs the solar plexus region and the middle back region, including the small intestines, as well as body vitality in general through the heart. It reflects the solar, fiery or Pitta energy in the circulatory and digestive system and Pitta's connection with the blood. The fifth house governs similar regions, but is also connected to the intellectual mind and to the reproductive system, the capacity to have children in either women or men, reflecting the child that is held in the belly.

6. VIRGO governs the middle and lower abdomen, including the colon. It also governs the hands. It rules over the digestive system in general, as well as bodily health as a whole. It reflects the Mercurial - earthy and Vata - energy in the large intestine, which is the main site of Vata in Ayurveda. The sixth house has similar associations relative to overall health, digestion and the lower abdomen.

7. LIBRA governs the lower abdomen and the lumbar region, including the kidneys and internal genitalia. It reflects the Venus, airy and Vata energy in the sex organs and more specifically the female reproductive system. The seventh house has similar associations to the reproductive system and sexuality.

8. SCORPIO governs the sacrum, rectum, bladder and external sex organs of the male. These reflect mainly a Mars energy, including male sexual vitality. The eighth house has similar indications of sexual vitality and governs the same regions of the body.

9. SAGITTARIUS governs the arteries, the lower back, hips and thighs. These are largely Pitta systems of action and expression but also sites where Kapha or bodily fat can accumulate. The ninth house has similar associations to the hips and surrounding region of the body.

10. CAPRICORN governs the bones and joints as well as the knees in particular. The bones and joints are mainly sites of Vata and reflect a Saturn energy. The tenth house also governs the knees and our standing in life.

11. AQUARIUS governs the power of exhalation and the skin, as well as the calves. It reflects the Saturn, airy and Vata energy that works through these regions. The eleventh house has similar indications.

12. PISCES governs the lymphatic system as well as the feet. It reflects the Jupiter, Kapha and watery energy that sustains the body. The twelfth house has similar indications.

An important principle of Vedic astrology is that if both the sign and house of the same number are afflicted, the corresponding bodily part suffers. For example, if Saturn aspects the ninth sign Sagittarius, the ninth house and their rulers, arthritis or paralysis of the hips is likely. If Saturn aspects the fifth house from the Ascendant, the fifth house from the Moon and their rulers, there is likely to be infertility in women, with possible surgery or hysterectomy. It is important to cross-reference signs and houses in order to verify the results of planetary influences.

Signs, Houses and Disease Tendencies

The signs and houses show potential health problems in the regions that they rule.

1. ARIES AND THE FIRST HOUSE indicate fevers, headaches, brain disorders, strokes, cerebral bleeding, injuries to the skull and head, as well as difficulties at the time of birth.

2. TAURUS AND THE SECOND HOUSE indicate swelling of the neck, sore throat, thyroid problems, obesity, injury to the face or throat, dental problems, or childhood diseases like colds, flu, mumps

and measles.

3. GEMINI AND THE THIRD HOUSE indicate cough, pulmonary disorders, asthma and injury to the shoulders, as well as nervous disorders, agitation and poor musculo-skeletal coordination.

4. CANCER AND THE FOURTH HOUSE indicate lung problems, dropsy and injury to the chest, breast tumors and breast cancer as well as emotional disturbances.

5. LEO AND THE FIFTH HOUSE indicate lack of vitality, weakness of the heart and solar plexus, stomach and digestive problems, and lack of fertility or menstrual problems.

6. VIRGO AND THE SIXTH HOUSE indicate poor digestion, malabsorption, gas, constipation, ulcers, food allergies, hypoglycemia, diabetes and appendicitis, along with immune system weakness.

7. LIBRA AND THE SEVENTH HOUSE indicate urinary disorders, infertility in women, venereal diseases and sexual vitality problems.

8. SCORPIO AND THE EIGHTH HOUSE indicate hemorrhoids, rectal cancer, blood disorders, impotence in men, and venereal diseases.

9. SAGITTARIUS AND THE NINTH HOUSE indicate obesity, arteriosclerosis, paralysis below the waist, arthritis in the hips or injury to the hips.

10. CAPRICORN AND THE TENTH HOUSE indicate weakness, injury or arthritis of the knees, as well as weakness of the bones in general.

11. AQUARIUS AND THE ELEVENTH HOUSE indicate poor circulation, skin disorders, weakness in the lower legs and nervous system problems.

12. PISCES AND THE TWELFTH HOUSE indicate lymphatic disorders, hypoglycemia, diabetes, tumors, trouble with the feet and fungal infections.

THE SIX/TWELVE AXIS

The sixth house and the sixth sign Virgo, which govern the lower abdomen, the colon and digestive nerves, are particularly important in determining a person's disease potential. The opposite twelfth house and sign Pisces, which govern emotional and metabolic balance, are also crucial. This means that the sixth house/twelfth house axis in the birth chart is very important for both physical and psychological health.

Virgo governs Vata, the biological air humor in the body, in general. As most diseases are of this humor, planets in Virgo tend to cause disease. On the other hand, planets in this sign can make one a healer if they are well disposed. Sometimes disease makes us turn to healing. Virgo shows service to the physical body, either our own or that of others.

- The Sun in Virgo makes a person prone to poor digestion, ulcers, constipation or appendicitis.
- The Moon in Virgo results in an emotionally sensitive digestion, food allergies and difficulty digesting dairy products.
- Mars in Virgo causes ulcers, intestinal bleeding, excessive appetite and sometimes diabetes.
- Mercury in Virgo is generally good for health as it is located in its own sign, but causes a nervous and sensitive digestion, particularly when afflicted.
- Jupiter in Virgo can cause obesity, diabetes or hypoglycemia, but can also aid in health and healing.
- Venus in Virgo causes hypoglycemia, diabetes and infertility and can render the emotional nature sensitive or vain.
- Saturn in Virgo causes constipation, distention, low appetite, malabsorption and arthritis.
- Rahu in Virgo causes nervous digestion or nervous weakness generally, with a weak immune system.
- Ketu in Virgo causes ulcers, intestinal bleeding, surgery on the intestines, and other problems similar in nature to those caused by Mars.

Planets located in the corresponding sixth house of disease can similarly cause weak health. Benefic planets suffer from location in the sixth, particularly if afflicted. The Moon in the sixth house causes weak digestion and emotional upset. Mercury in the sixth gives sensitivity in the nervous and digestive systems. Venus causes weakness to the urinary and genital tracts. Jupiter gives trouble with the liver and pancreas, though it can promote healing and support one in becoming a medical practitioner.

Malefic planets – the Sun, Mars, Saturn, Rahu and Ketu – are not bad for health if located in the sixth house (which is an upachaya house good for malefics) and not afflicted. They give a good immune system and the ability to overcome disease. Malefics when afflicted in the sixth house, however, can cause much harm. In this regard, one malefic when unafflicted in the sixth is usually good for health, but more than one can cause disease. Also if a malefic afflicts both the sixth house and its lord it can also cause trouble, even if by itself in the sixth house.

HOUSES OF HEALTH AND DISEASE

For examining overall health, the first house or Ascendant is the most important factor because it is the house of the body (Tanur-bhava). The fifth is the house of positive health, creativity and sexual vitality. The ninth is the house of the overall good fortune that improves the health as well.

An important rule in Vedic astrology is that benefic planets (Moon, Jupiter, Venus and Mercury) perform best when located in angular or trine houses (1, 4, 5, 7, 9 and 10), the main positive houses in the chart. In such positions they aid in health, physically or psychologically. It is said that Jupiter in angle will protect us even from all manner of diseases. Venus has a similar effect, although not to the same degree, as does Mercury or any natural benefic.

On the other hand, malefics in angular or trine houses damage the body, reduce our good fortune and weaken our health. Saturn or Mars in angles, for example, often cause health problems, particularly if they also aspect the Ascendant or its lord.

The main houses of disease in the chart are houses 6, 8 and 12. The sixth indicates diseases that arise mainly through faulty digestion or weak immunity. The eighth indicates congenital or vitality problems, including catastrophic or debilitating diseases and epidemics. The twelfth is the house of loss and indicates weakness, debility or hospitalization. Planets located in these houses in the birth chart, particularly benefics, make a person prone to diseases.

The lords of these three houses, particularly the rulers of houses 6 and 8, have the power to cause disease by their aspects or association, especially with the Ascendant and its lord. The lords of houses 3 and

11 can also cause health problems.

Upachaya Houses, Houses of Resistance to Disease

Houses 3, 6 and 11 are houses of resistance to disease and relate to the immune system. Malefics here destroy disease and increase our immunity. Benefics do not do well in the sixth, but are not bad in the third and eleventh.

Such houses are called upachaya or increasing houses in Vedic astrology as their strength, like that of the immune system, increases over time. Saturn, Mars, the Sun, Rahu or Ketu do well in these houses. In fact these malefics placed in upachaya houses can be stronger in protecting our health than can well-placed benefics. Whenever we examine the chart, we should not overlook the strength of malefic planets in upachaya houses for protecting the health and overcoming disease.

Houses of Longevity and Maraka Houses (Death-causing Houses)

The first is the main house of longevity as it represents our overall vitality. The eighth is also a house of longevity (ayus), in that it indicates our term of life. The third house relates to longevity as well as to vitality. As the eighth house by position from the eighth house, the third house shares in eighth house indications. Longevity is indicated by the first, third and eighth houses.

Houses two and seven are special maraka or 'death-causing houses', because as the twelfth from the third and eighth houses of longevity, they represent their negation, which is death. Planets located in these houses as well as their lords have the power to cause death during their planetary periods. However, their negative effects will only occur if the rest of the chart is weak. Otherwise their influence will only show in old age (after the age of 65). Yet their health related influences should not be overlooked.

Effects of the Ascendant Lord in Different Houses

The Ascendant lord (planet ruling the rising sign) is the main significator of the body and the outer self. Its position is a key to the overall health and well-being of a person. Generally, it adds strength to any house in which it happens to be located, but when afflicted, particularly if located in difficult houses like 6, 8 and 12, it can cause significant health problems.

Ascendant Lord in the First House

Located in its own sign, the Ascendant lord is good for health and vitality as well as for overall expression and achievement in life, adding energy to the body and strengthening congenital vitality. However, if afflicted by malefics in this location, it can cause significant health problems from birth because both the Ascendant and its lord will be compromised. If aspected by Saturn or Rahu, long term Vata problems or degenerative disorders are possible. If afflicted by Mars, long term Pitta problems are likely, not only infectious conditions but also accidents and injuries.

Ascendant Lord in the Second House

The Ascendant lord in the second house makes a person expressive and creative with speech. It also gives a good appetite and discrimination about food. However, if the chart is otherwise weak, this is not a good position for health as the second is a maraka or death-causing house. If afflicted, it gives poor eating habits or lack of taste for food, as well as possible health problems in childhood.

Ascendant Lord in the Third House

The Ascendant lord in the third house is generally good for vitality as the third is a house of vital energy. It gives the person a strong curiosity along with many hobbies, interests and activities in life. This placement is good for sports, the fine arts, or other activities using the hands and senses. However, the third has some limitations for health and give a person an unhealthy or indulgent life-style or otherwise make them reckless and prone to accidents.

Ascendant Lord in the Fourth House

The Ascendant lord in the fourth house endows a person with an emotional bent of mind, creating a heart centered temperament deeply concerned with home and happiness. Yet this placement can also render a person emotionally sensitive and if afflicted can make a person prone to psychological disorders. Then the person will take whatever happens to them in an emotional manner for good or ill. The Ascendant lord in the fourth generally connects the person strongly with the mother and her psychology.

Ascendant Lord in the Fifth House

The Ascendant lord in the fifth house is generally favorable for health and creativity as the fifth is a house of positive health. It also gives a strong creative intelligence, good judgment and discrimination in life. Yet when afflicted it brings about wrong values and bad choices that can lead to health problems and the wrong use of our vitality.

Ascendant Lord in the Sixth House

The Ascendant lord in the sixth house of disease can indicate a congenitally weak or sickly constitution and have an overall reducing effect on immunity and longevity. If unafflicted, however, it provides a strong immune system and the ability to ward off disease or to recover from disease if the person falls ill.

Ascendant Lord in the Seventh House

The Ascendant lord in the seventh house gives the person a powerful expression and a strong capacity for relationship, although it generally makes them more career or public oriented rather_than personal or marriage oriented. As the seventh is also a maraka or death-causing house, this is not a good position for health if the chart is otherwise weak.

Ascendant Lord in the Eight House

The Ascendant lord in the eighth house, if afflicted, makes a person prone to severe or catastrophic diseases or accidents that involve a collapse of vitality or even early death. Unafflicted, however, it provides a good longevity and a strong immune system. It can also indicate a person with profound research ability and deep insight. As the house of longevity (ayus), it can give knowledge of Ayurveda or other medical skills.

Ascendant Lord in the Ninth House

The Ascendant lord in the ninth house is a helpful position for overall health and good fortune. It opens a person up to a positive flow of grace and good karma from God, family (father particularly) and society. It is excellent for educational and religious gains and increase of reputation.

Ascendant Lord in the Tenth House

The Ascendant lord in the tenth house gives prominence in career and a strong active energy that is generally good for overall health and vitality. The person likes to be a leader, prominent in the public and successful in career. However, the person may sacrifice health for career or suffer health problems if the career does not go well.

Ascendant Lord in the Eleventh House

The Ascendant lord generally does well in the eleventh, which is a house of abundance and achievement. It affords power and influence along with the fulfillment of ones goals in life. But as a secondary house of disease (sixth from the sixth), this position can also indicate health problems, if other factors show the same.

Ascendant Lord in the Twelfth House

The Ascendant Lord in the twelfth house makes one prone to low vitality, chronic fatigue, weakness and depression. It can show time spent behind the scenes, out of ones country, in a hospital or in convalescence. On the positive side, it can indicate work as a healer or a doctor and gives a generous and compassionate nature with a strong spiritual inclination.

Timing of Disease

The birth chart indicates the basic potentials of our life. When these potentials will manifest is dependent upon timing that is reflected through astrological indications. In Vedic astrology there are three main factors of astrological timing: 1) planetary periods, 2) annual charts and 3) transits. As this is a matter of technical astrology, we will only examine it briefly.

Planetary Periods/Vimshottari Dasha

Special planetary periods are one of the hallmarks of the Vedic system and its predictive accuracy. Most important among the Vedic systems of planetary periods is the Vimshottari or 120-year cycle, which is based upon the Moon's degree within the Nakshatra (lunar asterism) at the moment of birth, which exactly determines the starting point within the cycle. Each planet governs a portion of this 120-year cycle with the Sun governing for 6 years, Moon for 10 years, Mars for 7 years, Rahu for 18 years, Jupiter for 16 years, Saturn for 19 years, Mercury for 17 years, Ketu for 7 years and Venus for 20 years – in that order. These major periods in turn are divided into minor periods according to the same proportions.

Planetary periods of malefic planets – Saturn, Rahu, Mars and Ketu – tend to cause disease for all charts. More specifically, the periods of lords of difficult houses, like houses 6, 8 and 12, have negative health implications. The period of the lord of the first house or Ascendant lord, if weak, can also cause disease because events relative to the body, which it rules, come out during its period.

The periods of the lords of houses 2 and 7 (maraka or death-dealing houses) can cause health problems, particularly if they occur later in life, or if the chart otherwise does not indicate good vitality. If the chart is otherwise strong, their periods will not usually result in health problems.

Other planetary period systems like Yogini Dasha, Jaimini Chara Dasha or Ashtottari Dasha (108-year cycle) may be examined as well. Many Vedic astrologers like to confirm their predictions by cross-referencing more than one Dasha system.

The Annual Chart or Varshaphal

The solar return, annual chart or Varshaphal in Sanskrit is an important indicator for all the events of the year, including health and happiness. It differs a few hours from the birthday time because it is based upon the actual return of the Sun to the same position in the sky at birth (its sidereal return), not simply the calendar time. This annual chart is called Varshaphal, which means 'the results of the year'. Astrologers should always examine it in relation to the timing of important issues.[24]

Transits (Gochara)

Transits are current positions of the planets. As transiting planets cross over positions in the birth chart, they trigger various events. Transits of malefic planets such as Saturn, Mars or Rahu and Ketu over sensitive points in the chart relative to physical or mental health like the Ascendant, Moon or Sun can cause health problems. This is particularly true if a planetary period that is adverse for the health is running at the same time, or if the Varshaphal overall is not strong.

Unlike Western astrology, which often looks at transits first, transits in Vedic astrology are employed at a tertiary level, after planetary periods and the annual chart, which itself marks the main transits for the year. Yet their influence cannot be ignored. While the general potential must be there in the Dasha system, the transits show when these are specifically actualized. Transits of or to the Dasha lord (planet ruling the current planetary period) are most important.

Health Potentials of the Nakshatras

Nakshatra	Starting Point	Ruler	Quality
1. Ashvini	00 00 Aries	Ketu	Quick
2. Bharani	13 20 Aries	Venus	Fierce
3. Krittika	26 40 Aries	Sun	Mixed
4. Rohini	10 00 Taurus	Moon	Fixed
5. Mrigashira	23 20 Taurus	Mars	Tender
6. Ardra	06 40 Gemini	Rahu	Harsh
7. Punarvasu	20 00 Gemini	Jupiter	Changeable
8. Pushya	03 20 Cancer	Saturn	Quick
9. Aslesha	16 40 Cancer	Mer-cury	Harsh
10. Magha	00 00 Leo	Ketu	Fierce
11. Purva Phalguni	13 20 Leo	Venus	Fierce
12. Uttara Phalguni	26 40 Leo	Sun	Fixed
13. Hasta	10 00 Virgo	Moon	Quick
14. Chitra	23 20 Virgo	Mars	Tender
15. Svati	06 40 Libra	Rahu	Changeable
16. Vishakha	20 00 Libra	Jupiter	Mixed

Nakshatra	Starting Point	Ruler	Quality
17. Anuradha	03 20 Scorpio	Saturn	Tender
18. Jyeshtha	16 40 Scorpio	Mercury	Harsh
19. Mula	00 00 Sagittarius	Ketu	Harsh
20. Purvashadha	13 20 Sagittarius	Venus	Fierce
21. Uttarashadha	26 40 Sagittarius	Sun	Fixed
22. Shravana	10 00 Capricorn	Moon	Changeable
23. Dhanishta	23 20 Capricorn	Mars	Changeable
24. Shatabhishak	06 40 Aquarius	Rahu	Changeable
25. Purvabhadra	20 00 Aquarius	Jupiter	Fierce
26. Uttarabhadra	03 20 Pisces	Saturn	Fixed
27. Revati	16 40 Pisces	Mercury	Tender

I will only give an introduction to the Nakshatras here as these will be the subject of a separate and more extensive study in an upcoming book. The Nakshatras are defined mainly in reference to the position of the Moon, which transits one Nakshatra a day, though they can be applied as well to the position of other planets. We can best understand the Nakshatras through examining them from three primary perspectives.

The first perspective is relative to the nature of the signs that they are a part of. The Nakshatras cover less than half a sign each (a total of 13 degrees 20 minutes). They reflect the portion of the signs that they constitute, adding specificity to the smaller area they cover but not contradicting the basic meaning of the signs and their ruling planets. For example, the first Nakshatra Ashvini will reflect the energies of the first section of the sign Aries in which it is located, and will further define the Aries qualities specific to this portion of the sign. This perspective is important for interpretive purposes.

The second perspective is relative to the planets ruling the Nakshatras, and this perspective is more important for predictive purposes. The

Nakshatras have their own ruling planets, which are different from the planets ruling the signs they are in and may even be inimical to them (for example, Venus ruled Nakshatras are located in fiery signs ruled by Mars, Sun and Jupiter, natural enemies of Venus). This is because the Nakshatra lord, unlike the sign lord that reflects interpretation based on location in space, reflects rather the unfoldment of planetary energies through the movement of time. This temporal influence of the Nakshatra ruler comes out mainly during the periods of planets located in the Nakshatra in the birth chart.

The Nakshatras form the basic underlying structure of the most important Dasha or planetary period systems used in Vedic astrology, such as the most commonly used 120-year Vimshottari Dasha cycle. For predicting the timing of the unfoldment of events, the Nakshatra and Nakshatra lord of the Dasha lord (planet ruling the on-going planetary period) are most important. For example, if one is running a Venus Dasha, with Venus located at 2 degrees of Leo, in Magha, a Nakshatra ruled by Ketu, one must carefully examine the position of Ketu as well as the Sun (lord of Leo) for determining how the Dasha is likely to unfold.

The third perspective is relative to the individual qualities of the Nakshatras themselves, and is a significant factor for interpretation. In regards to this, there are both general and specific ways in which the Nakshatras are described in Vedic astrology. I am emphasizing the most basic and important such consideration, which divides the Nakshatras into seven types.[25]

1) Fixed (Dhruva) Nakshatras grant enduring positive results for actions performed under them. In terms of the birth chart, they give strength of character and physique and are good for both physical health and emotional well-being. They are generally the best of the Nakshatras.

Dhruva Nakshatras include the three Uttaras (Uttara Phalguni, Uttarashadha and Uttara Bhadra) as well as Rohini, which is regarded as the most favorable single Nakshatra for outer actions. A well-positioned Moon in these Nakshatras (strong in brightness, in a good house and under good aspect) is a great aid to the overall well-being of a person.

2) Harsh (Tikshna) Nakshatras are good for aggressive, assertive and destructive actions, but are unfavorable for creative and constructive matters. They often bring enmity and disease to those born under them,

giving harshness to the emotions and even to the body.

Tikshna Nakshatras include Aslesha, Mula and Jyeshtha, generally considered the three most inauspicious Nakshatras, and Ardra, which is also a difficult Nakshatra. A poorly placed Moon in these Nakshatras (weak in brightness, in a bad house or under malefic aspects) presents many challenges for the happiness and longevity of a person, starting with difficulties in childhood. This is particularly the case for people born with the Moon in the first quarter (three degrees twenty minutes) of Mula and the last quarter of Aslesha or Jyeshtha.[26]

3) Fierce (Ugra) Nakshatras are also good for aggressive and assertive actions but not to the same degree as Sharp Nakshatras. They give an edge to the character of a person and create some possibility of disease, but also make a person competitive and grant success through action.

Ugra Nakshatras include the three Purvas (Purva Phalguni, Purvashadha and Purva Bhadra) as well as Bharani and Magha. A poorly placed Moon (weak in brightness, in a bad house or under malefic aspect) augments the difficulties of these Nakshatras, but a well-placed Moon in them grants a person a good deal of strength and endurance. The placement of the Moon in the first quarter or three degrees twenty minutes of Magha is the most problematical of these.

4) Quick (Kshipra) Nakshatras are swift to bring positive results for actions performed under them but these results are not as enduring as those gained under Fixed Nakshatras. So while they are very auspicious, their results can be limited. They also afford quickness, agility and flexibility of body and mind and are good for health and movement.[27]

Kshipra Nakshatras consist of Ashvini, Hasta and Pushya (which, with the exception of the timing of marriage, is considered to be the best Nakshatra, particularly for spiritual matters). A well-placed Moon in a Kshipra Nakshatra grants a good deal of energy, creativity and vitality.

5) Tender (Mridu) Nakshatras are good for relationship, communication and artistic ventures. They give softness, sweetness, tenderness or sensitivity of the body and mind and are generally good for health and longevity.

Mridu Nakshatras consist of Mrigashira, Chitra, Anuradha and Revati. These Nakshatras are generally good for health although they may, in similarity to an afflicted Moon, give some degree of emotional vulnerability.

6) Mixed or Both Harsh and Tender (Mridu-Tikshna) Nakshatras

combine the qualities of both groups. They consist of Krittika and Vishakha only. They give competitive strength to a person but can make one vulnerable to disease, particularly during childhood.

7) Moveable (Chara) Nakshatras grant quick positive results but are temporary or superficial in their effects. They grant speed, adaptability and quick movement for both body and mind and so are not bad for the health, but can cause psychological instability, if afflicted. They are not as favorable as Quick or Kshipra Nakshatras which they resemble, but are generally good overall. Chara Nakshatras consist of Punarvasu, Svati, Shravana, Dhanishta and Shatabhishak.

In addition to this classification, certain Nakshatras are particularly good for healing. These include Ashvini, which is good for starting healing practices and for revitalization and rejuvenation; Shatabhishak, which is good for administering medicines, for cleansing and catharsis; Mrigashira, which is good for nurturing, tonifying and rejuvenation practices; Rohini, which is good for healing of wounds and tissue growth; Pushya, which is good for nurturing and building therapies; and Shravana, which is good for counseling and psychological healing.

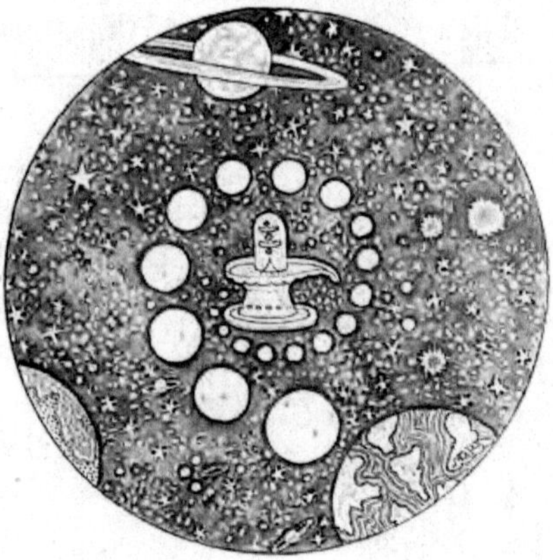

Vedic Astrology and Vedic Psychology

6

OUR mind and senses, much like the Sun, Moon and planets externally, serve to bring light into our inner world. In Vedic thought, the seven sensory openings in the head (the two eyes, two ears, two nostrils and mouth) correspond to the seven suns, the seven Adityas, which are also the seven planets. At other times they are called the seven seers or rishis. More specifically, the perceptive or intellectual mind (buddhi) is our inner Sun, while the reflective or emotional mind (manas) is our inner Moon.

The entire birth chart, including all the planets, has ramifications on our psychology and reflects how we feel about our life experience. Each position in the birth chart not only affects us outwardly but also inwardly, shaping external events and our subjective responses to them.

Both the planetary type and the doshic type of a person have important psychological indications. They are not simply physical types but psycho-physical types, reflecting not only the condition of the physical body, but how we think and feel as well. In addition, there are other forms of typology in Vedic astrology, which can also be important relative to psychology. These include classifications of people by their rising sign or Ascendant type, their Moon sign type and their Moon Nakshatra type. In addition there are other more specific astrological indicators of the mind, intelligence and emotions and their conditions.

I. Key Factors of the Psychology

1. The Ascendant or Rising Sign

The Ascendant or rising sign represents the basic presentation of a person in the external world. It indicates the manifest self or ego, the outer expression and body of a person. Each Ascendant from Aries to Pisces has its characteristic temperament and qualities based upon its elements and other factors. We can classify people into 'Ascendant types', reflecting these qualities.

From the standpoint of psychology, the first house is the house of the ego (ahamkara), the 'I am the body idea' or self-image upon which the ego is based. It is a crucial indicator not only for determining psychological health but also for career, relationship and general happiness, which are the main issues of the self in this world. The Ascendant and the influences upon it show the ego and its projects in life.

Ascendant types generally reflect the nature of the planet ruling the Ascendant sign. In the case of planets ruling two signs of the zodiac, the odd sign will reflect more the active or masculine side of the planet, while the even sign will reflect more the receptive or feminine side of the planet.

While people do not always have the bodily type of their Ascendant ruler, particularly if other planets are stronger in the chart, the nature of the Ascendant will always affect their psychology. As I have already discussed these Ascendant types in detail in my previous book Astrology of the Seers, I will not repeat that material here but refer the reader to it for that information.[28]

2. The Moon

The Moon indicates the basic emotional state of a person, their feeling nature. This is revealed astrologically by the Moon sign, the house location of the Moon, planetary aspects or influences on the Moon, and the extent to which the Moon is waxing or waning.

A strong Moon endows a person with a strong and steady emotional nature that will aid them in all endeavors in life. A weak Moon will make one prey to emotional disturbances and imbalances, and can cancel or render ineffective the other strengths and benefits in the chart. Generally a strong Moon will bring out the positive effects of the Moon sign, while a weak Moon will reflect its weaknesses.

In Vedic astrology, the Moon sign is used for personal indications— such as given in daily and monthly astrological forecasts in newspapers—rather than the Sun sign as is the case with western astrology. The term Janma Rashi or 'Birth Sign' refers to the Moon sign. The term Janma Lagna means Birth Ascendant or the rising sign. The Vedic system also considers transits from the Moon as much as it does transits from the Ascendant because these show how events affect us personally. Transits from the Ascendant more clearly show outer effects or material results.

The qualities of the Moon sign reflect not only the planet ruling that sign but also the nature of the particular house that the Moon rules relative to the sign it happens to be located in. (For this, we count the Moon sign itself as the first house.)

Moon Sign Types

1. ARIES MOON shows a direct, impulsive and expressive temperament, with the emotions driven by the will and vitality. It gives qualities of leadership, ego drive and a striving for preeminence. The person's emotional sensitivity will revolve around issues of independence, control and assertion, with a tendency to anger or domination. As the Moon rules Cancer, the fourth house from Aries, the emotional nature will be deep and intense and everything will likely be taken personally.

2. TAURUS MOON, reflecting the sign of the Moon's exaltation, creates a strong and determined emotional nature, with a need for stability, security and material success. The artistic and poetic side of the Moon often comes out in this sign of Venus. As the Moon rules the third house from Taurus, this position gives the person vitality, curiosity, creativity and many interests in life.

3. GEMINI MOON shows an intelligent, expressive, sensitive and changeable emotional nature. The person's emotions will be closely tied to the mind and the nervous system, making it difficult for them to discriminate between thoughts and feelings. As the Moon rules the second house from Gemini, this position affords good powers of speech and communication.

4. CANCER MOON, reflecting the Moon's own sign, makes a person friendly, caring and emotional, with a strong lunar nature and a life centered on human relationships. Generally, the personal and domestic side of life will dominate but if there is an influence of Saturn on the Moon, the public or political side can also be strong. The individual is likely to be a Moon type person.

5. LEO MOON provides strength, nobility and character to the person's emotions and psychology. The person will like drama and prominence, much like the Sun in Leo but also seek an emotional recognition and regard for what they do. As the Moon rules the twelfth house from Leo, their emotional nature often gets subordinated to their strong personality. Yet they often have a capacity for renunciation and spirituality (twelfth house) in order to uphold their high Leo principles.

6. VIRGO MOON endows a person with many interests, hobbies and pursuits, with a curious but practical bent of mind. The digestion may be sensitive and easily upset by nervous or emotional disturbances. This position is good for artists, craftsmen, healers and yogis, for developing finer and more sattvic vibrations. As the Moon rules the eleventh house from Virgo, a Virgo Moon can give many outer achievements, goals and good business skills.

7. LIBRA MOON marks a person with a strong social consciousness, idealism and a good artistic or creative expression. It is better for the public or intellectual side of the Moon rather than its domestic or emotional side. As the Moon rules the tenth house of career from Libra, it causes a person to seek recognition and gives them a desire to influence the masses. It makes the person diplomatic and is also often good for business activities and trade.

8. SCORPIO MOON, reflecting the sign of the Moon's debilitation, endows a person with a deep and secretive psychology, with strong and sometimes troubled emotions and some degree of anger and frustration in life. Yet it can indicate a profound or spiritual psyche, with interest in subjects like psychology, Yoga or Tantra. This is reinforced by the fact that the Moon rules the ninth house, the house of spirituality, from Scorpio.

9. SAGITTARIUS MOON shows an ethical and principled, but sometimes self-righteous personality, with a strong sense of good and evil or law and order, to which the emotions are subordinated, if not sacrificed. It can create the zeal of a crusader, priest, lawyer or reformer, sometimes even a fanatic. As the Moon rules the eighth house from Sagittarius, it can give an interest in deep spiritual and psychic issues, or healing and research.

10. CAPRICORN MOON, under the influence of Saturn, brings out the public side of the Moon, augmenting the intellectual, social, political or business acumen of a person. The individual will have a

practical bent of mind and emotions, with a strong sense of tradition and a need to produce material results. As the Moon rules the seventh house from Capricorn, it can give strong ties to the partner, particularly in the public or work sphere.

11. AQUARIUS MOON provides a self-effacing, idealistic and spiritual side to the personality. It is a common Moon for healers, monks and yogis on a higher side, but also for criminals, drug addicts and underworld figures on a lower side, depending upon whether Saturn has a detaching or debasing influence. As the Moon rules the sixth house from Aquarius, the health implications of this position are important, with an emotional vulnerability to disease.

12. PISCES MOON is highly emotional, poetic and romantic, in harmony with this sensitive, watery sign. When afflicted, emotional imbalance is likely, but when strong, an almost psychic sympathy or empathy prevails. The Moon here has a certain vulnerability and impressionability that should be protected, not only for the psychology but also for the health. It can cause a weak immune system or metabolic disorders, when afflicted. As the Moon rules the fifth house from Pisces, this position is good for creativity and for children and has a Jupiterian expansiveness that is emotional in nature.

3. Mercury and Jupiter

As the two main planets governing the rational mind, Mercury and Jupiter must be carefully examined to determine our psychology, intelligence and mental acuity.

Mercury is examined along with the Moon and the fourth house for determining our overall state of mind. While the Moon is the general indicator of our personal consciousness in life, the planet Mercury is the specific indicator of the intellect. The relationship between the Moon and Mercury in the chart shows how our emotional and intellectual natures interrelate. Mutual aspects between the two, particularly if afflicted, can cause a confusion of reason and emotion that can make for poor judgment, difficulty in communication and emotional imbalance.

Mercury indicates our basic mentality, rationality and power of perception, as well as our capacity for communication, specifically speech. Mercury also relates to education, particularly our schooling during childhood. Its position in the chart is an important indicator for determining these factors.

Jupiter is the planet of the higher mind, abstract intelligence and conscience. Its influence brings higher values including religious, ethical, philosophical or charitable considerations. It connects us with our soul, while Mercury is more connected to the informational aspect of the mind. Jupiter is examined along with the fifth house for determining the qualities and strength of our deeper mind and creative intelligence, including the capacity we have to learn on our own. It is also connected to education at a college or career level.

4. The Fourth House

The counterpart of the Moon among the houses is the fourth house, which relates to the home, mother, heart and emotional nature (manas). Along with the Moon and Mercury, the fourth house represents our basic psychology and our happiness or sorrow in life. This is also reflected by the planets influencing the fourth house.

If the fourth house is influenced by the Sun, the person will be independent, self-willed, detached and not emotionally sensitive. They will stay away from their home or turn it into a place of privacy and personal work.

If the fourth house is influenced by the Moon, the person will have a strong emotional nature, emotional sensitivity and a good connection to mother, family and ancestry. Love, devotion and loyalty will prevail in the heart. If the Moon is afflicted in the fourth house, however, one may suffer from loneliness, depression and various emotional disturbances.

If the fourth house is influenced by Mars, the person will have an emotional nature characterized by passion, anger and aggression, with a violent disposition in extreme cases. There will be little happiness in the home, which will at best be a place of work and at worst a place of conflict.

If the fourth house is influenced by Mercury, the person will have an expressive speech, mind and emotions. While the intellect may be strong, it is often tinged with emotion, which can bring out its artistic side but can weaken its power of judgment. The mind can have an introverted tendency and some degree of self-involvement.

If the fourth house is influenced by Jupiter, a balanced emotional nature with happiness, contentment and an ethical disposition will generally prevail. Jupiter located in the fourth house shows a spiritual grace and guidance that can protect the life, home and welfare of a person. It indicates the power of the guru to help a person inwardly and outwardly.

If the fourth house is influenced by Venus, the emotional nature will be romantic and expressive, with artistic tendencies like music or dance. Generally this position gives emotional stability and grace, but can dispose a person towards pride or vanity.

If the fourth house is influenced by Saturn, the emotional nature will likely be detached, cold or even depressed. Expressing emotions will be difficult and slow. One will stay away from home or turn it into a place of work. While good for spiritual detachment, this position is not good for ordinary happiness and often indicates psychological suffering.

If the fourth house is influenced by Rahu, the emotional nature will be sensitive, volatile and easily disturbed. Insomnia or emotional agitation can occur or even more serious mental and nervous system problems. On the positive side, healing energies can be developed as well as a deep emotional sympathy for others.

If the fourth house is influenced by Ketu, the emotional nature will be self-centered or self-focused, with limited expression or response to others. A martial energy can develop, with deep-seated anger, or a person may seek to leave the emotions behind. The mind will be sharp and critical but not very sensitive or broad.

5. The Fifth House

The fifth is the house of creative intelligence (Buddhi), indicating our values, goals, aspirations and judgments as well as our creativity, progeny or legacy. A good fifth house shows good intelligence and perception, counseling abilities, good creativity and clear expression. An afflicted fifth house shows wrong values, impaired judgment, wrong beliefs or destructive opinions. Note the effect of different planets dominating the fifth house by their influence.

If the fifth house is dominated by the Sun, the person will have a powerful and independent but self-focused mind. Creativity will be internalized, with a strong sense of ones own identity that can include a connection with the higher Self.

If the fifth house is dominated by the Moon, the person will have a creative but emotional mind, with a strong sense of family, communication or public affairs. There may be a good contemplative or reflective aspect to the mind.

If the fifth house is dominated by Mars, the person will have a sharp, perceptive and logical but perhaps aggressive and competitive mentality. This position can be good for science, law and debate. A malefic Mars influence on the fifth house and its lord makes a person violent, cunning and deceitful.

If the fifth house is dominated by Mercury, the person will have a quick, communicative and expressive mind, with a good intelligence and strong learning capacity. However, there may be a tendency towards superficiality and shifting of points of view.

If the fifth house is dominated by Jupiter, the person will have good judgment, a sense of ethics and conscience and devotion. The creative intelligence will be strong but directed toward public or spiritual, rather than family affairs. One can easily develop the higher mind through study and meditation.

If the fifth house is dominated by the influence of Venus, there will be an emotional, romantic or artistic bent to the intellect and its interests. The creative intelligence will be strong but with feeling and imagination dominating over logic.

If the fifth house is dominated by the influence of Saturn, the intellect will be profound, detached and philosophical. If afflicted, however, intellectual powers may be impeded, with dullness and slowness of thought and some tendency towards selfishness and narrow mindedness.

If the fifth house is dominated by the influence of Rahu, the mind will be sensitive, with a strong imagination but some tendency toward morbidity. The creative intelligence will be many sided but often diffuse or superficial.

If the fifth house is dominated by the influence of Ketu, the person will have a perceptive, intuitive and insightful mentality. If afflicted, the judgment will be poor, self-destructive and tending towards violence, much like the position of Mars.

6. Additional Considerations

Each house and planet has its psychological dimension of interpretation.[29]

The tenth house is often crucial for the psychology because it marks the career, vocation, status and social recognition of a person. Many people, in terms of their outer expression at least, are dominated more by the psychology of the tenth house than that of the fourth house, particularly men. We might say that the tenth house governs the 'public psychology' of a person, while the fourth governs the 'private psychology'.

The ninth house, along with Jupiter and the Sun, are significators for the Self or Soul (Atman). A good connection between the Ascendant or its lord and the ninth house or its lord provides a good ethical and spiritual disposition with a fair amount of Divine grace in life. Planets in the ninth house will help raise us up educationally, religiously and spiritually, and this will have its affect on the psychology and temperament of a person, bringing in higher values and pursuits.

The seventh house of relationship, as part of the one-seven axis or self-definition in life, is another important emotional indicator. Strong afflictions to the seventh house deny happiness and disturb the emotions. The seventh as the fourth house from the fourth house also reflects fourth house matters of home and emotion and should be examined accordingly.

The second as the house of speech and of childhood has an impact on the psychology as well. Strong malefics here make for a harsh expression and a difficult childhood. Benefics here make the expression pleasing and usually indicate a happy childhood as well.

II. Factors that Disturb the Psychology

Many astrological factors can disturb our psychological well-being. Most important are afflictions to the Moon, which is the primary indicator of our emotional nature. These are reinforced by afflictions to the fourth house and its lord, which like the Moon govern over our emotional nature.

Malefic influences to the Moon from Mars, Saturn, Rahu and Ketu disturb the psychology. Aspects of malefic house lords, like lords of the sixth, eighth or twelfth have a similar negative effect. Each of these influences has its own characteristics with anger most commonly associated with Mars, depression with Saturn, psychic vulnerability with Rahu and psychic sensitivity with Ketu. If two or more of these influences affect the Moon, then personal happiness will be very difficult. For example, domestic happiness is likely to be impaired if both Mars and Saturn aspect the Moon. Moon-Rahu combinations also can cause severe psychological and health disturbances, particular if aspected by Saturn.

However, while combined Mars-Saturn influences can destroy emotional happiness, they can lead to spirituality and are found in the charts of many great yogis. Without some detaching influence on the Moon, which represents ordinary happiness and attachments, the spiritual life is not easy. The same type of malefic aspects on the fourth house and fourth lord must also be considered.

Malefic aspects to Mercury, like those to the Moon, are disturbing to the mind, particularly if more than one is operative. These will result in wrong judgment and poor communication and other complications of the affairs ruled by Mercury. While not as harmful as aspects to the Moon relative to emotional happiness, they have their negative consequences on the intellect. Mercury-Rahu influences are well known to cause wrongful communication, if not deception. Mercury-Mars can cause a critical mentality, if not anger and aggression.

As the first house or Ascendant is that of the ego and our basic self-expression, afflictions to it can cause ego and personality problems. For example, malefic aspects to the Ascendant and its lord will give a person a harsh nature. Saturn influences on the first house can make a person selfish; Mars influences can render them aggressive; Rahu can make them unstable; and Ketu withdrawn as per the usual effects of these planets.

Certain Ascendants have more psychological sensitivity than others, particularly those ruled by Mercury (Gemini and Virgo) and also Pisces, which is an emotionally sensitive sign. Afflictions to these are more likely to result in psychological imbalances. The Virgo-Pisces axis is important for both physical and mental health, as already noted.

Malefic influences on the fifth house of intelligence, particularly if more than one, can impair our power of judgment and cause us to make wrong choices in life. Such bad judgment can extend to health, career, relationship, children or spirituality. Note the influences of malefic planets on the fifth house as discussed above.

Planets in difficult houses (six, eight and twelve) cause emotional upset, suffering and unhappiness, particularly psychological planets like the Ascendant lord, Sun, Moon, Mercury or Jupiter. But these positions can also give spiritual aspiration, renunciation and the capacity for yogic practices. What negates the ordinary psychology can take us to a higher psychology, if we learn to use these influences with a higher awareness.

Timing of Psychological Problems

The same techniques can be used for the timing of psychological imbalances and disturbances as for physical diseases, starting with the primary method of the dasha sequence (planetary periods). Generally, any difficult planetary influence will have its affects on the mind, even if the difficulties primarily relate to other aspects of life. Disease, career failures, financial losses or relationship breakups all tend to disturb the mind as well.

1. Planetary Periods

As the Moon is the general indicator of our emotional nature, its periods (dashas) will bring our emotions out for good or ill, depending upon its placement in the chart. If the Moon is afflicted, its periods are likely to be those of emotional disturbance, unhappiness or suffering. This is particularly true of malefic subperiods in the Moon's greater period like Moon-Rahu, Moon-Saturn, Moon-Ketu and Moon-Mars. Moon-Rahu is usually the most difficult. Moon-Mercury can be difficult because of the conjoint influences of two planets of the mind.

Mercury as the significator of the intellect will give mental issues and psychological problems during its periods, if it is afflicted. The subperiod of Mercury-Rahu is well known for bad judgment, including among astrologers and doctors. Combined Moon-Mercury periods can be challenging as noted.

Rahu is the general indicator of psychological, psychic or spiritual unrest or agitation, which can display itself during its periods. Within its larger cycle, subperiods of malefic planets or planets that relate to mental factors can be problematical, particularly Rahu-Moon, Rahu-Mercury, Rahu-Saturn, Rahu-Ketu and Rahu-Mars. Rahu subperiods that involve the fourth or fifth lords also bring challenges to these houses and their emotional and intellectual potentials.

Saturn's periods often cause delays, obstructions, stress and depression. These disturbances will occur relative to the mind during the subperiods of planets that affect the mind, like Saturn-Moon and Saturn-Rahu. Saturn-Mercury is usually not as difficult, however, because the two planets together often create a stabilizing influence on the mind.

The periods of the lord of the fourth house, if afflicted or in bad subperiods, also have their potential for emotional disturbances and psychological trauma. Similarly, the periods of the lord of the fifth house, if afflicted or during bad subperiods, cause wrong judgment, wrong ideas and a misguided will power.

Any combination of two malefics influencing the fourth or fifth houses will be particularly bad during their periods. For example, if Rahu is in the fourth house and Mars aspects the fourth house, then Rahu-Mars would likely result in anger, conflict and emotional unrest.

2. Difficult Transits

The same factors that relate to planetary periods are true relative to transits, though the results experienced will be weaker or of shorter duration (unless occurring during unfavorable planetary periods as well).

The seven and a half years of Saturn's transit to the Moon called sade-sathi, is famous for causing emotional hardship and mental unrest. It commences when Saturn is forty-five degrees before the Moon in the zodiac and continues until it is forty-five degrees past the Moon. Should the Moon be in mental signs like Gemini or Virgo, its impact on the mind will be stronger. Transits of other malefics to the Moon like Rahu, Ketu and Mars can similarly be difficult.

Mercury does not suffer as much from difficult transits as the Moon, but is still disturbed by malefic transits, particularly those of Rahu and Mars. Malefic transits to the first, fourth and fifth houses also have their affect in disturbing our sense of self (first house), heart and emotions (fourth house), and reason and intellect (fifth house).

The Chakras and Yogic Astrology

7

ASTROLOGY is more concerned with the subtle astral body than it is with the gross physical body. The astral forms the energy matrix for both body and mind and helps project the soul's karma into the material world. This 'astral' body or body of the stars reflects our 'astrology'. The planets and signs exist within us as the main energetic factors behind the astral body.

Besides our 'outer birth chart' relating to the physical body is an 'inner birth chart' of the astral body that reveals the life pattern of our soul. The main factors that make up the astral body are the seven chakras from the root to the crown. The chakras have detailed astrological equivalents in Vedic astrology, which has its own special way of examining the astral body through the birth chart.[30]

According to the science of Yoga, our life-energy or Prana is our inner Sun. Our internal Prana is the light that gives life and energy to all that we do, just as the external Sun energizes the outer world. This inner Sun of Prana follows a similar movement as does the outer Sun in the sky. It circulates through the chakras of the subtle body just as the Sun does through the signs of the zodiac. The spine and chakra system constitute this inner zodiac.

Besides the outer solar system that regulates the outer forces in the natural world, we have an 'inner solar system' that guides our inner being and self-expression. Many of us would consider the idea of an inner solar system to be just a metaphor. But from a deeper vision, it is the outer solar system that is the reflection of the inner, with the light of the physical universe being a visible reflection of the deeper light of consciousness. In other words, the inner zodiac is the main factor with the outer zodiac being its corresponding external form. Inner astrology is more important than outer astrology and forms the basis of many powerful yoga practices.

Our inner Sun of Prana moves up and down the spine and the chakra system along with each breath, traversing our inner zodiac along the way. Each breath constitutes a day for our inner Pranic Sun, with our inhalation as the day time and our exhalation as the night time. This is the astrological basis of Yoga Pranayama techniques that aim at moving the awakened or spiritually energized Prana up and down the spine during the practice. If we can do this, then each one of our breaths will have a great power for activating the chakras and arousing the Kundalini, the serpent power that opens the chakras, and which itself is the awakened energy of our inner Pranic Sun.

Not only the Sun but all the planets move through our subtle body or inner zodiac. They can be located in the chakras of the subtle body and their corresponding signs of the zodiac. The six chakras or energy centers of the astral body reflect the seven planets and the twelve signs that they rule. This sequence follows the orbits of planets around the Sun from the Sun as the third eye or head center, with the Sun and Moon considered as two aspects of one planet in terms of sign and chakra rulership.

Chakra	Planet	Solar Sign	Lunar Sign
1. Third Eye (Ajna)	Sun/Moon	Leo	Cancer
2. Throat Chakra (Visshuddha)	Mercury	Virgo	Gemini
3. Heart Chakra (Anahata)	Venus	Libra	Taurus
4. Navel Chakra (Manipura)	Mars	Scorpio	Aries
5. Sex Chakra (Svadhishthana)	Jupiter	Sagittarius	Pisces
6. Root Chakra (Muladhara)	Saturn	Capricorn	Aquarius

The Sun and Moon are well known in yogic thought as the right and left eyes of the Cosmic Person (Purusha) and relate to the two petals of the third eye center (Ajna chakra). They show our consciousness in its masculine and feminine, or will and feeling sides as activated through the right and left, the solar and lunar, pingala and ida nadis that traverse the entire chakra system from the base of the spine to the nostrils.

Mercury is the well-known ruler of speech and intellect, which relate to the throat chakra. Venus relates to love and affection and to the heart chakra. Mars rules the navel or fire center, our energy, drives and passions. Jupiter rules the reproductive system and the creative energy, our potential to expand. Saturn rules elimination and support and is the coarsest of the planetary influences, our potential to contract and the root chakra. Rahu and Ketu, in their role of shadowing the Sun and Moon, relate to the ida and pingala, the left and right nadis.

The Prana or life-energy moves up the spine following the six signs of the zodiac from Aquarius to Cancer. This ascending movement relates to the process of inhalation and the development of lunar or cooling energy. It builds up the fluids and tissues of the body. We could call this "the lunar half of the zodiac." The energy moving down the spine follows the six signs from Leo to Capricorn. We could call this "the solar half of the zodiac."[31] It relates to exhalation and the development of solar energy and is warming in nature. It promotes functional activity including digestion, circulation and mental acuity.

- Cancer and Leo, as the signs of the Moon and the Sun, show the basic polarity of our mind in terms of emotion and reason.
- Virgo governs our intake of impressions and Gemini our expression of ideas - the factors of the throat center.
- Taurus governs our emotional receptivity and Libra our capacity to express emotions - the factors of the heart center.
- Aries governs our projection of vitality and Scorpio its preservation - the factors of the navel center.
- Pisces governs our creative energy in life and Sagittarius its manifestation - the factors of the sex center.
- Capricorn governs our stability or conservative force in life and Aquarius its expression - the factors of the root center.

The seventh or head center (Sahasrapadma or thousand petal lotus) transcends the six chakras and the movement of time. It is the state of the Sun beyond time when it no longer rises or sets, the state of Samadhi in which the breath is suspended, the perpetual day of pure consciousness spoken of in the Vedas and Upanishads. "For him the Sun does not rise, nor does it set, it is a perpetual day for he who knows the secret spiritual teaching."[32]

The ancient Vedic yoga and the solar religions of the entire ancient world speak of the resurrection of the Sun out of darkness, or the building up of the circle of the Sun. This is the process of taking our life-force and intelligence, our soul or inner Sun, out of the cycle of ignorance, death, time and breath and into the superconscious, breathless states. It can be approached in several ways. Yogic practices direct the prana or life-force through the different chakras with mantra, pranayama and other energetic practices. Meditation or knowledge teachings (Jnana Yoga) build up the different aspects of direct perception. Devotional teachings (Bhakti Yoga) approach the chakras through the worship of or devotion to different deities.

Chakras and the Exaltation Points of the Planets

This relationship between the signs and the chakras also helps explain the exaltation of the planets.

Signs	Ruler	Chakra	Exalted
Leo, Cancer	1. Sun, Moon	Head	Jupiter
Virgo, Gemini	2. Mercury	Throat	Mercury
Libra, Taurus	3. Venus	Heart	Saturn, Moon
Scorpio, Aries	4. Mars	Navel	Sun
Sagittarius, Pisces	5. Jupiter	Sex	Venus
Capricorn, Aquarius	6. Saturn	Root	Mars

Jupiter is exalted in Cancer, the sign of the Moon and the head chakra. This shows the spiritual side of Jupiter and its function as the guru or guide, the teacher of the solar system. It is the point of maximum aspiration in life. Jupiter in the head center gives wisdom, peace and delight.

Mercury is exalted in Virgo, its own sign, and is the planetary ruler of the throat chakra. This is the place of speech. It is also our place of greatest vulnerability and shows how we take in and release things through the mouth. Mercury relating to the throat chakra gives intelligence, speech and mantric powers.

The Moon is exalted in Taurus, a sign of Venus and the heart. The Moon's connection with the emotional heart is well known. This is the place of greatest receptivity and openness. The Moon in Taurus gives devotion, loyalty and care.

Saturn is exalted in Libra, the other sign of Venus and the heart chakra. Here Saturn represents the higher dharmic principles of justice, order and detachment, which are necessary in using our heart energy in the right way, providing detachment and principled idealism in human relationships.

The Sun is exalted in Aries, the sign of Mars and the navel center or solar plexus, well known as a site of solar and fire energy. The solar energy of the head must be integrated with the vital will in the belly. The Sun in Aries gives the power to align the ego or personal will (third chakra) to the inner Self or Atman.

Venus is exalted in Pisces, the sign of Jupiter, and the sex center. While Jupiter governs the general energy of creation and expansion, Venus reflects the more specific energy of love and reproduction. It is important that we align the Venus and Jupiter aspects of sexuality. In Vedic thought, Venus is the significator of the partner for the male, while Jupiter is the significator of the partner for the female. We need to keep our creative energy in harmony with love and idealism. Venus in Pisces gives a Divine love to transmute the energy of the sex or water chakra.

Mars is exalted in Capricorn, the sign of Saturn, and connects to the root center. As the end of the solar half of the zodiacal cycle, this is the point of maximum potential of expression of the fire energy. It is here on the most outer level of our being that we need energy to work and accomplish things. On an inner level, Mars in Capricorn in the root or earth center gives the awakening of the Kundalini to set the inner transformation process in motion.

In this system of planetary exaltations, the Sun and the Moon are located in the center, the navel and heart chakras, along with Saturn, the planet whose signs are opposite them in the zodiac. These are the central powers in the chart, representing the basic dualities of self and not-self or spirit and matter. Above them in the throat and head are Mercury and Jupiter, representing the mind in its abstract and concrete, general and specific function, also opposite each other in the zodiac in terms of signs. Below them in the sex and root centers are Venus and Mars, representing the emotional, vital and sensual nature, also opposite each other in terms of the zodiac. The two planets (the Sun and Moon considered as one planet), the Sun and Saturn are in the center.

The exaltation status centers on the heart and the solar plexus, two energy centers that function as seats of the individual self. The sign ruling status, on the other hand, is a vertically oriented symbolism reflecting the flow of prana from the lower to the higher chakras. The exaltation order reflects how the planets function once their energy is integrated within us. The solar energy from the head needs to be integrated into the vital energy in our navel or fire center (Aries). The martial energy of the navel center needs to be made concrete in action in the root center (Capricorn). The lunar receptive mind from the head needs to be integrated into the love energy in the heart (Taurus). The Venus love energy in the heart needs to be integrated into the Jupiterian creative energy in the sex center. The Jupiter creative energy in the sex center needs to be brought to the top of the head. The Saturn detaching or negating energy in the root center needs to be brought up into the heart.

Finally, we should recognize that the actual opening of the chakras is a matter connected to the practice of the higher limbs of yoga. The chakras cannot be fully activated by the usage of gems, herbs or external influences, however helpful these may be for ordinary health purposes. The yogic powers of the chakras are only unfolded by Pranayama, Mantra and Meditation. Such an inner experience of the chakras requires a concentrated spiritual practice (sadhana) grounded in inner peace and connected to an authentic guide and enlightenment tradition.[33]

PART TWO

Astrological Treatment Measures

Outer Remedial Measures: Herbs, Aromas and Colors

8

VEDIC astrology is not just a system for reading our future; it is also a means of changing it. Besides its predictive side, Vedic astrology has an equally effective therapeutic aspect, which is particularly important to integrate when exploring its connection with Ayurveda.

According to Vedic astrology, astrological indications are only probabilities capable of some degree of alteration. Vedic astrology is not a fatalistic science, which chains us to a fixed destiny according to some rigid karmic determinism; it is a creative science for developing our karmic potential in the best possible manner. In this regard it is a humanistic science, recognizing our ability as conscious beings to shape our destiny. However, altering planetary influences requires both expertise and effort. The remedial measures of Vedic astrology give us the special tools with which to do this.

Vedic astrology employs many different types of astrological healing and protective measures. All aspects of Ayurvedic therapy have at least an indirect application to planetary healing because they can be used to balance the excess doshas created by poorly placed planets in the chart. All aspects of Yoga have relevance as well, including pranayama, visualization, mantra and meditation, which can be used to help correct negative planetary influences on the psyche. Various 'karmic' therapies like rituals, sacrifices, charity and service also have their place, countering the negative karmic consequences of difficult planetary placements. These treatments all have special astrological methods of assessment and timing connected to them. We will examine these methods in this second section of the book starting with the outer measures that are characteristic of Ayurveda.

1. Herbs, Foods and the Planets

The Sun is the power which causes plants to grow, while the Moon rules over their sap, the material substance through which they live and are nourished. Yet plants are also affected by the influences of all the planets at a subtler level.

According to Ayurveda, there are six tastes called rasas in Sanskrit, relative to which it classifies all herbs and foods. Each taste is composed of two of the five elements of earth, water, fire, air and ether, through which its properties can be understood. In Vedic astrology each planet relates to one of these six tastes. This allows us to correlate planetary and plant energies in a simple but effective manner. Each taste also has its specific action, increasing or decreasing the three doshas.[34]

The Six Tastes and Their Correspondences

Tastes	Elements	Energy	Doshas Increased	Doshas Decreased
Sweet	Earth & Water	Cooling	Kapha	Pitta & Vata
Salty	Water & Fire	Heating	Kapha and Pitta	Vata
Sour	Earth & Fire	Heating	Pitta and Kapha	Vata
Astringent	Air & Earth	Cooling	Vata	Pitta & Kapha
Pungent	Fire & Air	Heating	Pitta and Vata	Kapha
Bitter	Air & Ether	Cooling	Vata	Pitta & Kapha

Sweet taste, such as occurs in sugars and starches, relates to Kapha planets, the Moon, Jupiter and Venus, which have an overall tissue-increasing effect upon the body. Classical Vedic astrology emphasizes the identification of Jupiter specifically with the sweet taste because it is the main planet creating weight and bulk in the body, which derive from this taste and its earth and water elements. However, Venus, the planet of love, a Kapha emotion, as is well known, is also fond of sweets.

Salty taste mainly relates to the Moon, owing to its correspondence with the water element, the ocean and the plasma in our bodies, our internal ocean.

Sour taste is classically ascribed to Venus in several Vedic astrological texts because of its stimulating and attractive nature, as well as its Kapha increasing properties. Yet sour taste, which has a heating energy, particularly that found in alcohol and other fermented items can increase Mars energy.

Astringent taste, such as found in tannins, is mainly Vata in its properties, increasing dryness and lightness in the body. In this regard it is sometimes related to Saturn, which like the astringent taste causes our energy to contract and has stopping or inhibiting action on such processes as sweating, bleeding or elimination.

Pungent or spicy taste, which has a heating and stimulating energy, relates mainly to Pitta planets, specifically to the Sun, but also to Mars. Spices like ginger, cayenne or black pepper are storehouses of solar energy.

Bitter taste reflects the qualities of Vata, being cold, dry, light and weight-reducing in its action. In this regard it resembles the planet Saturn which rules over Vata dosha in general, but reflects other Vata planets as well. Bitter taste can stimulate the mental activity of Mercury because it increases the air and ether elements operative in the mind. Classical Vedic astrology relates bitter taste to Mars because bitter is the most effective taste for controlling Mars energy, reducing the heat and toxicity associated with it, not because it is similar in nature or energy to Mars.

When Vata is too high – or when the influence of Vata (airy) planets like Saturn, Rahu and Mercury predominate in the body – the use of sweet, sour, salty and pungent tastes is recommended, including a nutritive diet of grains, beans, root vegetables, seeds, nuts and dairy products. Mild spices (like ginger, cinnamon and cardamom) and tonic herbs like ashwagandha and shatavari or the Ayurvedic formula Chyavan prash are the main herbal therapies.

When Kapha is too high – or when the influence of Kapha (watery) planets like the Moon, Jupiter and Venus predominate in the body – the use of pungent, astringent and bitter tastes is indicated, including a light diet that avoids sweet, salty, sour and oily foods, as well as dairy products. The use of hot spices (like ginger, pepper or cayenne or the Ayurvedic formula Trikatu), and bitters (like gentian or aloe) that aid in weight reduction are the main herbal therapies.

When Pitta is too high – or when the influence of Pitta (fiery) planets like the Sun, Mars and Ketu predominate in the body – the use of bitter, astringent and sweet herbs and foods is recommended, including less use of salt, spices and sour articles, along with a cooler and blander diet in general with more raw food. Mild bitters are recommended like gotu kola (brahmi) and cooling spices like turmeric and coriander are important herbal therapies.

It is possible to more precisely equate individual foods and herbs with the planets and use astrology to aid in both dietary and herbal treatment, but this is a complex matter and is best left more for an advanced study of medical astrology, particularly for those who are trained in Ayurveda.[35]

2. Aroma Therapy and the Planets

Plant fragrances share the same basic properties as the herbs from which they derive. Yet they have a subtler energy that is better for transmitting planetary influences. Aromas, one could say, stand intermediate between gems and herbs in strength of influencing and altering planetary energies. They can either be used as aromatic oils or as incense.

- Best for increasing the energy of the Sun are hot, spicy aromas like ginger, cinnamon, heena, camphor, and sage.
- For increasing the energy of the Moon, use cool and calming aromas like jasmine, lotus, gardenia, and sandalwood.
- For increasing the energy of Mars, best are stimulating fragrances like musk, floral musk or camphor.
- For balancing the energy of Mercury, use calming and mind-clearing aromas like sandalwood, basil, mint, and wintergreen.
- For increasing the energy of Jupiter, best are strengthening aromas like sandalwood, frankincense, and lotus.
- For increasing the energy of Venus, sweet fragrances are important like rose, saffron, jasmine, lotus, nag champa, and plumeria (fran-

gipani).

- For Saturn, healing fragrances are indicated like myrrh, frankincense and cedar.
- Many aromatic oils and incenses are good for Rahu because they clear the troubled psychic air caused by this shadowy planet. Calming and clearing fragrances like sandalwood, frankincense and myrrh are particularly good for it.
- Perceptive Ketu energy is increased by light, penetrating fragrances like camphor, bayberry, thyme and sage.

3. Color Therapy and the Planets

Each planet relates to a certain color of the cosmic rays that serve to make up our auras or energy fields. The influence of each planet can be increased by exposure to its corresponding color, or decreased by exposure to opposite colors.

Color therapy is particularly good for targeting emotional and psychological imbalances but can be used for physical diseases, particularly those involving the blood, nerves or reproductive system. Many fiery Pitta disorders (infections and inflammations) can be reduced by the usage of cooling colors like blue, white and green.

Color therapy is also the foundation for Vedic gem therapy and its principles should first be learned before prescribing gems. The basic colors of the planets are:

- SUN – Red (transparent)
- MOON – White (opaque)
- MARS – Red (opaque)
- MERCURY – Green
- JUPITER –Yellow
- VENUS – White (transparent)
- SATURN – Blue

The red color of Mars is an opaque, dark or blood red, while that of the Sun is bright or transparent red. The Moon relates to white like snow or opaque white, while Venus is lighter white or transparent (which may be tinged a little with blue). Venus also rules variegated or rainbow-like colors, which are produced by reflecting light through a transparent stone. Jupiter in its higher quality is golden. Saturn in its lower quality is dark, and also black. In its higher quality it is more like a sky blue or azure.

The lunar nodes can also be related to special colors outside the ordinary spectrum: Ketu is infrared, while Rahu is ultraviolet. Rahu is also smoky or black; Ketu a bright red or orange. Rahu has a shadowy effect, while Ketu produces a strange illumination around things.

Generally, pure shades of the different colors will increase the higher influences of the planets, while coarse shades will increase their negativity. For example, dark colors like black or gray will increase the negative side of Saturn, while deep blue will increase its positive energy.

Astrological color therapy can be applied by using colors that are opposite to the colors of the planets, in order to counter their excess. We need to be careful in our choice of colors because we gravitate towards the colors of the planets that dominate us, which can be negative. For example, individuals under the influence of dark planets like Saturn and Rahu tend to live in dark places and wear dark clothes, which increases the malefic power of these planets. To counter this negative influence, they should live in a bright environment and surround themselves with bright colors. Those under the influence of hot planets, like Mars, Ketu and the Sun, should avoid too much bright color and light, particularly warm colors like red and orange.

Yet in addition to the principle of using opposite colors in order to balance excessive influences, color therapy can also be applied by directly using the planet's own color to strengthen the influence of weak planets or to otherwise augment the power of the planets one wants to strengthen. To increase Venus energy, for example, bright, variegated and pastel colors are good. To develop a higher Saturnian detachment, dark blue is good. For a positive, creative and stimulating Jupiterian energy, yellow or gold are helpful. For a soothing and calming lunar energy, the color white works well.

Methods of Color Therapy

There are many methods of astrological color therapy. One very direct method is to increase exposure to the planet's color in your environment. This may involve changing the colors of your home or office walls, particularly the room in which you spend most of your time. You can paint your rooms according to astrological principles. Having a meditation room in a certain color can be very important. If you are a health practitioner, the right colors in the healing room are very helpful.

The colors of our clothing are another factor. A simple method used in Vedic astrology is to wear a colored thread corresponding to the planet we are seeking to increase. Such fabric should be made with natural fibers.

We can also open up to the appropriate planetary colors in nature, like those that occur in the landscape around us or in the colors of certain flowers. Each natural environment, like mountains, rivers, valleys or the ocean, possesses its own potentials for color therapy. Spending time in a green forest, for example, will help stimulate the intellect (Mercury). Gazing at the blue sky will aid in a higher Saturn energy (detachment).

A good rule to remember is that colors produced through natural impressions are better than those produced artificially. Artificial colors, like neon or fluorescent lights, or mass media impressions, tend to be unwholesome and disturb the nervous system and our vital energy field.

More specific color therapy involves using colored lights to bathe the body. Special colored lamps or special lamps with different colored filters can be used for this purpose. As color therapy is used in other healing fields, such lamps are available from a variety of sources. There are also special color therapy devises that project color through gems, combining both color and gem therapy. These are particularly useful astrologically.[36]

The internal visualization of color is another important approach. The color or quality of our thoughts and emotions strongly affects the color of our aura. Our thoughts are affected by external factors, particularly sensory impressions, but we can also change them directly on an internal level. We can meditate upon specific colors or visualize them around us. In this regard it is helpful to first concentrate on an external source of the color in order to saturate the mind in its energy, like gazing at the blue sky before visualizing that blue color within the mind. Statues of deities or yantras of specific colors can be used on our altar or in our meditation area to assist us with our internal color therapy.

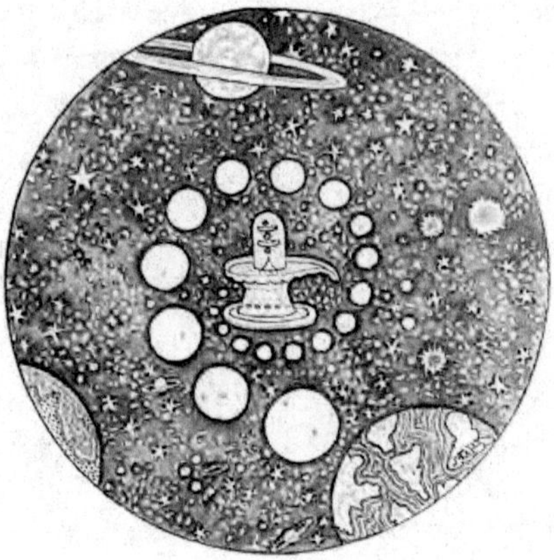

The Main Astrological Remedial Measure: Vedic Gem Therapy

9

GEMSTONES are the most important remedial measure used in Vedic astrology, which emphasizes gem therapy above all other astrological therapies. Gems possess the greatest power of any substances found on Earth to transmit planetary influences, both to counter negative planetary energies and to promote those which are positive. Most people who receive a Vedic astrological reading come away with a gem recommendation and think that without it the reading is not complete.

Gemstones are formed by the cosmic rays transmitted through the planets. They represent the energies of the planets deposited on Earth, their counterparts on this earthly plane of existence formed in the mineral matrix from which all life arises. They are like fragments of the planetary lights placed here on Earth in order to link us up to the greater universe beyond. In fact, the Earth itself is like a gigantic gemstone, with its silica-rich, quartz-like crust that supports life, and its many minerals that form crystals of various types. Gems are the ultimate concentration of light energy in the mineral kingdom, a kind of condensed light that can hold and reflect the light of the stars.

Gems work on an etheric plane, bringing the astral light of the planets into the physical realm. They carry the influences of the planets into our energy field to help balance our own aura or pattern of light. In this regard certain gemstones, like ruby for the Sun or pearl for the Moon, correspond with particular planets and can serve as conduits for their energy.

Vedic gem therapy is primarily an astrological measure, though gems are also used in Ayurveda, Yoga and other Vedic disciplines. In the Vedic view, without first understanding the astrological affects of gems, it is not possible to use them in the best possible manner. While much new information on gem therapy has come out in recent years, particularly in New Age publications, much of it remains speculative. The Vedic system of gem therapy, on the other hand, has proven itself through both astrological and Ayurvedic applications over a period of several thousand years. It can help us use gems with greater beneficial effect, however we approach them.

Western astrology has used gems for balancing planetary influences, particularly during the Middle Ages. While this use of gems fell out of favor in later western astrology which took a more psychological orientation, it is coming into vogue again with the new emphasis on natural healing that often includes gems and crystals. The Vedic use of gems has similarities with this older western astrological use of gems but some differences as well, particularly as to which particular gems and metals correspond to individual planets. Above all, Vedic astrology has its own complex yet precise system for determining which gems to wear, how to wear them and what their effects are likely to be.

Gems for the Planets

Each planet has its own gemstone, which are of the highest quality of gems:

SUN — Ruby
MOON — Pearl
MARS — Red Coral
MERCURY — Emerald
JUPITER — Yellow Sapphire
VENUS — Diamond
SATURN — Blue Sapphire
RAHU — Hessonite Garnet
KETU — Cat's Eye

Substitute Gem-Stones

While the stones listed above are the most powerful (and most expensive), the following less expensive but less powerful substitutes are allowed.

SUN	Spinel, garnet, sunstone, red zircon, red tourmaline
MOON	Cultured pearls, moonstone
MARS	Carnelian, red jasper
MERCURY	Aquamarine, peridot, jade, green zircon, green tourmaline
JUPITER	Topaz, citrine, yellow zircon, yellow tourmaline
VENUS	White sapphire, clear zircon, clear quartz, white coral
SATURN	Lapis lazuli, amethyst, turquoise, blue zircon, blue tourmaline
RAHU	Any golden grossularite garnet
KETU	Other cat's eye (mainly quartz)

As a substitute gemstone for the Sun, I recommend garnet, which is not expensive and is commonly available. For the Moon, cultured pearls or moonstone are good. As red coral is abundant and not expensive, substitutes for it are seldom necessary. For Mercury, peridot, which relates to deeper volcanic rocks, is probably the best substitute gem. For Jupiter, citrine is an easy to acquire substitute. For Venus, clear quartz crystal can be used as an inexpensive substitute, while white sapphire is almost as good as diamond in its effects. For Saturn, amethyst is excellent for general usage.

Stones for Rahu are of three types: The first is a golden grossularite garnet of the hessonite type. The second is a light red or cinnamon stone. The third is a very dark red or purple garnet. The third is not a true hessonite garnet but an almandine garnet. Some consider that the almandine can be a useful substitute for hessonite (but I prefer to avoid it as it is a dark stone). The main Cat's eye for Ketu is Chrysoberyl. Crystal cat's eye can be used as a substitute. Tiger's eye is not strong enough to effectively serve as a substitute for cat's eye.

Metals for Setting Gem-Stones

Some astrologers consider that gold is the best metal for setting all expensive stones because it is the metal of the Sun from which all the planets derive their light. Their view is that the energetics of the metal are overcome by the power of the stone and it serves a more or less neutral role to transmit the gem's influence.

Other astrologers point out that the heating nature of gold must be considered in its usage with gemstones. They hold that white gold (gold with silver) or gold with copper are better when the properties of gold may be inappropriate for a gemstone that is cooling in nature. Or they may recommend silver, which is a cooling metal and has lunar qualities opposite to the solar nature of gold. In this way the effects of gemstones can be modified according to the metals used to set them, which have their own properties. I think the second view is more accurate. Yet we must also remember that the colors of certain gems inherently go better with different metals. For example, pearl usually looks better with white gold or silver than with gold.

Gold promotes the stimulating, heating and fiery properties of gems. It increases the Agni (fire) in the gem and makes it more suitable for Vata and Pitta constitutions in terms of Ayurveda. It is better for ruby, cat's eye, yellow sapphire or hessonite garnet and aids in their heating and expansive energy. It can be used for emerald and blue sapphire, which tend to be cooling, but only if we want to help balance their effects.

White gold has a more cooling effect. Many regard it as preferable to silver, if one wants a good metal conductor that is less heating than gold. It is better for pearl or diamond. Gold with copper has a neutral nature and can be used for settings in which we do not want to overly increase Pitta, particularly red coral for Mars.

Silver increases the sedating, cooling and watery properties of gems, but is not as powerful a conductor of planetary energies as gold. It makes gems more suitable to Pitta constitutions. Substitute gemstones, as their influences are weak, do not require gold and can usually be set in silver.

Vedic astrologers may also modulate the effects of gems according to their color. For example, a lighter red colored ruby may be used when one wants to increase solar energy but not aggravate Pitta. Or pink coral may be used if one wants to increase Mars energy but guard against overheating the person.

Where to Place Gemstones on the Body

High quality gems are most effectively worn as rings. The fingers have a special capacity to conduct the influence of gems into the rest of the body because they are connected to the subtle channels of the mind and nervous system. Note the following table for the relationship of the planets, the fingers of the hands and the five elements.

Fingers and the Planets

Index finger	Ether	Jupiter
Middle finger	Air	Saturn
Ring finger	Fire, Water	Sun, Moon
Little finger	Earth	Mercury

The right thumb also relates to the Sun and the left thumb to the Moon. But generally it is not advisable to wear rings on the thumb as this is not only cumbersome but can block the flow of energy into the body.

Rings should generally be worn upon the fingers of their respective planet or of its natural friends. In this regard, planets come in two groups or camps. The first camp or group of friends consists of the Sun, Moon, Mars, Jupiter; the second is comprised of Mercury, Venus, Saturn, Rahu and Ketu.[37]

Gemstones for the Moon function well on the fingers of the Sun or Jupiter, the ring and index fingers. Stones for Mars can also be worn on the fingers for Jupiter or the Sun. Gems for Venus can be worn on the fingers of Saturn or Mercury, the middle or little fingers. Stones for Rahu and Ketu can be worn on the fingers of Saturn or Mercury (note that Ketu is sometimes considered along with Mars and its gem often worn like a gem for Mars).

The middle finger, the finger of Saturn, is usually better for gemstones than the little finger, the finger of Mercury. It governs a more central pranic flow and interferes less with the movements of the hand. Many men do not like to wear rings on the little finger and find it inconvenient. Similarly, it is easier for most people to wear rings in the ring finger (hence its name), than the index finger.

The right hand has a more solar and spiritual force and is generally preferred for all astrological rings, but the left hand can also be used. On the left hand, gems increase the cool, watery, lunar, receptive and feminine properties and work on the left nadi (Ida nadi). On the right hand, they increase the warm, fiery, solar, active and masculine properties and work on the right nadi (Pingala nadi).

As many people work with their right hands, gems may be more conveniently worn on the left hand. It is better to wear them on the left hand or to take them off during work than not to wear them at all. The same principles can be extended to wearing bangles or bracelets on the right or left wrist or arm.

Necklaces

Necklaces hanging around the neck and touching the throat area have an effect more on the throat chakra. They are good for gemstones for Mercury, which relates to the throat chakra, for improving powers of speech, communication, nervous or respiratory functioning.

Necklaces hanging to the heart have more an effect on the heart chakra. They are preferable for gems for the Sun, Moon and Venus, which have heart energies. They increase will, emotion, love, vitality and circulation. Necklaces, pendants and strands are helpful for wearing weaker quality or substitute gemstones, which require more weight of stone to have a strong influence.

Another method is to use one's planetary gemstone as the central bead in one's mala or rosary for reciting prayers or mantras. Such a setting helps conduct the power of the gemstone inwardly to higher levels of consciousness. Or one can have an entire rosary made of a secondary gemstone. This is particularly good for doing mantras to the planet involved, like using a mala of quartz crystals for propitiating Venus through Venus mantras.

Gemstones can be kept on altars, in healing rooms, in vehicles or other external places where one wants to specially benefit from their protective energy. For such purposes, larger masses of substitute gems like quartz clusters are sufficient or other uncut gems in larger sizes.

Placing Gemstones on Different Parts of the Body

Gems can be placed temporarily on different parts of the body to order to aid in their treatment. If Venus is weak and there is a kidney problem, for example, a gemstone for Venus like a white sapphire can be placed (taped) over the kidney region, particularly during sleep. In this regard, the placing of gems on chakras (either on the front or back of the body) or on marma points (Ayurvedic energy points) can be very helpful.[38]

Using More Than One Gem

Generally it is best to wear one primary gemstone that is good for the chart. A single powerful stone will usually provide the strongest results. However, not everyone has one specific planet in their chart that needs strengthening, so for them more than one gem may be helpful. If this is the case, one can wear different gemstones on different fingers. Usually three rings are the maximum in this regard or the energy becomes too complicated. Or additional gems can be used in necklaces and bangles.

Another method is to wear more than one gemstone in a single setting on a ring, but the most important gemstone should be larger, with the others serving a secondary or support role. When two stones are set together, the larger stone should usually be placed on the bottom. Or smaller gems can be mounted around the larger gem. However, remember that the use of multiple stones on the same setting is a complex matter and more likely to require advice from an astrologer or gemologist. Some stones are incompatible and rather than simply balancing each other out, may weaken each other.

A special combination of all nine planetary gemstones exists called a Navaratna. It has the gemstone for the Sun in the center. The stone for Venus is at the top, with clockwise those for the Moon, Mars, Rahu, Saturn, Ketu, Jupiter and Mercury. A Navaratna can be worn by anyone for general balancing of planetary influences. Sometimes it is made with the stone of the main planet that needs to be strengthened in the chart in the center.

Mounting of Gem-Stones

All gemstones should be mounted so as to touch the skin. Otherwise, the energy from the planet will not be effectively transmitted. One can wear gems without the stone touching the skin but the effect will be reduced and remain mainly ornamental, not therapeutic in nature. This is not only essential for rings but best for necklaces, bangles and all other settings. Some people turn necklaces over so the gem can touch the skin when the setting is not open to the back. But they often forget to do so, or the pendant swings around and the energy of the setting itself is not helpful.

Gem Quality and Size

The ability to determine which gemstone a person should wear is based upon a precise astrological analysis. Yet it is equally important to use a good quality gemstone, for which a good knowledge of gemology is necessary, such as may require a consultation with a trained gemologist. Not all astrologers are good gemologists, though some may be. If your astrologer is not also a gemologist, make sure to have your gemstone examined by a qualified gemologist to ensure it is of the best quality, particularly if it is an expensive stone. One should use unheated, natural stones, without significant flaws, preferably of the primary gemstones for the best astrological gem therapy.

Primary planetary gemstones should be at least 1.5 carats in size, preferably over 2 carats (3 carats is a good size if one can afford it; 5 carats is optimal). Substitute gems require larger settings because their power is not as strong. Quartz crystal, amethyst and citrine are best worn as strands or as large stones around the neck (at least 5 carats).

While gemstones can be expensive, they are a one-time expense that, if properly prescribed, can be useful for the entire life. Gems also retain their value or increase in value over time. Therefore, we should consider using them, in spite of their cost, and make sure to get a good size and good quality, if at all possible.

Effects of Gemstones

Some stones have possible side-effects and should be prescribed with care. This is particularly the case with the primary gems for malefic planets like blue sapphire for Saturn, cat's eye for Ketu or ruby for the Sun (yet not so much in the case of red coral for Mars). Getting a good gem prescription and making sure that the stones are right for you before using them is particularly important in the case of such stones for malefic planets.

Note that the following positive effects of gems are only likely to occur if the correct gem is prescribed and in the right size, setting and circumstances as well as with the right intentions on the part of its user. While some gems may yield immediate good results, often it takes time, sometimes a period of months for the effects of gems, which are subtle, to fully manifest.

Such results are owing to the positive influences of the planets received and amplified through the gem. They are not a result of the gem itself which is merely a transmitter. You cannot simply put on the gem, expecting to get such results, if the chart does not warrant it. Wrongly prescribed gems can cause disharmonies, excesses or imbalances of various types that will become evident over time.

Ruby

Physically
Ruby increases Pitta and Agni and decreases Kapha and Vata. It improves overall vitality, digestion and circulation. It is good for strengthening the functions of the heart, small intestine, brain and eyes. It aids in physical revitalization and rejuvenation and counters debility and fatigue.
Psychologically
Ruby strengthens ones sense of self, destiny, leadership and com-mand. It aids in self-confidence, self-expression and self-discipline. Generally it helps elevate a person in life, endowing one with the character and will power necessary for great achievements.
Spiritually
Ruby can put one in touch with ones soul and higher self (Atman). It can improve meditation, perception and insight, and help pro-mote Self-knowledge and Self-realization. It is particularly good for the Yoga of knowledge (Jnana Yoga), connecting us with the light of consciousness within.

Pearl

Physically
Pearl increases Kapha and Ojas (primary vitality) and decreases Pitta, Vata and Agni. It increases the water element in the body as a whole, strengthening the plasma, lymphatic system and skin. It is good for the stomach and lungs and for the reproductive system, improving fertility.

Pearl (cont'd)

Psychologically
Pearl brings calm and contentment to the mind and emotions. It is good for creative expression, especially poetry and music. It is par-ticularly soothing and supporting for the feminine psychology and helpful for countering any emotional afflictions in the chart, including fear, anger and hatred.
Spiritually
Pearl helps develop the devotional side of the heart and the con-tem-plative aspect of the mind, including higher virtues of peace, charity, friendliness, equanimity and non-violence. It is good for the Yoga of devotion (Bhakti Yoga) and makes us receptive to higher influences, grace and guidance.

Red Coral

Physically
Red coral increases Agni and Pitta (but usually not excessively) and decreases Vata and Kapha. It strengthens the blood, marrow, bones and the reproductive system (particularly for men). It aids in digestion and circulation and also helps build up the muscle mass.
Psychologically
Red coral increases ones resolve, will power and work capacity. It helps calm the emotions and creates motivation and determination so that we carry our actions out to the end. It increases the warrior spirit within us.
Spiritually
Red coral can be used to promote energetic yogic practices like mantra, meditation and pranayama. It provides motivation and vitality to pursue the spiritual path and gives the self-discipline and self-examination necessary to take this pursuit to a deeper level.

EMERALD

Physically
Emerald is in general a balanced stone in terms of the doshas but can decrease Agni or the digestive fire. It strengthens the nerves, lungs and vocal organs, improving perception and respiration. It aids in balancing endocrine function and helps promote growth and development in children.
Psychologically
Emerald improves the mind and emotions and stimulates the senses. It provides us better powers of speech, communication and expression, aiding in the learning process, particularly for children. It grants acuity of perception and gives speed, agility and comprehensiveness to our mental work.
Spiritually
Emerald sharpens the mind for yoga, mantra and meditation. It helps us develop the higher or spiritually discriminating aspect of the mind (buddhi) for the Yoga of knowledge and aids in teaching spiritual subjects. It is also good for developing Prana and healing energy.

YELLOW SAPPHIRE

Physically
Yellow sapphire increases Kapha and Pitta, but not usually exces-sively, and decreases Vata in a major way. It helps develop Ojas (pri-mary vigor), strengthens the immune system, and aids in overall growth and development. It is particularly good for the liver, spleen and pancreas. It promotes growth and healing of the tissues and helps balance the functions of the endocrine system.
Psychologically
Yellow sapphire improves our outlook in life, grants enthusiasm, and gives us courage and generosity to pursue our goals. It aids in positive emotions generally and makes us happier, more joyful and more content. It strengthens our judgment, raises our values and brings calm and steadiness to the mind.

YELLOW SAPPHIRE (cont'd)

Spiritually
Yellow sapphire increases our overall spiritual aspiration and motivation, connecting us with our higher purpose as a soul. It is good for meditation in all of its forms and for karma yoga. It puts us in touch with our dharma and helps us follow an uplifting and ethical lifestyle. It connects us with the energy of the guru.

DIAMOND

Physically
Diamond decreases Pitta and Vata and mildly in-creases Kapha. It strengthens the reproductive system, the bones and Ojas and helps promote overall strength, beauty and vitality, aiding in longevity. It is particularly good for women in developing female energy.
Psychologically
Diamond increases creativity and passion in general, whether in terms of art or in terms of sexuality, but gives fortitude, steadiness and resolve as well. It strengthens vision, imagination and insight.
Spiritually
Diamond is good for promoting devotion, Divine love and Bhakti Yoga. It also improves higher perception, opens us up to subtle energies and is good for Tantric practices, not just sexual but practices using the creative imagination and subtle perception including astrology.

BLUE SAPPHIRE

Physically
Blue sapphire reduces Pitta and Agni but increases Kapha and Vata. It aids in detoxification and in weight reduction, helping to reduce infection and inflammation, aiding in immunity and longevity.

BLUE SAPPHIRE (cont'd)

Psychologically
Blue sapphire helps control of the emotions, reducing desire and anger, improving our resolve to face and overcome obstacles. It grants calmness of mind generally, countering anger and aggression and promoting mental steadiness and emotional endurance.
Spiritually
Blue sapphire is good for detachment, renunciation, retreat and her-mitage. It puts us in contact with the void, the infinite and the eter-nal. At the same time it increases our capacity for spiritual work and service. It helps us transcend the world and our attachments to it.

HESSONITE GARNET

Physically
Hessonite garnet increases immunity, strengthens the endocrine system, calms the senses, deepens the breath and protects the ner-vous system. It aids in sound sleep and helps reduce stress, envi-ronmental sensitivity and sensory overload.
Psychologically
Hessonite garnet increases our capacity for empathy and deeper feelings, but at the same time it affords us emotional strength and endurance. It allows access to the positive forces in the subcon-scious mind as well as supporting our connection with the collec-tive consciousness and the masses of people.
Spiritually
Hessonite garnet opens us up to higher powers of service and devo-tion, putting us in contact with positive karmic trends in the envi-ronment and new energies of consciousness and creativity. It allows us to externalize our spiritual path into some helpful work in the world, including healing practices.

Cat's Eye

Physically
Cat's eye improves circulation through the brain, senses and ner-vous system. It aids in coordination of the muscles and motor organs. It improves our resistance to disease and our ability to handle environmental stress.
Psychologically
Cat's eye increases acuity of both the mind and the senses. It gives control over the emotions and the subconscious mind and makes the will stronger. It gives resolve, determination, focus and endu-rance..
Spiritually
Cat's eye helps awaken our higher perceptive abilities and stimu-lates our seeking for liberation and Self-realization. It can put us in touch with the guru, without or within. It is good for meditation of an introspective nature, like the Yoga of knowledge. It helps us un-derstand our karma in life and is a good aid for the practice of astrology.

1. Which Gemstones to Wear: Basic Rules

To determine which gemstones are best for a particular birth chart, we must first understand how to determine the status of planets in Vedic astrology as both 'natural' and 'temporal' benefics or malefics. Natural benefics are the Moon, Jupiter, Venus and Mercury. Natural malefics are the Sun, Mars, Saturn, Rahu and Ketu – as explained earlier in the book.

'Temporal benefics' are planets that rule good and helpful houses from the Ascendant like houses one, five and nine. 'Temporal malefics' are those that rule bad and challenging houses in the chart like houses six, eight and twelve. All planets work to strengthen the effects of houses that they rule, but not all houses are good for the chart overall. We generally do not want to strengthen the power of malefic houses.

Temporal status is a complex matter for which I have provided a simple table below.[39] It's logic follows the division into two planetary camps with the Sun, Moon, Mars and Jupiter forming one group of friends, and Mercury, Venus and Saturn forming the other, with some minor variations. Because all planets, except the Sun and Moon, rule two houses from the Ascendant – which may include both a good house and a bad house, determining the overall effect of a planet can sometimes in the end be a judgment call. The table is general and may require some modification as per individual chart.[40]

Table of Temporal Rulership

ASCENDANT	Generally Benefic	Neutral or Mixed	Generally Malefic
ARIES	Mars, Sun, Moon, Jupiter	None	Mercury, Venus, Saturn
TAURUS	Venus, Mercury, Saturn	Sun	Moon, Mars, Jupiter
GEMINI	Mercury, Venus	Saturn	Sun, Moon, Mars, Jupiter
CANCER	Moon, Mars, Jupiter	Sun	Mercury, Venus Saturn
LEO	Sun, Mars, Jupiter	Moon	Mercury, Venus, Saturn
VIRGO	Mercury, Venus	Saturn	Sun, Moon, Mars, Jupiter
LIBRA	Mercury, Venus, Saturn	None	Sun, Moon, Mars, Jupiter
SCORPIO	Mars, Sun, Moon, Jupiter	None	Mercury, Venus, Saturn

Table of Temporal Rulership (cont'd)

ASCENDANT	Generally Benefic	Neutral or Mixed	Generally Malefic
SAGITTARIUS	Jupiter, Sun, Mars	Moon	Mercury, Venus, Saturn
CAPRICORN	Saturn, Venus	Mercury	Sun, Moon, Mars, Jupiter
AQUARIUS	Saturn, Venus	Mercury	Sun, Moon, Mars, Jupiter
PISCES	Jupiter, Moon, Mars	Sun	Mercury, Venus, Saturn

Several conflicting opinions exist among Vedic astrologers regarding the prescribing of gemstones. These mainly fall into two opposing camps. The first group consists of those astrologers who recommend gemstones for weak planets in the chart in order to make them stronger. Their theory is that gems work primarily to increase the power of the planet that they relate to. This is the 'safe school', which I usually follow and will primarily examine in this book. According to it, the weakest benefics (figured both naturally and temporally) should be strengthened with the appropriate gemstones.

The second group consists of astrologers who recommend gemstones for the planets causing trouble in the chart, which are usually the malefics. Their logic is that it is best to propitiate the planet causing the problem, even if it is a malefic like Saturn or a lord of difficult houses like the eighth house. By removing the cause, the problem will be corrected. However, strengthening malefic planets increases their influence upon us and can cause dangers. Because of this, I recommend not to wear the gemstone of malefic planets unless you are really prepared to work with their energy on an inner level, doing extensive mantra and meditation practices. It is also best to have the ongoing help of a good astrologer or spiritual guide, if you want to follow this approach.

I will explain the rules for the first school of thought (the 'safe school'):

Rule 1 for Prescribing Gemstones

Use gemstones to strengthen the influence of weak benefics in the chart, particularly rulers of prime benefic houses 1, 5, and 9.

This is an important rule to consider for the lord of the Ascendant, the ruler of the chart as a whole, and for the lords of the fifth and ninth houses, the houses of grace and fortune. Gems for the planets ruling these houses are usually safe to wear, particularly if their lord is weakly placed in the chart. Such conditions include the planet located in its sign of debility, in difficult houses like 6, 8 and 12, under strong malefic influences like Mars, Saturn, Rahu, Ketu or the sixth or eighth house lords, or if the planet is combust or retrograde. If the planet is also a natural benefic, it is even safer to wear its gem.

If the house itself (1, 5 or 9) is under the influence of natural malefic planets (Saturn, Mars, Rahu, Ketu, Sun), that is another factor for strengthening its lord, even if the particular planet ruling that house is not itself afflicted. For example, if the Ascendant is under double malefic influences of Mars and Saturn it can be good to wear the gemstone for the planet ruling it, even if that planet itself is free of such afflictions. The same rule can be extended for temporal malefic influences on good houses. Aspects of the sixth, eighth or twelfth lord on such good houses can be similarly weakening.

The gem of the lord of the ninth house, the best house in the chart, is usually the safest to wear (with the possible exception of Gemini, where Saturn also rules the difficult eighth house). Many astrologers consider that the gem of the ruler of the Ascendant is also good for everyone to wear because it represents the 'self' of the person. But some caution should be taken if the Ascendant ruler is a temporal malefic (also ruling difficult houses like 6 and 8 apart from its rulership of the Ascendant, like Mars for Aries and Scorpio Ascendants).

Rule 2 for Prescribing Gemstones

Avoid gemstones of planets that are already strong in the chart, particularly if they rule malefic houses. To wear the gemstone of a strong malefic may only increase its power to do harm.

If planets are already strongly placed in the chart we ordinarily do not need to wear gems for them. If they rule malefic houses like 2, 3, 6, 7, 8, 11 and 12, we may only increase their capacity to cause harm. If the planet is also a natural malefic one should be doubly careful.

For example, if Saturn is located in Capricorn for a Cancer Ascendant, a strong position in an angle and in its own sign, we usually would not recommend a gem for it. This would increase the power of Saturn, which is both a natural and temporal malefic for Cancer.

If a temporal benefic is already strong in the chart, like a planet ruling houses 1, 5 and 9, its gem can usually be safely used but it may not be necessary or may not be the best gem to wear, if there are other temporal benefics in the chart that are more weakly placed.

Rule 3 for Prescribing Gemstones

Gemstones of natural malefic planets (like Saturn) should only be worn if the planet is a temporal benefic (ruler of good houses) and also weakly placed in the chart.

For example, if Saturn is located in its debility in Aries for a Libra Ascendant, its gemstone can be worn because it is a Raja Yoga Karaka (a ruler of good angular and trine houses that gives power and success in life). On the other hand, if Saturn is positioned in Aries for a Leo Ascendant, it would be better to wear a gemstone for Mars (the ruler of Aries) instead if one wanted to compensate for the weak Saturn because Saturn is not a good planet for Leo.

Rule 4 for Prescribing Gemstones

Gemstones of temporal malefic planets (lords of malefic houses like 3, 6, 8 and 11) are not usually worn.

This is a clarification of the previous rules. Rulers of these houses cause harm in the chart. If a planet is a natural benefic but a temporal malefic, like Jupiter for Libra Ascendant ruling houses 3 and 6, we would usually not recommend a gemstone for it, even if it is weak in the chart. If a planet is both a natural and a temporal malefic, like Mars for Gemini Ascendant ruling houses 6 and 11, its gemstone could be quite harmful.

Possible exceptions are the Moon and perhaps the Sun if they are especially weak in a chart because they represent Ascendants in their own right.

Rule 5 for Prescribing Gemstones

If using the gem is warranted by other factors, it becomes more favorable to wear it if its major or minor period is transpiring.

Some Vedic astrologers recommend wearing the gem of whatever planet is ruling the current planetary period (dasha). I would not go that far, but if there are several planets whose gem would be good to wear, one should give preference to the planet running the period involved.

Such a temporary use of gems can be done for planets that one might not normally want to use to strengthen the chart as a whole. For example, one might wear the gemstone of the ruler of the tenth house of career during its period, if it is weak and finding a good job is a problem.

Rule 6 for Prescribing Gemstones

If using a gem is warranted by other factors, one should grant special protection to a planet undergoing difficult transits.

This is particularly true for the Moon, which can bring a lot of suffering when transited by Saturn or Rahu. If the Moon is an important benefic in the chart, like for Cancer Ascendant, even if it is not otherwise very weak, we might want to recommend its gemstone during the period of Saturn's transit as a protective measure.

Rule 7 for Prescribing Gemstones

For gems, as for all affairs in the chart, examine houses from the Moon as well as houses from the Ascendant.

If both the Ascendant and the Moon are ruled by friendly planets (Saturn, Mercury and Venus are one camp; Jupiter, Sun, Moon and Mars are the other), the prescription of gems is easier. For example, if the Ascendant is Taurus and the Moon is located in Capricorn, since both Venus, the ruler of Taurus, and Saturn, the ruler of Capricorn, are natural friends and Mercury is a friend of both, should any of these three planets be weak either from the Ascendant or the Moon, its gem would usually be appropriate.

Conversely, we should be careful if planets belonging to unfriendly groups rule the Ascendant and the Moon. For example, if Gemini is rising but the Moon is in Sagittarius, the planets that will rule good houses from the Ascendant will rule difficult houses from the Moon. To deal with this, an important method is to see which is stronger, the Ascendant or the Moon, and prescribe the gems according to the stronger. To determine this, however, one must examine the chart carefully.

Rule 8 for Prescribing Gemstones

The positions of planets in divisional charts, particularly the navamsha, should be examined in a secondary way.

In determining whether to use the gem for a planet we should look at the navamsha chart as well and other divisional charts.[41] This helps us fine tune our prescription because the navamsha represents the fruit of the rashi or basic birth chart.

Rule 9 for Prescribing Gemstones

Another factor to bear in mind, though a secondary consideration, is that masculine gems – those for the Sun, Mars and Jupiter – are generally better for men and feminine gems – those for Venus and the Moon – are better for women. Here Mercury is considered to be androgynous.

For example, gemstones for the Moon may be helpful for women, if the Moon is afflicted in the chart, even if it rules difficult houses from the Ascendant.

Advanced Rules of Prescribing Gemstones

There are many other special rules for prescribing gemstones that go beyond the basic principles just indicated. These principles are mainly for gems that aim at improving the overall health and well-being of a person. Gems can also be prescribed for more specific issues and for particular domains of life. These considerations are outside the main scope of this book, so I will only provide a general indication of them here.[42]

Planetary gems generally strengthen the houses a planet rules or the house it is located in. This means that we can use gems to strengthen other affairs of life like wealth, vocation, education, relationship or spirituality relative to the planets influencing these houses in the chart. The down side of this option is that houses that may be good for such particular factors may be detrimental for general health and well-being of the person.

We may use gems to strengthen weak houses in the chart like wearing a gem for the ruler of the seventh for promoting marriage. But we must remember that the seventh house, though bringing marriage, can also hasten disease and death as a maraka or death dealing house.

When a planet rules two houses, its gem will strengthen both. For example, Venus rules the fifth and the twelfth houses for Gemini Ascendant. If we use its gem to promote the fifth house, say to benefit children, we must also consider its twelfth house or loss potential. In such instances of dual rulership we usually consider the overall favorability of the planet relative the Ascendant. In this example, because Venus is a friend of Mercury, the Ascendant ruler, we would put more weight on its positive fifth house rulership than its negative twelfth house effect.

If we use gems for planets that rule negative houses, we should do so only as a temporary measure or as balanced out by other gems which protect the health of the person. It is a little safer if the planet involved is also a natural benefic.

There are certain instances when we might prescribe the gem of a planet that is already strong in the chart, if occupationally the planetary energy is highly stressed. This rule is particularly helpful when a chart has no planets that are particularly weak and the person has an active career. To give an ancient example, Kings were often advised to wear rubies, even if the Sun was strong in their charts because of the demands made upon them for leadership. Astrologers and healers benefit from wearing gemstones while giving consultations or treatments to bring a healing or guiding energy in for their clients. For example, a healer may wear a gemstone for Mercury during treatments to increase the flow of Prana, even if the gem is not otherwise the best gem for them.

But please remember, all such rules remain general. One must examine the chart as a whole and not simply follow a mechanical means of prescription. And remember that even when you may have determined the best gem for the chart, the gem will require a good quality, the proper location on the body, a good setting and a special energization to become really effective.

Finally, always consider that gemstones are not indicated for all charts. Not every chart has one or two planets that can be conveniently strengthened with a gemstone. Spiritually advanced seekers may also not want to wear any gemstones as these can increase karmic involvements. And if one cannot afford a gemstone, there are effective alternative measures like the use of mantras to counter negative planetary influences. However, gemstones overall are the most direct, effective and easy to use of all astrological healing measures and should always be carefully considered.

Purification of Gem-Stones

All gemstones are receptors and take on the influences around them, whatever these may be. They reflect and hold the strongest energy that they are exposed to. Gemstones of sensitive or mutable planets, like the Moon and Mercury, are more susceptible in this regard.

All gems need, first of all, an initial purification to clear out such influences. This cleanses them of any impurities that may have attended their production or their sale. Purification is more important if the gem was previously worn by another person as gems will absorb much from a person over time.

Certain substances in nature have the power to clear negative influences from gems. Water is the most basic. Immersing a gem in ocean water or in water from a mountain stream is good. Soaking a gem overnight in a copper vessel filled with pure water is another method. Water from silver and gold vessels is yet stronger. Special Ayurvedic nervine herbs like tulsi (holy basil), brahmi (gotu kola), calamus, sandalwood or small amounts of camphor are particularly useful for making gems receptive to higher influences. Small amounts of these herbs can be added to the water used to purify gemstones.

Another simple method is to soak gems overnight in raw milk, which has a strong absorptive property itself. More preferable is a fivefold mixture of raw milk, yogurt, ghee (clarified butter), honey and raw sugar. This mixture is particularly useful for opaque stones like pearl or red coral.

One can also use internal methods, like clearing a stone through meditation; focusing ones awareness on the stone while allowing the mind to come to a state of complete calm and rest. It is good to chant the appropriate mantra for the planet as well, meditating on the planetary deity. We should meditate upon the gem as located in the heart chakra, third eye or on top of the head, wherever we want its higher influences to manifest.

Gems can be taken to temples or other holy places and blessed by spiritual teachers. They can be empowered through planetary rituals like pujas and yajnas. Note the following chapters for more information on these procedures. In short, gems should be treated as sacred objects. They should not be looked upon as mere possessions or ornaments but as tools of bringing our lives in harmony with the greater powers of the universe.

It is best to choose a good time (Muhurta) for the moment one first puts on the gem. It is best to chose the day ruled by the respective planet or a day ruled by one of its friends (here the days of Rahu correspond to Saturn and those of Ketu to Mars). The Moon should be waxing, between the third day after the new Moon to the day of the full Moon. A good lunar day or tithi is important like the fifth, tenth or eleventh. The Moon should be in a good sign and Nakshatra. The Moon should not be near malefics and there should not be planets in bad houses like 6, 8 and 12.

The Ascendant should be auspicious and harmonious to the planet whose gem is being selected, such as the sign that occupies the ninth house in the birth chart, signs ruled by the planet, those in which it is exalted, or the signs of its friends. The planet itself should be auspiciously placed and not in the sign of its debility. Naturally, not all these factors may be found during any particular muhurta but one should strive to have as many of them as possible.

Gemstones should be purified the evening before one chooses to put them on. One should rise before dawn on the appropriate day, perform a morning meditation and then put on the stone at the time of sunrise, repeating the appropriate planetary mantra at least 108 times, while meditating on the planetary deity.

While gems naturally transmit the energies of the planets, what we are seeking from them has some influence on how they affect us. For example, a yellow sapphire for Jupiter may only give material abundance if used with purely materialistic intentions. If used with spiritual motivation and aspiration, however, it can give wisdom and Divine grace. For this reason, try to seek what is highest with the gem, not simply what you would personally like. It is also best to use your planetary gemstone as part of regular mantra and meditation practices. This will help maintain its ability to aid in your spiritual life.

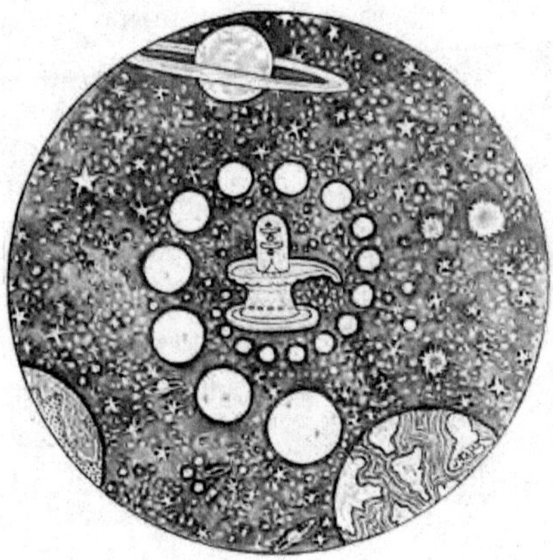

Planetary Deities: Communing with the Cosmic Powers

10

THE planets are among the foremost of the great Gods (Devas) or cosmic powers behind this vast universe. As the planets represent the forces of time that govern all things, all the Gods can be said to work through the planets in one way or another. The planets are an integral part of the cosmic Lord's self-expression and creative power through which the eternal order of karma and dharma is maintained.

As the Brihat Parashara Hora Shastra, the main classic work on Vedic astrology clearly states: "There are many incarnations of the unborn Supreme Self. To grant the results of karma for the souls of creatures, he takes the form of the planets. To reduce the strength of evil forces and to increase the strength of the Devas, to uphold dharma, He is born in many auspicious incarnations (avatars) from the planets." Planetary Devas can help their devotees like any other forms of God, granting them well-being, grace and wisdom. In addition God can take birth on Earth with the power of different planets. In Vedic thought, the Divine incarnations known as avatars carry such higher astrological forces.

The Gods represent the divine aspect of planetary energies, while humans and other creatures represent the karmic aspect. As creatures of karma we ourselves are products or children of all the planets. At death, the souls of humans go back to the planetary spheres that their karma is most strongly connected with, and through the planetary rays they are able to move as far into the divine light as their soul has evolved. From the worlds of the planets advanced souls can enter into higher worlds of the Sun and stars beyond.

Planetary Deities East and West

In the West, we are suspicious of the idea of many Gods, associating this idea with some primitive nature worship, if not idolatry. This is a misinterpretation of the nature of God whose unity does not exclude a variety of manifestations, assuming many names, forms and functions in His/Her cosmic play. The Gods or Devas represent the living powers of the conscious universe working behind the great forces of nature, of which the stars and planets are central conduits. We could say that the planets are merely transmission devices, like telephones, whereas the deities are the beings who operate and communicate through them. These different divinities are not separate Gods but different facets of the cosmic being, like the limbs and organs of the human body.

We might also consider Hindu forms of planetary deities to be strange, with their unusual appearances, gestures and ornaments. We should recognize that these images are not designed to communicate to our outer or superficial mind but to our inner mind and heart. The worship of planetary deities is a type of 'cosmic communication' in the universal language of mantra, symbol, story and ritual – which is the language of the soul. The deity so portrayed is an archetype for the mind to work with on a meditational level. For example, many planetary deities relate to different forms of the Divine Father and Mother, probably the two most important of all archetypes.

Ancient religions both East and West had a planetary side to their deities which, after all, represented the great powers of Heaven. This is obvious in the Roman names for the planets (Jupiter, Mars, Mercury, Saturn and Venus), which were also the names of their most important Gods and Goddesses. While such planetary deities became obscured by the advent of Christianity in the West, the Hindu religion—which has much in common with the older pagan religions of Europe—has continued to honor them.

Ritual worship of the planets is common in Hindu temples today, particularly in South India, where there are special altars for the navagrahas or nine planetary deities. While circumambulating the main shrine of the temple, the worshipper performs a smaller circuit of a platform on which statues for the nine planetary deities are placed, which is located in a corner of the temple room. In this way astrological worship remains an integral part of Hindu temple worship.

In the Greco-Roman system, general and planetary deities were equated. Roman Jupiter, for example, is not simply the deity of the planet Jupiter, but more primarily the great Lord of Heaven and the King of the Gods, a major deity for which the planet Jupiter, as the brightest of the nighttime stars, is only the planetary counterpart. The same is true of the other planetary deities in their pantheons. The astrological side is just one aspect or expression of a vast cosmic symbolism.

The Vedic system shares this basis, but is more complex in that it discriminates between the specific planetary deity, which is identified primarily with the planet, and general Divine powers ruling over the planet, which have broader indications and correlations. For example, the Vedic God Indra, who much like Roman Jupiter wields the thunderbolt and is King of the Gods, is not a specific planetary deity. Rather, he is a general deity ruling over not only the planet Jupiter, but also, in one of his other forms, the planet Venus, relating him to the two brightest of the planets.

Vedic thought evolved beyond simply identifying its great Gods with the planets to a more detailed set of correlations. In the Vedic system there are three levels of planetary deities. First, each planet has its own specific deity (devata). This is the deity relating directly to the planet and expressed by its name, like Surya for the Sun or Chandra for the Moon. These planetary deities are mainly astrological in nature.

Second, the Vedic system recognizes another deity that stands above the planetary ruler, a kind of overruler (adhidevata), like Agni, the Fire God, for Surya, the Sun. This overruler represents general qualities and energies associated with and ruled by the planet, like the Sun and fire.

Third, each planet has a supreme deity (pratyadhidevata) whose power lies behind the other two. This is the aspect of God or the cosmic Lord (Ishvara) working through the planet, like Lord Shiva, the deity of pure existence, for the Sun, or his consort the Goddess, Shakti, the great Goddess, for the Moon. There is even a fourth level of planetary deities hidden in this third level. At this fourth level all planets represent one or more aspects of the Godhead, Brahman, and the higher Self, Atman or Purusha, which is the highest light.

In the older Vedic period, the planets were generally referred to by their overrulers, rather than by their specific planetary deities, a practice which probably arose later. This is the same condition that existed in Greco-Roman thought in which an astrological symbolism was just one aspect of the Gods and Goddesses. This usage, of course, makes it difficult to determine whether a deity name like Jupiter or Indra refers to a planet or to just to a God, or at what point in history the planetary side of its symbolism arose. But it does show the organic connection of astrology to the ancient worship of the Gods in all their forms.

Three Levels of Vedic Planetary Deities

Planet	**Deity**	**Overruler**	**Supreme Deity**
Sun	Surya	Agni, Fire God	Shiva, Supreme God
Moon	Chandra	Apas, Water Goddess	Parvati, Supreme Goddess
Mars	Kuja	Bhumi, Earth Goddess	Skanda, War God
Mercury	Budha	Vishnu, Maintainer	Narayana, Cosmic Person
Jupiter	Brihaspati	Indra, King of the Gods	Brahma, Law giver
Venus	Shukra	Indrani, Queen of the Gods	Indra, King of the Gods
Saturn	Shani	Yama, GoD of Death	Prajapati, Creator
North Node	Rahu	Durga, Goddess of Power	Serpent God
South Node	Ketu	Chitragupta, God of Karma	Brahma, God of Knowledge

While the above system is the most common, several variations do exist. This is because the greater deities of the universe have many sides and cannot simply be reduced to a single planetary influence.

The nature of these deities can be examined in more detail through various books on the Hindu religion, particularly the Puranas, which provide much information about them, from myths and stories to mantras and details of their worship. There is often a specific Purana emphasizing each one of these deities, like the Shiva Purana, Vishnu Purana, and Skanda Purana. Others are mentioned in special sections of the Puranas, including those dealing specifically with the planets. The Puranas are an important set of esoteric encyclopedias from a yogic perspective and should be studied carefully by all those who follow Vedic astrology. Many Puranas also contain important information on Ayurveda, Vastu and other Vedic sciences.

However, the more specifically Vedic and Nakshatra deities, like Indra and Agni, are demoted in the Puranic scheme and cannot always be understood through their depictions. An examination of older Vedic texts is required to truly understand them.

Vedic Deities for the Planets

The Sun

The main Vedic name for the Sun is Surya, which means the energizer, inspirer, enlivener and transformer. Surya is the deity (devata) for the Sun. It is he who sets all things in motion as the guiding force behind the universe, the executive cosmic intelligence and power. Surya is the great god who directs the cosmic movement, the solar logos or indwelling cosmic being. He represents the cosmic will in life towards growth, evolution and the development of consciousness.

The Sun has many names in Vedic thought including Savitar (inspirer), Aditya (primal intelligence) and Bhaskara (maker of light). Many different forms of the Sun Gods or Adityas (like Mitra, Varuna, Aryaman and Bhaga) rule over different Nakshatras, months, seasons, times of the day, and other time cycles. For example, Mitra is said to be the name of the rising Sun, Indra for the Sun at noon, and Varuna for the Sun at setting. Generally Surya is more the deity of the solar disc, while Savitar is more the being or consciousness, the Purusha in the Sun.

Agni or Fire is the overruler (adhidevata) of the Sun. Agni is the God of fire on all levels, representing fire as a cosmic power. He is not simply the material fire but also the life fire, the fire of the soul and the Divine or spiritual Fire behind the entire universe. This cosmic fire manifests through the Sun who transmit fire, heat, light and color in all their forms.

The Sun represents God or the Cosmic Lord in general, the cosmic masculine principle. In Hindu Dharma, the main form of the great God is Shiva, Mahadeva. Shiva is the supreme deity (pratyadhidevata) of the Sun. Shiva means what is auspicious, tranquil, peaceful or at rest. It also refers to the states of death and liberation (moksha). Shiva is called Sham-bhu or Sham-kara, the giver or maker of what is auspicious or of peace, as well as Sada-shiva, the one who is eternally or perpetually Shiva or auspicious. Astrologically, the Sun is the original light and final abode of all.

Yet not only Shiva but also Vishnu can be seen as the supreme deity for the Sun. Vishnu is the preserver of the universe, the maintainer of the cosmic order. He is a form of the Sun god, much like the Greek god Apollo. In this regard, he is usually called Surya-Narayana, the Sun as the Cosmic Person who dwells on the cosmic waters of space. Vishnu represents the Sun as the power of love, beauty, inspiration and protection. He is also the Sun as the abode of the cosmic waters (the ocean of space). While Shiva represents the transcendent Sun or the light beyond time, Vishnu represents the immanent Sun or the light involved with and directing the cycles of creation.

The deity Brahma, the Creator among the Hindu trinity, is also sometimes portrayed as another form of the Sun God. In this regard Brahma, Vishnu and Shiva represent the creative, preservative and transformative aspects of solar energy and of Divine light. Brahma is the creative aspect of solar energy. He holds the Vedic mantras, which are said to dwell in the Sun's rays, through which all life is produced and organized.

The Sun ultimately symbolizes the Atman, the higher Self, the God of all the Gods. He represents our highest conception of the deity or truth, which may be abstract and formless, a principle or law, not necessarily a devotional image. The Sun is the dharma, the power that upholds all the laws of the universe. Brahman itself, the Vedantic term for the Godhead and absolute, originally referred to the expansive eastern light of the Sun. All the other planetary Gods can be seen as forms of the Sun God, just as all lights are manifestations of the supreme light of consciousness.

The Moon

Chandra, the main Sanskrit name for the Moon, means the giver of delight. It refers to beauty, passion, quick and changing rhythmical movement and reflected light. Chandra is also the Moon as the ruler of the month and the dispenser of the seasons. Inwardly it relates to the Moon as the ruler over our emotions, feelings and creativity. Like the Sun, the Moon has many other names relative to its different qualities and actions.

Apas, the Water Goddesses, is the overruler (adhidevata) of the Moon. Just as the Sun governs fire as a cosmic element, the Moon rules over the complementary principle of water —from the material waters, to the biological waters of life, to the transcendent waters of consciousness. Apas is also Soma, the nectar or nourishment principle complementary to Agni as the eater or the energizing principle. Agni and Soma represent the basic duality of fire and water, male and female, dry and damp, hot and cold – the prime duality behind the universe. Sometimes the water God is called Varuna, the ruler of the heavenly ocean, which relates not only to the setting Sun but also to the Moon.

The Moon represents the Goddess in general, the cosmic feminine force. In Vedic thought, the great Goddess (Mahadevi), the supreme power or Shakti, is the wife of Lord Shiva or the great God (Mahadeva). She is often called Parvati as the power of Divine love, beauty and delight.

Parvati means 'she who has parts.' Her name refers to the rhythms of nature through which the Goddess dances, the rhythms that follow the phases of the Moon, and support the ebb and flow of all of life. Parvati also means the 'daughter of the mountain', which here refers to the mountain of the sky. Parvati in her many names and forms (Shakti, Uma, Gauri, Durga, Kali, Tara, Sundari) is the supreme deity for the Moon.

Just as is the case with the Sun God, Lakshmi, the consort of Vishnu, like Parvati, Shiva's wife, is often regarded as a form of the Moon Goddess, representing fertility, beauty, fortune and happiness. Sarasvati, often compared to the autumn moon, is another moon Goddess as well. As the consort of Brahma, the lord of knowledge, she governs poetry, music and dance, the creative powers of the Moon.

The Moon, we could say, is the feminine aspect of the Sun and the three great Goddesses of Sarasvati, Lakshmi and Kali (Parvati) portray the three complementary aspects of lunar energy in its creative, preservative and transformative aspects. All the other planetary Goddesses can also be seen as forms of the Moon Goddess.

Mercury

Budha, which refers to the power of perception, is the main name for the planet Mercury in Vedic thought. Budha also means awakening and is associated with the early light of the Dawn. It is related to the term Buddha or the enlightened one, who is often associated with this planet. Budha is also the name of one of the great early human kings of the lunar dynasty, who was born as the son of the Moon. He resembles the God Hermes of the Greeks and Egyptians.

Vishnu is the overruler of Mercury, relating to the planet as the power of intelligence, reason and discrimination (buddhi). Vishnu is the power that measures out and regulates the cosmos. He is the indwelling cosmic intelligence that is the power of communication, love and healing. He grants discernment, detachment and clarity to his devotees. Note that this is a more specific Mercury function of Vishnu than his supreme power that is connected to the Sun. It relates more to his Trivikrama or three striding form.

As Vishnu, Mercury relates to Narayana, the cosmic form of Vishnu that enters into the hearts of all creatures, as its supreme deity. Mercury on the higher level is the cosmic intelligence that is closest to the Sun of truth. For this reason, Narayana, which is often connected to Surya, relates to Mercury as well. Through the intelligence of our soul, the Divine light enters into us.

Venus

The Vedic name for Venus is Shukra and means shining, luminous and bright. It also refers to a seed and to the reproductive fluid, showing its connection with love and sexuality. Shukra is also the name of one of the great primal rishis and gurus of the world. He is the main seer of the Bhrigu family, well known for their knowledge of astrology, Ayurveda, Vastu, martial arts and Tantra. Specifically, Shukra is the guru or guide of the Asuras or anti-Gods, and can bring the undivine forces over to the Divine. As the morning and evening star, Venus has the powers of reproduction, regeneration, rebirth and transformation.

Indrani, the Queen of the Gods, is the overruler of the planet Venus, just as Indra, the King of the Gods, is the overruler of Jupiter. Indrani here does not just refer to a particular Goddess but to the ruling power and beauty of all the Goddesses, and the Goddess in all her love, bliss and delight forms, much like the Goddess or beauty Sundari in later Tantric thought.

As Venus is the brightest of the planets and stars, it connects to Indra, the king of the Gods, as its supreme deity. This refers to Indra as the lord of the senses (Indriyas), which Venus controls. The senses are the Gods and the creative/delight urge of Venus is their ruler. Indra rules the cosmic Prana or life energy through which all the senses operate and which comes to us through Venus.

Yet Venus relates to many other forms of the Goddess. Lakshmi, the wife or consort of Lord Vishnu, corresponds to Venus as the Goddess of love, beauty, and abundance. Like the Greek Goddess Aphrodite, she is born of the ocean. On a higher level, Lakshmi represents Divine love and devotion (Bhakti). She gives both human comforts as well higher attainments. As a power of Maya, we can easily get caught in her glamour. Her favor, particularly at a mundane level of wealth and happiness, has always been most sought after by human beings.

Mars

There are many names for the planet Mars in Sanskrit including Angaraka, the radiant one and Mangala, the giver of good fortune. But perhaps most important is Kuja, he who is born – 'ja', of 'ku'– the Earth, a common epithet for Mars who is the son of the Earth in Vedic thought. As the son of the Earth, Mars is called Bhumi-ja and Bhauma as well. Kuja represents the fire force at work in the field of the Earth, from the fire at the core of the Earth, to the volcanic fire, to the fire in plants and animals, to the fire of human will power.

While the Sun and the Moon relate directly to fire and water as elements, Mars relates to the earth element_in a more indirect way. As the fire hidden in matter, Mars grants us the energy to accomplish our labors on the physical plane. For this reason the Earth Goddess or Bhumi Devi is the overruling deity of Mars. Sometimes in her stead, the overrulership of Mars is ascribed to the Earth God or lord of the field (Kshetrapati), who is a form of Vishnu and Rama. In this regard, Mars is a God of agriculture or of tilling the Earth. At other times, Kshetrapati is ascribed instead as the supreme ruler of Mars.

Usually however the supreme deity of Mars is said to be Skanda, the second son of Shiva and Kali (born after Ganesha) who, like the Greek god Mars, is the war god and the leader of the Divine army. Skanda represents the Divine will in manifestation through which truth conquers falsehood. Anger and violence are distortions of this energy on the physical plane. Skanda holds all spiritual powers but we must undergo purification (tapas) in order to receive them. He is also called Karttikeya, the one born of the Pleiades or Krittika Nakshatra, and Subrahmanya, the good priest. He is Kumara or the Divine child to the Sun and Moon who are his father and mother. He is most popular in South India, where he is called Murugan in Tamil.

In addition, the planet Mars relates to Hanuman, the monkey God and head of the Divine army of Lord Rama. Hanuman is generally worshipped on Tuesdays, the day of Mars.

Jupiter

Brihaspati, the main Vedic name for the planet Jupiter, means 'the lord (pati) of the vast or the profound (Brihat)', which indicates his role as the lord of the night sky, the brightest of the nocturnal stars. Brihaspati is the priest or guru of the Devas or Gods, the cosmic powers of light. He is the first and foremost of the human rishis, the great seers and sons of Agni or fire, who guide humanity spiritually. He is famous for his knowledge of mantra, ritual, yoga and Vedanta. Jupiter is also called Guru owing to his overall knowledge-giving and teaching role. As guru, one honors Jupiter by honoring one's guru.

Brihaspati in the Vedas is also called Brahmanaspati, or the lord of Brahman, the universal creative power and lord of the ritual order of the cosmos. In this regard he has connections both with the later God, Brahma, the creator among the Hindu trinity, and Ganesha, the lord of time and karma.

The Vedic God Indra is the overruler of the planet Jupiter. Like the Roman God Jupiter, he is the Lord of Heaven who wields the lightning and thunder, the divine weapons which destroys the titans, Asuras or anti-Gods. In this regard Jupiter is the planet of justice, law and dharma.

Jupiter relates to the Creator Brahma as his supreme deity – the cosmic law giver, the upholder of Dharma, and the giver of the Vedas or the Divine books of truth. Sometimes Jupiter is associated with Brahman in the neutral gender which indicates the Godhead, absolute or supreme reality, the higher truth behind all the Gods, as he holds the keys to spiritual knowledge.

Jupiter also relates to Ganesha or Ganapati, the Elephant God, the first son of Shiva and Parvati. Ganesha, like Jupiter, is the great god of wisdom through whom we overcome all obstacles. He grants knowledge of Yoga, Astrology, Vastu, science and mathematics. He is the Divine teacher and guide and represents the cosmic intelligence working behind the world. The first and most famous Vedic Ganapati mantras are part of hymns to Brihaspati.[43]

Saturn

The main Sanskrit name for Saturn is Shanischarya, which means 'he who moves slowly', often reduced to Shani for short. Shani is the son of the Sun, but in the negative sense. He represents the shadow of the Sun, the powers of death, time and decay. He is the darkness that is born along with the light. True to his name Saturn slows us down and teaches us through patience and endurance.

Saturn relates to Yama, the God of death as his overruler. Yama is sometimes regarded as the first man like Manu, himself a solar figure, or as Manu's twin brother, the death born as the shadow or background companion along with human life. Yet Yama can also grant us the power to transcend death and gain immortality, which comes through self-discipline, self-sacrifice and voluntary death while living – the spiritual qualities of Saturn which represent the practice of Yoga.

Saturn relates to other forms of Death, including Lord Shiva and his consort Kali, who rule over death, destruction, eternity and transcendence as cosmic principles. Death is the great teacher or guru in many spiritual teachings, including the Upanishads (notably the Katha). In this regard, Saturn like Jupiter is the guru but represents learning through work and suffering, while Jupiter indicates learning through inspiration and effort.

Saturn relates to the God Prajapati, 'the lord (pati) of creatures (praja)', particularly in the form of the Divine grandfather as his Supreme deity. Also called Brahma, Prajapati represents the creative urge that contains inherent within it both the shadow of death and the secret desire to go beyond death to the deathless.

Owing to his dark nature, Saturn corresponds to dark forms of Shiva and Shakti, much like Rahu and Ketu. This is particularly true when Saturn is malefically disposed in the chart. Saturn often requires special Tantric propitiation through dark forms of worship, honoring the Divine presence in death, suffering and deprivation. He requires that we face our fears and challenge and overcome our negative emotions. In this regard, Saturn may be propitiated through Kali or through Aghora, the darker forms of Shiva and his consort, sometimes also called Bhairava and Bhairavi. Prajapati is ruled over by Shiva, just as Saturn is under the rule of the Sun.

Rahu

Rahu means 'what hides, covers or obscures', including a cave. It refers to the darkness of the eclipse that hides or swallows the Sun or Moon. Rahu indicates secrecy, profundity and the abyss. He is the bodiless part of the severed serpent, the cut off head which indicates the way beyond body consciousness.

Rahu's overruler is the great Goddess Durga, who represents the Divine Mother in her protective and saving role. She is also called Tara or the saviouress. Durga is fierce relative to the demons or negative forces that threaten her children, but loving and protective of her devotees. She is the Goddess who takes us over all difficulties and destroys all the demons or obstacles that beset us. These demons are often represented through the form of various serpents. Durga rules over Maya, the power of illusion that is often associated with Rahu.

Rahu's Supreme deity is the Serpent God (Sarpa Deva). Serpents represent energy, which flows in currents and through channels and holes, just as a serpent moves. All forms of energy from the Kundalini, the serpent power of consciousness, down to Prana and even wind power are symbolically represented as such serpents. Rahu reflects the supreme serpent force that can even swallow the Sun. Shiva is the lord of serpents, the foremost of which are Rahu and Ketu. In this regard the serpent God that rules over Rahu is himself under the rule of Shiva.

Ketu

Ketu means 'a flag, a sign, a symbol, intimation or indication'. It refers to the smoke that is the indicator or precursor of fire. It indicates the first light of the dawn or the first rays of the Sun. Ketu also refers to comets (upaketu), which were often regarded as omens of misfortune. Ketu indicates secret knowledge, including symbols, secret languages and ancient teachings. Ketu is the cut off body of a serpent and represents going beyond the mind.

Ketu is ruled over by Chitragupta who is the God of karma, connected to Yama or the God of death. Chitra means 'a picture', and gupta means 'hidden'. Ketu reflects the karmic residues that are present like pictures in our deeper subconscious mind. These come out in sleep, death or deep meditation when the ordinary mind ceases its activity.

The supreme deity of Ketu is Brahma as the giver of spiritual knowledge, much like Jupiter. While Jupiter is the outer guru, Ketu is the inner guru. At a higher level Ketu relates to the formless Brahman or transcendent reality. Ketu, which is outwardly karma, is inwardly spiritual knowledge or Jnana.

Ketu is also connected to Ganesha who is Dhumaketu or smoky Ketu. Ganesha, like Ketu, has his head cut off but replaced with that of en elephant (who has a serpent-like trunk). Ganesha, like Ketu, rules over both karma and spiritual knowledge and is also the main deity of Vedic astrology, which is the science of karma. Sometimes it is the skinny or thin Ganesha that relates to Ketu, while the fat Ganesha relates more to Jupiter.

Meditation on Planetary Deities

Meditation on planetary deities attunes our consciousness with the higher awareness within the planets, promoting both psychological and spiritual healing. It is best used with mantra as explained in the next chapter. Please note Astrology of the Seers for more information on the traditional forms of the Vedic deities and how to visualize them.[44] Of main importance is to contact the living energy of the planets; the forms that we choose are secondary. In addition, in our general worship of God or the Goddess, for whatever purpose, we should not forget astrological forms and energies, which are among the most powerful.

Deities for the Planets, a Universal View

Looking behind the meaning of these planetary deities, we get the following system:

Sun	Divine Father	**Moon**	Divine Mother
Mars	Divine Son or War God	**Venus**	Divine Daughter or Goddess of Love
Mercury	Divine Child	**Jupiter**	Divine Teacher or Guru
Saturn	Divine Grandfather or Grandmother	**Ketu**	Divine Father in Wrathful or Transformative Energy
Rahu	Divine Mother in Wrathful or Protective Energy		

Each planet represents an inner archetype that we must integrate within ourselves for wholeness and transformation. Each represents a particular part of our psyche that we must understand and honor with its appropriate place within us. Each represents a certain stage in spiritual growth and a particular approach along the path of Yoga. Until we have mastered the forces and qualities of all the planets, we must be bound to the cycle of time, death and rebirth (samsara).

Weakness of the Sun can be countered by worship of the Divine Father; that of the Moon by worship of the Divine Mother. Weakness of Mercury can be countered through the energy of the Divine child. Weakness of Mars can be balanced by the Divine warrior or hero, weakness of Venus though the Goddess of beauty and delight.

Jupiter energy can be strengthened by the archetype of the Divine teacher and giver of wisdom. Positive Saturn energy can be strengthened by the archetype of the Divine Grandfather, the lawgiver and ancestor spirit, or by the Divine Grandmother. Afflictions of Rahu and Ketu can be overcome by understanding our shadow and by learning how to bring the light out of darkness. The dark forms of the Father and the Mother can help us do this.

The Ten Avataras of Lord Vishnu

The ten avatars of Lord Vishnu have planetary correspondences, through which we can also propitiate the planets. This is the main method used in the classic astrological text, the Brihat Parashara Hora Shastra.

Lord Vishnu, by the power of compassion, voluntarily takes birth through the planets in order to guide the souls of creatures, who themselves are compelled by karma to take birth through the planets. All births, Divine and ignorant, occur through the planetary rays. When the solar system comes to an end, the souls of creatures merge into the planetary deities, which in turn merge back into Vishnu, who in his highest nature as the Supreme Person, Purushottama, transcends all time and space, birth and death.

Matsya – Fish

Ketu relates to the fish incarnation of Lord Vishnu. This is the fish that saves Manu – the original man, a kind of Adam and Noah figure – from the great flood, after which begins a new cycle of creation on Earth. Ketu relates to destruction that is the prelude to and foundation for a new creation.

Worshipping Matsya avatara grants us a new creative force and allows us to find a fresh and higher karma to move our lives forward to the Divine, transforming and uplifting our Ketu energy.

Kurma – Turtle

Saturn relates to the turtle or tortoise incarnation of the Lord Vishnu. This is the great tortoise of the directions that carries the universe on his back. Saturn is a strong and hard planet, which serves as a great support in life if we know how to use its energies.

Worshipping Kurma avatara grants us the strength and support of the foundational powers of the entire universe, transforming and uplifting our Saturn energy.

Varaha – Boar

The Varaha or boar incarnation of Lord Vishnu relates to Rahu. The boar saves the Earth and lifts it out of the cosmic marsh. Rahu in its higher form has a saving and redeeming energy as manifested by the Goddess Durga, its overruler, and by the boar incarnation of Lord Vishnu.

Worshipping Varaha avatara allows us to overcome the marshland of our own ignorance and the many negative serpents that inhabit it, transforming and uplifting our Rahu energy.

Narasimha – Man-Lion

The man-lion as a symbol of courage, strength and will-power naturally relates to the martial planet Mars. Narasimha shows the Divine wrath necessary to overcome the forces of ignorance and evil.

Worshipping Narasimha avatara helps us turn our anger into Divine righteousness and protection of dharma, transforming and uplifting our Mars energy.

Vamana – Dwarf

One might consider it odd that Jupiter, the largest of the planets, is identified with the dwarf among the avatars of Vishnu. However, Vamana is only a dwarf in his initial appearance. He expands in size to become a great giant and measures out the entire universe by his three steps.

In this regard, Vamana represents the wisdom-power of Jupiter that comprehends the entire universe in a threefold law. Worshipping him puts us in contact with Jupiter's power to organize our lives in a cosmic way, transforming and uplifting our personal Jupiter energy.

Parashurama

Parshurama relates to the planet Venus. He is the Brahmin warrior who destroys the negative forces that rule over us in our ignorance. Venus in Vedic thought is the guru or guide of the Asuras, the negative/undivine forces in the universe. Parashurama represents the martial side of Venus as the Asura-guru who must chastise these negative forces. When these negative forces submit to his guidance, he can lead them to the path of the Gods.

Worshipping Parashurama helps us to transform and uplift our Venus energy from a power of self-indulgence to one of self-discipline.

Rama

Rama is the great dharma king, the foremost prince of the solar dynasty, and the representative of the cosmic order of Dharma on Earth and in society. His rule, Rama Rajya, is the rule of truth and the Divine light. His association with the Sun is, therefore, quite apt. Rama can even be a name for the Sun.

Worshipping Rama helps us increase the solar light in our lives as a power of truth, righteousness and compassion, and helps us to transform and uplift our Solar energies.

Krishna

Krishna relates to the Moon as the great planet of beauty, delight, love and devotion, the pastimes for which Krishna is well known. He was also a great prince of the lunar dynasty. Like the Moon, Krishna has great popularity and the ability to move the masses.

Worshipping Krishna helps us transform and uplift our lunar energy into one of Divine devotion and delight.

Buddha

Buddha not surprisingly relates to the planet Mercury or Budha in Sanskrit. Buddha is the avatar of reason, logic, intelligence and discrimination (buddhi), which are the gifts bestowed by a strong Mercury in the chart.

Worshipping Buddha puts us in contact with the higher spiritual power and meditative insight of the planet Mercury, helping us to transform and uplift our Mercury energy.

Kalki

Kalki as the tenth avatar represents all nine planets conjoined. Some see him as representing the new planetary dharma that is emerging in the world today. Worshipping him can help us energize all the nine planets in a positive way for inner transformation and upliftment.

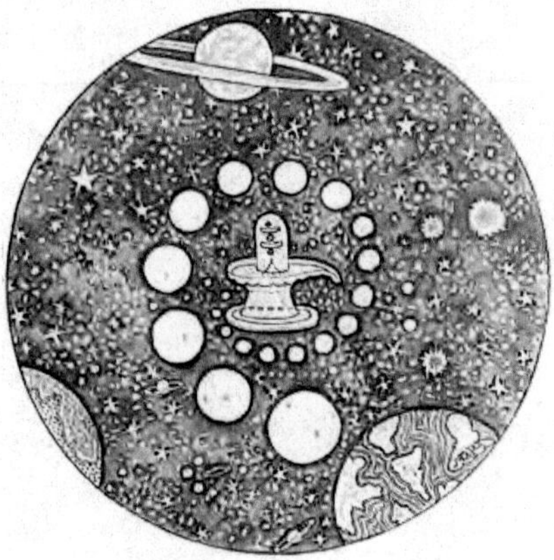

Planetary Mantras

11

MANTRA is the main tool for working on the mind in Yoga, Ayurveda and Vedic astrology. It is perhaps the most important technique of all Vedic sciences. Mantra is the basis of the entire Vedic language and way of thought, which is mantric in nature.

Mantra is not just a means of gaining knowledge; it is a powerful technology for bringing about positive changes in both the conscious and subconscious mind. Mantra can alter deep-seated emotional patterns probably better than any other method of working with the mind. It can increase mental abilities and open higher intuitive faculties, unlocking potentials of awareness that otherwise might remain dormant. It can help erase negative karmic tendencies, including those that have their roots in previous births.

Yet the influence of mantra goes beyond our personal mental activity to the level of the cosmic mind.[45] It can link us up to God (Ishvara), the inner guru, whose indicator is found in mantras like OM. Mantra reflects the vibratory knowledge that creates the universe. Through mantra we can learn to work with all the forces of nature at an inner level. Mantra can be used for controlling the five elements out of which the universe is composed. It can harmonize us with the cosmic powers of creation, modulating the energies transmitted through the stars and planets, the great lords of time that help unfold the cosmic movement.

In yogic thought, the sense quality of sound relates to the element of ether, the first of the cosmic elements. The field of ether vibrates as the cosmic sound OM which upholds all the worlds. The planets not only reflect the seven rays of creation in terms of gem therapy but also the seven primal cosmic sounds that go with these in terms of mantra. The influence of each planet can be harmonized by the right use of sound and mantra.

Mantra is probably the most direct way to balance the energy of the planets within us—in effect attuning us to the music of the spheres. It can reach planetary forces hidden behind our mind and life energy, down to the deepest layers of our being. Mantra is always worthy of consideration when we are seeking how to balance planetary energies. Astrological mantras are something we can do for ourselves, with no expense and with little in the way of side effects, unless we try to use them for selfish or harmful purposes.

Yet mantra, though seemingly the easiest astrological remedial measure, can be the most difficult to effectively implement. While one can simply wear a gem, or have a ritual performed, one has to repeat the mantra oneself, with deep feeling, motivation and attention regularly for a long period of time. Most mantras require repetitions in the tens of thousands in order to become fully effective. Their complete empowerment requires awakening the power or shakti of the mantra, which is like an explosion of the mantra's energy within us. This can take years of practice to arrive at, though for some individuals with good insight or good karma it can happen quickly.

The astrological use of mantras is best done as part of a practice of mantra yoga, including chanting, mental repetition of mantras, pranayama and meditation. We should aim at feeling the mantra vibrating behind our every thought and working in every cell of our bodies.

Application of Astrological Mantras

The planets project powerful cosmic forces, both positive and negative, which influence us on all levels. They are not just material or chemical sources of light, but the source of subtle mental and emotional energies. They are lords of fate, karma and destiny that we must approach with reverence and respect. Their mantras are their names through which we can connect to their inner being. Their mantras are not simply sounds to repeat or formulas that work of their own accord. They require deep regard for, if not devotion to, the Divine forces working through the planets, the Planetary Gods and Goddesses. So please bear in mind our discussion of these planetary beings when you consider the role of mantra.

There are certain formalities traditionally associated with taking up any mantra. Initiation into astrological mantras usually follows a ritual worship of the planet and is done at a favorable time and place. Mantras are usually given as part of a spiritual tradition or lineage and received from a guru. It is best to receive astrological mantras from yogis and astrologers who have used the mantras as part of their lifelong practices. A mantra from one who has not practiced it or who does not have the shakti (power) of the mantra is not likely to yield its full effects.

Astrological mantras, however, do not have as many restrictions in their usage as do spiritual mantras aimed at gaining higher spiritual aims. Astrological mantras are part of astrological treatment methods with a limited and specific application that depends mainly upon the planet needing propitiation in the chart. Yet the more we empower the mantra and the more it is grounded in an authentic tradition, the stronger it becomes.

A well trained Vedic astrologer should know both the mantras for the planets and how to adapt them to their clients. Yet he should also know his limitations, particularly if he is just learning these mantras himself. He should not use them beyond their scope, claiming that the mantras will give magical results or of themselves solve a person's problems without any examination of the karmas involved.

A good astrologer should work with mantra as part of their personal spiritual practice, building up their mantra shakti in a consistent manner. A Vedic astrologer should practice Vedic planetary mantras on a regular basis, preferably every day before seeing clients or studying charts. Planetary mantras stimulate the right perception and intuition required to learn the secrets of Vedic astrology. Planetary mantras should be done along with other spiritual and yogic mantras, like those to Ganesha, ones guru or the form of God one worships.

Mantras have more latitude in their application than gemstones, which are mainly used for strengthening weak planets in the chart. Mantras can be used to increase the positive influence of benefic planets, yet can also serve to decrease the negative influence of malefic planets. Mantra works either way while gems are more safely used to increase positive planetary influences.

Yet besides their usage as a remedial measure in their own right, mantras are an integral part of all other astrological remedial measures. They are essential to properly empower planetary gemstones.

The appropriate mantras awaken the subtle power of the gems and help us use them in a more conscious manner. They form the basis for propitiatory rituals for the planets like pujas or yajnas. Without some knowledge of mantra, it is difficult to apply any astrological treatment measures effectively.

Bija Mantras

The most important and powerful of all mantras are single syllable or bija (seed) mantras like OM. Bija mantras are primal sounds that carry an integrated concentration of both sound and meaning from which all language and the very forces of creation arise. They can create a great force of transformation that penetrates deep into the subconscious mind, reaching the very causal body or karmic sphere of the soul. Bija mantras have an energetic effect that works well with pranayama and silent meditation. As such, they can be more powerful than prayers, which rely more on thought and intention. Bija mantras may be used by themselves or combined with other mantras, in which case they serve to energize them more strongly.

The Astrological Usage of OM

OM is the foremost of all bija mantras and has a wide astrological application. OM in the Vedas relates to the Sun and to light in general. The Upanishads say that the Sun chants OM as it moves in the sky.[46] OM is the sound of the essential cosmic vibration transmitted through the Sun and all the stars. It also relates to the planet Jupiter as the cosmic guide or guru and to the Moon as the light of the mind.

OM is the syllable of 'assent' that allows us to harmonize with everything. In this regard, OM in Sanskrit also means 'yes'. Chanting OM allows us to affirm any planetary influence that we want to bring into our lives. Whatever planet we chant OM to, we energize its light and affirm its power.

OM is also the syllable of 'ascent' through which the upward movement of awareness occurs. Whatever planet we chant OM in regard to; we enter into its upward movement and contact its evolutionary force. Our energy goes to that planetary deity, power or consciousness in the higher worlds.

In addition, the mantra OM clears the mind at a deep level, making it receptive to higher influences. That is why all longer mantras begin with OM; it creates the foundation for them to truly create results.

All planetary mantras should similarly start with OM. OM puts us in touch with the higher Self or Purusha, the Cosmic Person manifesting through the different planets.

Ganesha Mantra

Ganesha, the elephant-headed God, the first son of Shiva and Parvati, is the main deity of Vedic astrology. He is the lord of time and karma as well as the deity governing all the occult sciences, including the usage of mantras. He holds the powers of all mantras within himself and can make them all work effectively.

Ganesha is usually propitiated at the beginning of any activity for protection and removal of obstacles. He is worshipped before any other deities, whether for external rituals or for internal yoga practices. For honoring Ganesha, one can use the following simple name mantra. Alternatively one can use the seed mantra GLAUM ('au' pronounced like 'ou' in 'sound') for Ganesha. It is good to do this mantra of Ganesha before the planetary mantras.

OM Gam Ganeshaya Namah!

Planetary Name and Bija Mantras

Certain seed syllable or bija mantras can be used for the planets. These come in two main groups.

- First are bija mantras based upon the names of the planets, like SUM for Surya (the Sun). They reflect the sound of the first syllable of the name of the planet.
- Second are special Shakti or Siddha mantras like HRIM. These have planetary connections but are not necessarily limited in usage to one planet.

We will discuss both types of mantras. Of the two, the name mantras are most commonly used and of easiest application.

The Sanskrit names for the planets are not merely incidental, but reflect the essential qualities of the planets, which they carry in their sound vibrations. The Sanskrit language has the power to convey astral energies, the foremost of which are transmitted through the planets. The planetary seed mantra brings the corresponding planetary ray into our minds and hearts.

Planetary influences can be balanced through chanting the names of the appropriate planets. OM is chanted at the beginning of the mantra because OM empowers all mantras. Then the specific name of the planet is chanted in the dative or 'to' case (Sanskrit is an inflected language, unlike English which relies on propositions for its case endings). It concludes with the word 'namah', which means offering reverence or respect. The bija mantra for the planet is generally used before the name. All bija mantras end with an 'm' sound called 'anusvara' in Sanskrit. It is pronounced with a nasalization of the vowel, ending in the closing of the lips.

The following are the main name mantras for the planets. Note the Sanskrit table in the Appendix for the correct pronunciation of the letters indicated. I have also discussed these mantras in Astrology of the Seers.[47]

- **Sun - Om S m S ry ya Namaha**
- **Moon - Om Cham Chandr ya Namaha**
- **Mars - Om Kum Kuj ya Namaha**
- **Mercury - Om Bum Budh ya Namaha**
- **Jupiter - Om Brim Brihaspataye Namaha**
- **Venus - Om Shum Shukr ya Namaha**
- **Saturn - Om Sham Shanaye Namaha**
- **Rahu - Om R m R have Namaha**
- **Ketu - Om Kem Ketave Namaha**

Usage of Planetary Mantras

Planetary name mantras are used to gain the powers of the planets for either spiritual or worldly goals. They aid in the fulfillment of the intention with which they are done. For example, if we repeat a mantra for the planet Jupiter to facilitate its wealth-giving properties, it will promote that for us. If we do one to it to facilitate its wisdom-giving power, it will aid in that direction. However, we must be careful what we seek through the mantra because we will energize our minds on that level of karma. Generally, we should primarily seek spiritual goals through mantras for the universal good.

Planetary mantras should be chanted 108 times (or 1,080 times) on a daily or weekly basis (on the day of the planet particularly). Generally, one should repeat them up to 100,000 times over a period of one to three months if one wants to effectively empower them. The mantra can be repeated mentally, though it is good to repeat it audibly at first until one is used to the sound, then to repeat it with a low voice, like a whisper until the sound is quite familiar.

Another method is to just use the bija mantra for the planet and not recite the full planetary name mantra, like repeating the bija SUM for the Sun. This is easier and quicker and yet remains very effective. Such name and bija mantras, which are easy to pronounce, are the best to give to clients who want to use mantras but find longer mantras hard to pronounce.

These mantras can be used to aid in the purification of gemstones or with rituals like yajnas and pujas. Besides focusing on a single planetary mantra, we can repeat the entire set of all nine planetary mantras as a way of increasing our inner growth and developing all the higher qualities that the planets can represent.

It is important to afford such reverence to the planets on a regular basis, particularly to those planets whose influence one most needs to harmonize. Being mindful of the planets is a yogic observance that has many benefits. That is why an astrologer is often blessed, for in giving reverence to the planets, the planets give their grace to the astrologer as well.

Shakti Mantras for the Planets

Besides the name mantras for the planets are certain powerful (Shakti) single-syllabled mantras. These Shakti mantras are special bija or seed mantras with a wide application in yogic teachings. Most have special planetary correspondences (like SHRIM and the Moon), but can be used for all the planets relative to the general qualities or connections that they invoke and create. As Shaktis or feminine energies, each connects to its own special form of the Goddess. Most are dominated by the sound 'ee' (Sanskrit long-I sound) which grants ruling power. Such powerful mantras should be taken up only with due care, proper guidance, suitable initiation and intuitive insight.

AIM – ऐं

AIM (pronounced as the English contraction 'I'm') is the seed mantra of Sarasvati, the Goddess of knowledge and speech, and the consort of Lord Brahma, the Creator in the Hindu trinity of great Gods. It relates primarily to the planet Mercury as a planet of speech, knowledge and guidance. It is sometimes used for the Moon and Jupiter, promoting their creative and expressive powers.

AIM is also the mantra of the guru and helps us access higher knowledge. It can be used to call or invoke the wisdom power of any planet that we direct it towards.

SHRIM - श्री

SHRIM (pronounced shreem) is the seed mantra of Lakshmi, the Goddess of Prosperity and Abundance, and the consort of Lord Vishnu, the Preserver in the Hindu trinity of great Gods. It relates primarily to the Moon as a planet of abundance, happiness and fertility. It is sometimes used for Venus as a Goddess Mantra for the heart, happiness and love. It is also used relative to Jupiter for its general benefic qualities.

SHRIM is the mantra of refuge or devotion. It can be used to take refuge or express devotion to any of the planetary deities, helping us to gain its favor.

KRIM - क्रीं

KRIM (pronounced kreem) is the seed mantra of Kali, the Goddess of time and transformation, and the consort of Lord Shiva, the Destroyer/Transformer in the Hindu trinity of great Gods. It primarily relates to malefic planets like Mars (destruction) or Saturn (death).

KRIM is a mantra of work, yoga and transformative energy. It can be used to connect us with the inner power of any planetary deity we wish to connect to.

HRIM - ह्रीं

HRIM (pronounced hreem) is the prime mantra of the Goddess in general in all of her three main powers. It is said to be equivalent to OM for the Goddess. It relates primarily to the Sun as the source of life and light and to the heart, the place of our inner Sun. It is sometimes used with Jupiter or the Moon to promote their benefic forces. As it represents the power of Maya that Rahu projects into the world, it can also ward off the negative effects of Rahu.

HRIM is a mantra of magical force, captivation and empowerment. It can be used relative to any planetary deity whose magic and presence we wish to access at the level of the heart.

KLIM – क्लीं

KLIM (pronounced kleem) is the seed mantra of desire, love and attraction. It relates to the God Krishna, who grants bliss (Ananda), and to Sundari, the Goddess of love and beauty. It is mainly used relative to the planet Venus, but sometimes relative to the Moon as well.

KLIM can be used relative to any planetary deity we would like to access in order to fulfill our wishes or express our devotion.

STRIM – स्त्रीं

STRIM (pronounced streem) is the seed mantra of the great Goddess Tara, who in Hindu thought is the wife or feminine form of Brihaspati, the planet Jupiter. Tara means 'a star' in Sanskrit and relates to the Nakshatra Rohini, the star Aldeberan, or alpha Taurus. As Brihaspati/Jupiter is the high priest or guru of the Gods, Tara is the high priestess. As a general mantra of the Goddess, particularly in her higher knowledge form, it can be used for the Moon and Venus as well.

STRIM can be used as well relative to any planetary deity whose energy we wish to expand or project in a creative manner. It also helps us overcome difficulties associated with the planets. This mantra of the Star Goddess attunes us to the benefic powers of the stars, particularly relative to the Nakshatra which she rules.

HUM – हूं

HUM (pronounced hoom as in English 'whom') is the main Agni or fire mantra. Astrologically it relates to fiery planets like the Sun, Mars or Ketu and increases their fiery properties. It is particularly good for bringing in the higher perceptive power of Ketu, which is a great aid in astrological research.

HUM can be used relative to any planetary energy whose light, warmth, power and insight we would like to activate.

A related mantra HAUM ('au' pronounced as 'ou' in sound) is specific for worshipping Lord Shiva and is good for the transformative aspect of solar energy ruled by him.

RAM – रां

RAM (pronounced rahm) is the mantra of Lord Rama, God in his protective, saving and compassionate form. It has already been mentioned as a seed sound for Rahu. However, it can also be used relative to the Sun, Mars, Jupiter or whatever planet whose saving power we wish to increase. It is most applicable to the Sun.

The Language of Shakti Mantras

Shakti mantras are woven into various combinations to access different deities and their specific qualities. For example, OM AIM HRIM SHRIM, means Om, I invoke (AIM), open my heart to (HRIM) and take refuge in (SHRIM). Or OM KRIM HUM HRIM means OM, I energize (KRIM), enkindle (HUM) and open my heart to (HRIM). These Shakti mantras allow us to energize our thoughts and feelings at a deeper level.

Instead of the bija mantras for the names of the planets, the Shakti mantras can be used instead, like OM HRIM Suryaya Namah! Or more than one bija can be used like OM AIM HRIM SHRIM Chandraya Namah. However, such combinations are extremely powerful and should be learned and practiced with the appropriate guidance.

Mantras for the Chakras and the Elements

LAM, VAM, RAM, YAM, HAM (all pronounced with a short vowel sound as the 'a' in the word 'father') are the bija mantras of the five great elements of earth, water, fire, air and ether and relate respectively to the five chakras from the root (Muladhara) to the Throat (Vishuddha). They strengthen their respective elements and chakras and can also be used for the planets connected to the elements. In addition, the mantra KSHAM rules the third eye or mind center and the mantra OM the crown chakra and center of consciousness.

- The mantra LAM (relating to earth and the root chakra) gives groundedness, stability and contentment. It strengthens the Venus and Mars and helps ward off the negative effects of a malefic Saturn.
- The mantra VAM (relating to water and the second chakra) gives movement, vibration and fluidity. It strengthens watery planets like the Moon, Venus and Jupiter.
- The mantra RAM (relating to fire and the solar plexus) gives fire and will power and strengthens the Sun, Mars and Ketu.
- The mantra YAM (relating to air and the heart center) gives power of movement, velocity and direction. It strengthens Mercury.

- The mantra HAM (relating to ether and the throat chakra) gives space, force and pervasion. It strengthens Mercury and Jupiter.
- The mantra KSHAM (pronounced "kshum") strengthens the third eye or Ajna chakra, the Moon and Mercury.
- The mantra OM strengthens the head or crown chakra and the Sun.

Prayers to the Planets

Besides the name and bija mantras, there are longer extended mantras, which are usually verses or parts of hymns. We could also call these 'prayers'. They aim at propitiation (prarthana) of the deity for general or specific results.

Such verses aim at warding off negative energies and promoting positive energies through an attunement of our speech, mind and will to the divine forces of the universe that work through the planets. To use them requires that we recognize the power of cosmic consciousness behind the planets, extending to our own higher Self or cosmic being.

These hymns are largely an expression of devotion and reverence for the planetary deities and their powers. By reciting them, we worship God through the planets, recognizing the planets as manifestations of a higher spiritual intelligence. The oldest of this type of chants come from the Rig Veda, the oldest of the Vedas. Note the next chapter for the Vedic Hymn or prayer to the nine planets, which is composed in Vedic Sanskrit. Another form of such planetary prayers comes from the Puranas, Hindu scriptures of the later ancient period, and are composed in classical Sanskrit.

The Vedic hymns are called Suktas, while the Puranic and later hymns are called Stotras. There are specific Stotras for each of the planets, with the largest number for the Sun. Special Navagraha Stotras or nine-planet hymns also exist for propitiating all the planets at once. Along with Stotras are special hymns that give the names of the deities from 12 to 108 to 1000 (Sahasranama). There are many such Name (Nama) Stotras to all the planets and to their overruling deities.

However, many people prefer to worship the planets through their own Ishta Devata, the particular form of God that they worship. Devotees of Lord Vishnu like to chant the thousand names of Vishnu (Vishnu Sahasranama) for astrological purposes. Devotees of Lord Shiva may use the thousand names of Shiva (Shiva Sahasranama) or Shiva Mahimna Stotra. Devotees of the Goddess may use the thousand names of Lalita (Lalita Sahasranama). There are special forms of

Vishnu (like the ten avatars) or of the Goddess (like the ten wisdom forms) which can be used for astrological purposes by corresponding them to the planets. Other chosen forms of God or the Goddess can be used from other traditions in similar ways.

Other special Vedic mantras can be used for astrological purposes. For example, the Mahamrityunjaya mantra to Lord Shiva is used specifically to ward off calamities, including those caused by the planets.

The Mantras of the Sanskrit Alphabet

The Sanskrit alphabet consists of fifty prime mantras, considered to be the 'mothers' or root powers behind the entire universe. They have special correspondences with the planets and signs as noted below.[48]

The Planets and the Sanskrit Alphabet

16 Sounds in the Head and Senses - Sun

अं	aṃ	Top of Head	आं	āṃ	Forehead
इं	iṃ	Right Eye	ईं	īṃ	Left Eye
उं	uṃ	Right Ear	ऊं	ūṃ	Left Ear
ऋं	ṛṃ	Right Cheek	ॠं	ṝṃ	Left Cheek
ऌं	lṃ	Right Nostril	ॡं	ḹṃ	Left Nostril
एं	eṃ	Upper Lips	ऐं	aiṃ	Lower Lips
ओं	oṃ	Upper Teeth	औं	auṃ	Lower Teeth
अं	aṃ	Top of palate	अः	aḥ	Bottom of palate

9 Sounds of Tissues – Moon

यं	yaṃ	Plasma	Heart or Air Chakra
रं	raṁ	Blood	Navel or Fire Chakra
लं	laṃ	Muscle	Root or Earth Chakra
वं	vaṃ	Fat	Sex or Water Chakra
शं	śaṃ	Bone	Retention of Breath
षं	ṣaṃ	Marrow	Retention of Breath
सं	saṃ	Reproductive	Inhalation
हं	haṃ	Prana	Throat or Ether Chakra/Exhalation
क्षं	kṣaṃ	Mind	Third Eye

25 Sounds of the Trunk and Limbs – 5 Planets

Right Side, Mars		**Left Side, Venus**		
कं	kaṃ	चं	caṃ	Shoulder Joint
खं	khaṃ	छं	chaṃ	Elbow Joint
गं	gaṃ	जं	jaṃ	Wrist Joint
घं	ghaṃ	झं'	jhaṃ	Base of Fingers
ङं	ṅaṃ	ञ	ñaṃ	Tip of Fingers

Right Side, Mercury		Left Side, Jupiter		
टं	ṭaṃ	तं	taṃ	Hip Joint
ठं	phaṃ	थं	thaṃ	Knee Joint
डं	baṃ	दं	daṃ	Ankle
ढं	bhaṃ	धं	dhaṃ	Base of Toes
णं	maṃ	नं	naṃ	Tip of Toes

Trunk, Saturn		
पं	paṃ	Right Abdomen
फं	phaṃ	Lower Abdomen
बं	baṃ	Left Abdomen
भं	bhaṃ	Base of Throat
मं	maṃ	Heart

The Sun relates to the vowels, which in Sanskrit are a group of sixteen. Vowels traditionally represent the spirit, soul our inner Self because they can be pronounced without the aid of consonants. Consonants in turn represent matter, form and limitation because they rest upon vowels for their expression.

The Moon relates to the nine semi-vowels and spirants (s and h sounds). These are intermediate between vowels and consonants in their sound quality. Like vowels their sounds can be drawn out over a period of time, but like consonants, is limited in duration.

Of the two groups, the semi-vowels govern the prime elements with Earth-lam, Water-vam, Fire-ram, Air-yam and Ether-ham. These relate to the five lower chakras of the subtle body, from the root or muladhara chakra to the throat. The sibilants govern Prana. The Sanskrit letter S governs inhalation, while the letter H governs exhalation. The letter

S governs time or duration, while the letter H governs space or prana (life-force). The Sanskrit Sh sounds govern the balance between these two forces.

Mars relates to the five guttural consonants (pronounced in the region of the throat). Venus relates to the five palatal consonants (pronounced in the region of the soft palate). Mercury relates to the five cerebral consonants (pronounced with the tongue curled back toward the roof of the mouth). Jupiter relates to the five dental consonants (pronounced with the tongue against the teeth). Saturn relates to the five labial consonants (pronounced using the lips).

The set of five planetary sounds also relate to the five elements but in a more general sense. The Mars group governs fire, the Venus group water, the Mercury group earth, the Jupiter group ether and the Saturn group air.

The Sun as the sixteen vowels, the Moon as the nine semi-vowels and spirants, and the five planets as the five sets of consonants (twenty-five total), make up the fifty letters of the Sanskrit alphabet.

These mantras make up the Mantra Purusha or cosmic being of mantra, which we can visualize in a planetary form. Astrologically speaking, the Sun and the vowels form his head. The Moon and its letters are his tissues and his Prana. Mars and its letters form his right arm. Venus and its letters form his left arm. Mercury and its letters form his right leg. Jupiter and its letters form his left leg. Saturn and its letters form his trunk.

We can visualize our own body as this astrological mantra Purusha and use the recitation of the Sanskrit alphabet as an astrological treatment measure.

The Signs and the Sanskrit Alphabet

Aries	aṃ, āṃ, iṃ, īṃ	**Taurus**	uṃ, ūṃ, ṛṃ
Gemini	ṝṃ, ḷṃ, ḹṃ	**Cancer**	eṃ, aiṃ
Leo	oṃ, auṃ	**Virgo**	aṃ, aḥ, śaṃ, ṣaṃ, saṃ, haṃ
Libra	kaṃ, khaṃ, gaṃ, ghaṃ, ṅaṃ	**Scorpio**	caṃ, chaṃ, jaṃ, jhaṃ, ñaṃ

The Signs and the Sanskrit Alphabet (cont'd)

Sagittarius	ṭaṃ, ṭhaṃ, ḍaṃ, ḍhaṃ, ṇaṃ	Capricorn	taṃ, thaṃ, daṃ, dhaṃ, naṃ
Aquarius	paṃ, phaṃ, baṃ, bhaṃ,maṃ	Pisces	yaṃ, raṃ, laṃ, vaṃ, kṣaṃ

Each sign of the zodiac similarly has corresponding Sanskrit letters. Note that OM corresponds to Leo, the sign of the Sun. Some people in India will name their children based upon these sounds of the signs, though most do so based upon the Nakshatra sounds. This system as a whole is not much used today, though it is emphasized in ancient texts on Mantra Yoga. The vowels begin with Aries as the first sign. The consonants begin with Libra as the first sign, with five per sign. The rest are counted off in the usual order of the Sanskrit alphabet.

Other Methods of Propitiating the Planets

Besides gems and mantras, which are the most important, many other remedial measures exist in Vedic astrology. We will examine these briefly.

Yantras

Yantras are special geometrical and numerical meditation devices, sometimes fabricated in the form of small copper squares, which help attune us to the underlying order of the cosmic mind. The universe itself is like a gigantic yantra, a multidimensional geometrical structure that embodies cosmic law or dharma. The mineral mass of the earth is composed of crystals that one could call embodied yantras. Gemstones themselves are like solid crystalline yantras. Each planet is a yantra, as it were, with its energy field circumscribing a special geometry and with the various minerals and gases within it creating various 'yantric fields'.

Just as each planet has its mantra or special sound energy, so too it possesses a yantra or special energy pattern. A yantra is the visual energy body of the mantra and of the planet that it corresponds to. It is usually abstract in form, though some contain small pictures of planetary deities as well. I have discussed the subject briefly in the Astrology of the Seers,[49] for those wanting more information on it.

Yantras magnify the energy of mantras and are used as part of meditation, particularly for developing concentration (dharana). One can use yantras as substitutes for gems but, like mantras, they require considerable attention in order to energize properly. In the use of a yantra, one meditates upon the geometrical form, transforming ones mind itself into the yantra. Yantras, like mantras, can also be used as empowerment devices for gemstones or can be used in rituals.

Yajnas

Yajnas are Vedic fire rituals. Special sacred fires are built for the planets and used for worshipping them with offerings of ghee, rice, sandalwood and other items. Mantras are used to sanctify the fire and accompany all offerings. The Vedic Hymn to the Nine Planets (Navagraha Sukta) is usually the main prayer used.

Yajnas are mainly prescribed for propitiating negative planets, particularly Mars, Saturn and Rahu. Yet special yajnas for all nine planets can be found like the Navagraha Homa. They are also used as shantis (propitiations) for unfavorable Nakshatra births.[50]

The best way of having a yajna performed is to go to a Hindu temple where these are offered and have it done there. Some Hindu temples in the West offer yajnas, particularly South Indian temples, which more commonly have this type of worship. It is best if one is physically present at the yajna. However, yajnas performed in important temples in India have been found to be effective, even when done for people in other countries.

Some Vedic astrologers swear by yajnas and their efficacy to help people on all levels. However, yajnas can be costly. If cost is an issue, you should probably first consider purchasing a gemstone that you can use for your entire life, as opposed to a yajna that is only performed once.

Pujas

Hindu texts like the Puranas outline pujas or devotional rituals to the planets. These usually require images or statues of the planetary deities, but certain grains may also be used to symbolize them. If your planetary yantras have pictures of the planetary deities, as many do, you can use them for pujas as well.

Many temples in India, particularly in the south, have statues of the nine planetary deities in a special shrine. In India, there are also special temples sacred to different planetary deities that are used specifically for propitiating these planets. Just as in the case of yajnas, pujas usually are performed by trained priests, but you can also learn to conduct your own pujas. Many Hindus perform daily puja, particularly to their chosen deity (Ishta Devata). Some Vedic astrologers perform daily pujas to the planets.

Pujas are of different types and can be simple or elaborate. They consist of offering flowers, fragrances, incense, ghee lamps, food or water to the statue of the deity along with the appropriate mantras. The puja brings the energy of the deity into the statue so that it can dispense its grace upon us. Generally, pujas are not as expensive to do as yajnas, but may not be as powerful in their effects.

Exotic Measures

Besides these systematic measures of balancing planetary energies, more exotic approaches exist as well. For example, one can feed crows, a Saturn bird, for propitiating a negative Saturn. There are many such arcane and folk methods of dealing with the planets in Vedic astrology, found in texts like Lal Kitab. Another method is to offer charities of various types in order to counter negative planetary energies. This method is mentioned in the Brihat Parashara Hora Shastra.

Such methods show us that there are many ways of propitiating the planets. While some are very formal, others are not. The important thing is to be aware of planetary energies and develop ways of harmonizing them that work for ourselves and for our communities. Without a harmonious relationship with the stars and planets, our efforts to achieve personal or social well-being may remain limited. If our lives are not in harmony with the great forces of the universe, starting with the planets, how can we expect them to bring real happiness or welfare?

The Vedic Hymn to the Nine Planets (Navagraha Sukta)

12

VEDIC mantras are the oldest and most powerful of all mantras. The following hymn presents the standard verses used for honoring the planets and their deities in Vedic rituals. Most of them derive from the *Rig Veda* but a few are from later texts. While such verses are hard to translate, hopefully these renditions can help the reader connect with them at least to some degree. The Sanskrit chanting of these mantras is available by tape for those who want to experience that.[51] Listening to such tapes helps us connect to the sound vibrations of the planets.

There are three sets of verses for each planet, one for the planetary deity (devata), the second for its overruler deity (adhidevata), and the third for its supreme deity (pratyadhidevata), much as has already been discussed, but the older Vedic scheme presents some slight variations.

Vedic Hymn to the Nine Planets

Meditation on Ganesha

OM! We meditate upon the pervasive God adorned in white, who has the color of the Moon, with four arms, whose face is peaceful, for the removal of all obstacles.

The invocation of the planetary deities, like that of any Hindu Gods and Goddesses, begins with the worship of *Ganesha*, the Elephant-headed God who grants skill and wisdom and removes any obstacles to the worship. As Ganesha is the lord of time, karma and calculation, he is also invoked as the main deity for Vedic astrology. Vedic astrologers should seek his blessings before beginning their work.

Gayatri Mantra and Invocation of the Seven Worlds

OM *Bhuh (the Earthly Realm)!*

OM *Bhuvah (the Atmosphere)!*

OM *Suvah (Heaven)!*

OM *Mahah (the Realm of Cosmic Law)!*

OM *Janah (the World of Origins)!*

OM *Tapah (the World of Yogic Power)!*

OM *Satyam (the Sphere of Truth)!*

We meditate upon the most adorable effulgence of the
Divine creative Sun (Savitar), that he may inspire our minds!

OM, *the cosmic waters, the cosmic light, the essence, immortality, Brahman, Bhur (Earth), Bhuvah (Atmosphere) Suvar (Heaven),* OM!

The invocation of the planetary deities is preceded by the Gayatri mantra to the Sun God as *Savitar*. This is the most important Vedic mantra for connecting us to the Divine light. Savitar represents not just the Sun but the supreme light of consciousness behind all forms of light – the radiance of the Atman (higher Self) that can inspire and illumine our minds so that the mantras we chant can be fully effective.

The Gayatri mantra is a powerful tool to help us learn Vedic astrology and for developing astrological insight. It is important for strengthening solar energy and connecting us to the spiritual heart, the seat of the soul or inner Sun.

In this version, the recitation of the Gayatri includes special mantras for all the seven lokas or planes of existence from the lowest earthly realm of physical matter to the highest realm of spiritual truth and pure existence.

Mantras for the Sun

1. Revolving through the realm of space by the power of truth, putting to rest both the mortal and the immortal, the Sun God Savitar travels in a golden chariot, illumining all the worlds.

2. We choose Agni, the sacred Fire, as our messenger, the invoker who carries all the treasures, the good will of the power of worship.

3. Pashupati, Lord of the animals both the two-footed and the four-footed, may your select sacred offering come to us; may there be wealth and growth for your worshipper.

The first verse is to the Sun's deity (devata) as Savitar. Savitar specifically is the form of the Sun God that governs all transformations of the light, including both the change from night to day (sunrise) and from day to night (sunset). He is the lord of all evolutionary changes, including the yogic process of Self-realization. Here he is worshipped mainly as the deity of the Sun.

The second verse is to the overruler (adhidevata) of the Sun, Agni or the Fire God as symbolic of all the powers of fire and light. Agni as the cosmic fire guides the cosmic ritual order of creation and evolution, of which the Sun is the prime driving force for life on Earth.

The third verse is to Lord *Shiva*, the power of pure consciousness as the supreme deity (pratyadhidevata) of the Sun. Here he is called Pashupati, the Lord of the animals, which esoterically means the Lord of the souls who are symbolically represented as various animals before the Divine. These animals are also found in the constellations, which reflect various animal symbolisms.

Mantras for the Moon

1. Overflow, O Soma. May all vigorous powers come to you from every side. Abide in the gathering place of power.

2. In the Waters, Soma has said to me, are all the medicines and the Fire that gives blessings to all, and the waters that are the universal medicine.

3. The Goddess Gauri has chanted, fashioning the waters. She has become onefooted, two footed, fourfooted, eightfooted, ninefooted and a thousand syllabled in the supreme ether.

The first verse lauds the Moon's deity (devata) as Soma, the fluid essence or vitality principle behind all life and form. This nourishing and rejuvenative force comes from the Moon and aids in all healing.

The Water Goddesses (*Apas*) are the overrulers of the Moon just as Fire is of the Sun. They carry all medicines and healing powers for both body and mind. They serve as a vehicle for the Cosmic Fire or life-energy which is their child.

Gauri is Lord Shiva's consort, also called Parvati and Shakti. The term additionally refers to a female buffalo, which symbolizes the power of the Divine Word as it roars. Gauri represents all the meters or powers of speech up to a thousand syllables, which represent the thousand petals of the crown chakra. The Moon's connection with the crown chakra is quite ancient and well known in yogic literature.

These verses show the importance of the Moon for all healing practices and for empowering all medicines. The Moon is also significant for empowering all mantras, which are seen as the vegetation of the inner mind.

Mantras for Mercury

1. Awaken, O Agni, recognize your worshipper. Direct him to the fulfillment of his wishes. Again making your father young, extend the thread in you.

2. Vishnu strode forth over this world placing his three steps, gathering all in his dust.

3. You are the crown of Vishnu, you are the back of Vishnu, you are the scissors of Vishnu, you are the thread of Vishnu, you are the enduring power of Vishnu, you are the offering for Vishnu.

The first verse is to *Budha*, the planetary deity for Mercury, who represents the youthful form of Agni, the early light of dawn and the awakened state of the mind. Mercury holds the power of renewal and has the power to make us young again. This refers to Mercury as relating to the individual mind.

The second verse is to *Vishnu*, the overruler of Mercury, in his form as *Trivikrama*, the maker of the three strides, which measure out the entire threefold universe of Earth, Atmosphere and Heaven or body, breath and mind. Mercury gives us the power to understand these underlying laws of the universe. This refers to Mercury as relating to the cosmic mind.

Vishnu is also the supreme deity for Mercury in his *Narayana* form or form of the Cosmic Person who pervades all the worlds. Mercury grants that humane intelligence and compassion that helps us become one with all. He is the Divine intelligence of the soul dwelling within us. This refers to Mercury as relating to the supreme consciousness.

Mantras for Mars

1. Agni is the head of Heaven and the mountain lord of the Earth. He invigorates the waters' seed.

2. O Earth, our place of dwelling, be auspicious for us and free of thorns. Grant us a wide peace.

3. With the Lord of the Field, as with a good horse, may we win cattle and horses that provide nourishment. May he be compassionate to such as we.

Mars is lauded in the form of the Fire God Agni as the lord of the Earth, Heaven and the Waters. This relates specifically to his name as *Angaraka*. The reproductive power of Mars is alluded to as well.

The overruler for Mars is the Earth Goddess (*Bhumi Devi*), in whose field he manifests as her son. Once we control our aggressive Mars energy we can create peace and growth for our lives on Earth.

The supreme deity for Mars is the Lord of the Field, *Kshetrapati*, as his main work on Earth is a kind of cultivation or agriculture. Kshetrapati is associated with Lord Rama and his consort Sita, who represents the cultivated field. Kshetrapati here takes the place of *Skanda* in the usual order of planetary deities or is another name for him.

Mantras for Venus

1. To the brilliant light (Shukra), to Agni, carry your purified thought offering, who with wisdom travels through all divine and mortal births.

2. I have heard that Indrani is the best wife among women. Her husband never experiences old age and death.

3. We call upon Indra from the peoples in all directions. For us may he be supreme.

The first verse is to *Shukra* (Venus) as Agni or the cosmic fire in its brilliant effulgence (the Sanskrit word Shukra also means brilliant). All the planets are forms of Agni, aspects of the cosmic fire which are the Divine children in creation. Venus as Shukra or the reproductive force is not only the power through which all creatures are born but also that which carries the wisdom that directs and guides these births.

The second verse is to *Indrani* or Shakti, the overruler of Venus, who is the queen of Goddesses as Indra is the King of the Gods. She grants the powers of longevity and rejuvenation that work through the planet Venus.

Indra, as the King of the Gods and the supreme ruler of the planet Venus, refers to the highest and unique Divine light just as Venus is the brightest of all the stars. Indra represents the creative, transformative force, the higher life energy that is connected to Venus. Venus can grant us that power and supremacy.

Mantras for Jupiter

1. Brihaspati, beyond our worthy foes, shine radiant and strong of will among the peoples. As you shine with strength born from truth, grant us that rich and lustrous light.

2. Indra with the Maruts, drink the Soma here, just as you drank the Soma of King Sharyata. By your guidance and in your protection, O hero, may the rishis, skilled at worship, come here.

3. Brahman was born originally from the East, as the adorable light revealed its radiance. The original foundation is his dwelling. He has revealed the origins of being and non-being.

The first verse is to the Vedic God *Brihaspati*, the priest of the Gods, through whom we can overcome all difficulties by the power of ritual, prayer, mantra and meditation. These powers are more potent than all worldly powers and grant a greater and more fulfilling and enduring reward.

The second verse is to the God *Indra*, the King of the Gods, along with his army of Maruts, wind and storm Gods. He is the overruling deity of Jupiter as the head of the heavenly army. This head of the hosts energizes the higher rishi or seer powers and puts us in touch with them. While the solitary form of Indra is associated with Venus, Indra as the group leader is connected with Jupiter. Later on this function of head of the group of the Gods was taken over by Ganesha.

The third verse is not to *Brahma*, the Creator, which is related to Jupiter in other accounts, but to *Brahman* or the Godhead, the Absolute within and beyond all creation, whose transcendent nature can be understood through the wisdom of Jupiter as the divine guru. The east is symbolic for the third eye.

Mantras for Saturn

1. May the Goddess Waters be auspicious for us to drink. May they flow peace and happiness to us.

2. Prajapati, all these creatures are not different from you, whom you surround on every side. Whatever wish we offer, may that come true. May we be lords of the treasure.

3. May you come to the sacred grass spread for Yama. Sit along with the our fathers, the great Angirasa Rishis. May the mantras uttered by the sages bring you here. King Yama, may you take delight in this offering.

The first verse for Saturn is the standard daily prayer used for the ritual drinking of water in Hindu practices. While one might find it odd to associate water with Saturn, a dry planet, Saturn is the lord of the great Prana or life-force of the waters of space, the cosmic waters. Saturn as *Shani* is related to the Vedic term Sham, meaning 'what is peaceful and auspicious', which is associated with Lord Shiva who is Sham-kara or Shankara, 'the maker of what is auspicious'. Through warding off negative Saturn energy we connect with these higher benefic forces.

In the second verse Saturn's overruler is the Divine Creator, Brahma or *Prajapati*, not simply as a cosmic ruler, but as the indwelling consciousness that has become the entire universe. This connects him to the supreme reality (Parabrahman). Saturn is also the grandfather principle here.

In the third verse Saturn's supreme ruler is *Yama*, the God of death, not in a mere outer sense of suffering but as the primal sage and leader of the ancient rishis, the supreme yogi. Yama or death as the great teacher shows us the path beyond death and mortality to deathlessness and immortality. These mantras show the spiritual side of Saturn, which is the main power behind the soul's inner growth.

Mantras for Rahu

1. With what special grace will Indra manifest for us brilliantly, our friend who ever helps us, with what powerful company?

2. The spotted cow has come and sat before the Mother again, extending beyond the Father to the world of light.

3. The rope that the Goddess Nirritti has bound around your neck; let that be loosened. We release you from that for greater longevity. May your happy life not be cut short.

In the first verse Rahu is referred to as the shakti or power of Indra, the supreme lord, that works along with the Maruts, the storm Gods or Gods of Prana. Rahu is called *Ka*, the feminine form of Who, referring to the power of the unknown deity behind all names and forms. It also relates to the Goddess Kali in later Hindu thought.

The second verse is the Divine Mother *Durga* as the overruler of Rahu, in the form of the spotted Cow (Prishni) who symbolizes the night sky. The cow is also the Prana or life force that extends beyond Heaven and Earth to the realm of the immortals. Rahu gives that power of transcendence.

The third verse is to the Goddess *Nirriti*, the supreme ruler of Rahu, who represents karma, bondage, disease and death. We can better understand her as the Goddess Kali in her grandmother or crone form. Propitiating her we can overcome disease, gain longevity and ultimately gain immortality.

Mantras for Ketu

1. Creating a ray (Ketu) where no ray existed, creating a form where there was no form, O youthful Indra, Lord of Life, you were born along with the dawns.

2. The Creator (Brahma) among the Gods, the master of the verse among the poets, the seer among the sages, the falcon among the birds of prey, the axe in the forests, Soma flows through the purification filter, singing.

3. May he radiant (Chitra), appear radiant to us, whose rule is radiant, the giver of life. May he, lustrous with his lights, grant to his worshipper a wealth of light that is vast and full of energy.

The first verse is to Ketu as a form of the God Indra, the King of the Gods, who brings the light out of darkness, the first intimation of which is Ketu as the initial ray of the dawn. Ketu symbolizes the initial light of any venture, including the yogic quest.

The second verse is to *Brahma*, the Creator, in the form of Soma, the delight or Ananda from which all creation springs. Ketu, which also means a 'symbol', grants us the knowledge of the essence of all things, their sign or symbol, which is ultimately Ananda. Those with a strong Ketu have a good sense of symbols, mantras and secret codes.

The third verse is to *Chitragupta*, the lord of karma, as the supreme Lord of Ketu. Our karmic code is the ultimate secret code that we must learn to decipher. Ketu is the main planetary force which helps us do that. Chitragupta is sometimes regarded as a form of Ganesha who is the lord of time and karma on a cosmic level. Ketu's ability to grant higher perception and meditational powers is clear from these verses.

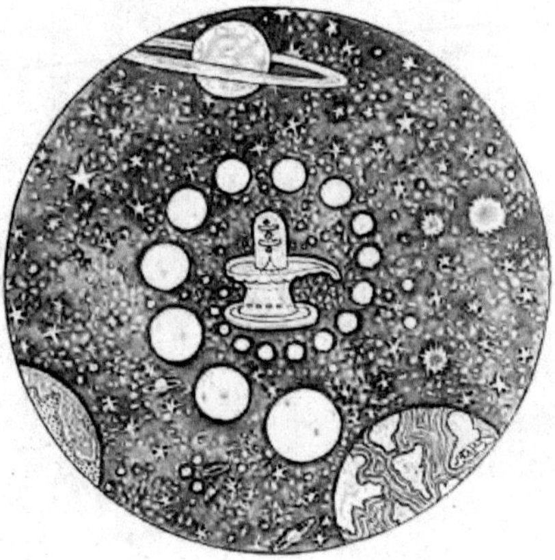

PART THREE

Example Charts

Example Charts

13

Keys to Reading Vedic Charts

The following are charts of famous people, whose life and appearance are well known and easy to reference. They cover a broad range of body types and temperaments including examples of good and bad health, short and long life. My main aim is to show how the Ayurvedic constitution is reflected in the Vedic astrological chart.

I have indicated how the Ayurvedic constitution or doshic type is reflected by the dominant planetary influences in the chart, with due consideration for both the Ascendant and the Moon sign, outlining on the basic physical and psychological nature of the person. I have kept the analysis simple for the benefit of readers who may not know the details of Vedic chart interpretation. I have emphasized charts where one dosha predominates. I have similarly tried to keep the planetary types simple, though there are many possible combinations in this regard.

I have generally chosen charts which are not too complex astrologically and where there is little doubt as to the birth time. I have relied upon the database of Lois Rodden for the birth data of most of the charts.

Primary Factors of Constitution in the Birth Chart

For determining the Ayurvedic type of a person through the birth chart, the following factors are most important:

1. The Ascendant and its lord, which rules the bodily self. This includes:

- The dosha ruling the Ascendant.
- The dosha of the planet ruling the Ascendant.
- The dosha of the sign in which the Ascendant lord is located.
- The dosha of any planet that may aspect the Ascendant or its lord.
- The disposition of the Navamsha and the same factors within it.[52]

2. The Moon sign and the Moon, which represent the psychology and impact the physiology.

The Moon also has a greater impact upon a woman's constitution, owing to the connection between the feminine nature and the Moon.

3. The Sun sign and the Sun, which represent the basic vitality and digestive power of the person.

The Sun is the general significator of the first house. Conjunctions with the Sun especially leave their mark on both the physical and mental energy of the person. Men reflect more of their Sun just as women tend to reflect their Moon.

4. The sixth and the eighth houses of disease and their lords, particularly when they impact the Ascendant and its lord.

While these factors reflect disease potential more so than constitution, they have an impact upon the constitution. They often hold the key to the constitution of the person when the main astrological factors don't seem to tally.

The planetary and doshic type is generally determined by the main planet that dominates these constitutional and health factors in the chart, whether by rulership or aspect. This main planet can generally be determined from overt planetary placements in the chart, but may require a more elaborate analysis of planetary strengths and weaknesses, which the Vedic system has several means of calculating.[53] The Nakshatras have an influence that can be important as well. Ascertaining health has the same degree of complexity in its determination as career, relationship, spiritual, finances and other domains of life in the chart.

In addition, for some people the dominant planet in the chart as a whole may be different than that which is most dominant for the factors of the body. Such people will have a psychology or career under a different planetary influence than that of their body type. These cases are exceptions but do occur.

Vedic Planetary Aspects

The Vedic system employs its own special set of aspects, which are different than those of western astrology and much simpler, as listed below. For more information on the mechanics of reading a Vedic chart, please consult introductory books on the subject like the author's own *Astrology of the Seers*.

- The Sun, Moon, Mercury and Venus fully aspect the signs in which they are located and the sign seventh from them.
- Mars, Jupiter and Saturn fully aspect the signs in which they are located and the sign seventh from them but have their own special aspects as well.
    - Mars also aspects the signs fourth and eighth from its position in the chart.
    - Jupiter also aspects the signs fifth and ninth from its position in the chart.
    - Saturn also aspects the signs third and tenth from its position in the chart.
- Rahu and Ketu have the first and seventh aspects. Some astrologers ascribe them fifth and ninth aspects like Jupiter as well.

Because Mars, Jupiter and Saturn have more aspects than the other planets, their influence in determining the doshic type of a person is usually more important because they are more likely to aspect both the Ascendant and its lord. Mars when aspecting both the Ascendant and its lord will usually create a Pitta type person. Jupiter when aspecting both the Ascendant and its lord will usually create Kapha. Saturn when aspecting both the Ascendant and its lord will usually create Vata. Of course, exceptions do exist.[54]

As a note of caution, it is not advisable to try to determine the Ayurvedic constitution from the chart alone unless one has a great deal of experience in this area. It is best to cross reference the chart with an actual examination of the person or at least some study of their appearance and medical history. Birth times may be inaccurate as well as astrological factors more complex than what appears. Whenever treating the health of a person we should gather all helpful data before we draw any conclusions or make any recommendations.

The Vedic South Indian Chart

Pisces	Aries	Taurus	Gemini
Aquarius			Cancer
Capricorn			Leo
Sagittarius	Scorpio	Libra	Virgo

The charts displayed will all be drawn in the South Indian format, which follows the above order of the signs. Because all these charts follow the same format, the signs will not be listed separately in each of them but can be inferred from the position of the planets in the chart.

For the same reason, the number of the house in which a planet is located will not be marked. The houses are counted off starting with the Ascendant as the first house. So, for example, if Gemini is the Ascendant then Gemini will mark the first house, Cancer the second house, Leo the third house and so on. If Cancer is the Ascendant, then Cancer will mark the first house, Leo the second house, Virgo the third house, and so on. Please bear this in mind while looking at the charts.

33 Example Charts

1. Mohammed Ali, Pitta

Birth Chart

	MA SA	JU	
KE			ASC
VE ME MO SU			RA

Navamsha

	MA SA	KE	MO JU
SU ASC			MA ME
VE ME MO SU			
SA	RA		VE

Jan. 17, 1942, 06 35 PM, Louisville KY, 85W46, 38N15

Ascendant – 26° 29' Can.	Sun – 04° 14' Capricorn
Moon – 19° 23' Cap.	Mars – 10° 00' Aries
Mercury – 20° 28' Cap.	Jupiter – 18° 54' Taurus Rx
Venus – 27° 37' Cap. Rx	Saturn – 26° 36' Aries Rx
Rahu – 22° 53' Leo	Ketu – 22° 53' Aquarius

Planetary Periods

Birth – Moon/Mercury	Mars – Jan. 3, 1945
Rahu – Jan. 3, 1952	Jupiter – Jan. 3, 1970
Saturn – Jan. 3, 1986	Mercury – Jan. 3, 2005
Ketu – Jan. 3, 2012	Venus – Jan. 3, 2019

Mohammed Ali was known for his aggressive and competitive urge as a fighter, but also for a volatile, expressive and charismatic personality, particularly his poetic self-eloquence. His Cancer Ascendant affords him sensitivity to the moods of the masses, along with a practical turn of mind with his Sun and Moon together in Saturn ruled Capricorn. This kept him in the public eye and gave him an almost political influence on people.

However, neither Saturn nor the Moon is his dominant planet. Ali's chart is dominated by a strong Mars in the tenth house in its own sign of Aries. Mars is located in its own sign in an angle not only from the Ascendant but also from both the Sun and Moon. This creates a powerful Yoga or positional combination for Mars, a Mahapurusha or great person Yoga for Mars called Ruchaka Yoga, making him a Mars type person and endowing him with a primarily Pitta or fiery mind-body type. Mars aspects the Ascendant with its fourth sign aspect, bringing its power to bear on the body and character of the person. It affords him great success and fame through its tenth house position. Mars is also the final dispositor of all the planets in the chart. This makes him a famous fighter and boxer.

However, Mars is not alone in the tenth house. A debilitated and retrograde Saturn is also there, casting its special tenth sign aspect on the Sun and Moon, which are located in Saturn ruled Capricorn. This Saturn in the tenth brings secondary Vata characteristics into Ali's character and physiology. It makes his career have several ups and downs. Saturn dominates the Navamsha chart, showing this hidden Vata behind the evident Pitta of his outer personality.

Such a malefic Saturn weakens Ali's overall health and vitality, afflicting both Mars and the Moon, being the main factor through which he contracted Parkinson's disease, a windy or Vata disease. Parkinson's disease is commonly connected to excess Pitta or fire that pushes Vata out of balance. Not surprisingly, the disease took off under Ali's Saturn major planetary period. His Ketu, which is poorly placed in the eighth house in Saturn ruled Aquarius, further contributed to the Ketu related nerve and muscle problems afflicting him.

Relative to gems, though Ali's chart is strong in terms of career, the Ascendant lord is notably afflicted. A gem for the Moon or a pearl would be very helpful for protecting his overall health and longevity.

2. John Belushi, Kapha

Birth Chart

	RA		
ME MA SU			SA
JU VE <u>ASC</u>	MO	KE	

Navamsha

SU		<u>ASC</u>	RA
			MA SA
			MO
KE		JU	VE ME

Jan. 23, 1949, 05 12 AM, Chicago IL, 87W39, 41N51

Ascendant - 04° 40'Sag.	Sun - 09° 59' Capricorn
Moon - 03° 28' Scorpio	Mars - 21° 35' Capricorn
Mercury - 26° 53' Cap.	Jupiter - 22° 23' Sagittarius
Venus - 19° 27' Sagittarius	Saturn - 11° 49' Leo Rx
Rahu - 07° 06' Aries	Ketu - 07° 06' Libra

Planetary Periods

Birth - Saturn/Saturn	Mercury - Nov. 13, 1967
Death - Mercury/Saturn	

John Belushi was a comedian and actor, well known for his heavy Kapha build and Kapha behaviors and acts, like his humorous overeating, as one of the original cast of Saturday Night Live. His Ascendant type is expansive Sagittarius and he took on its more jovial characteristics. Kapha Jupiter dominates the Ascendant as its lord along with Venus, another Kapha planet, located very close to it. There are no other aspects on the Ascendant or its lord. Taurus, a Venus ruled Navamsha, also dominates. So Kapha prevails in his physiology as the dominant dosha.

This combination of Jupiter and Venus together in Sagittarius grants Belushi charisma, humor, a partying tendency and a capacity for self-indulgence that eventually proved destructive with his early death at the age of 33 that occurred from a drug overdose. His planetary type is Jupiterian but lacking in discrimination (or we could say is a Jupiter-Venus type).

In Vedic astrology Jupiter-Venus combinations, though both benefic planets in themselves, are not always good because the two planets are regarded as natural enemies. Venus tends to bring out the lower side of Jupiter energy leading to excess or dissipation. Yet, although often negative for the character of a person, the effects of this combination can bring wealth, popularity and other material rewards.

Belushi's chart is a good example of the potential destructive effects of Jupiter-Venus combinations. For Sagittarius Ascendant, Venus is the malefic sixth lord, showing enemies and diseases and reducing longevity, adding to the difficulties of the chart. Yet there are other notable afflictions.

The Moon is waning and near its maximum point of debility at 3 degrees of Scorpio in the difficult twelfth house and receives no benefic aspects. This can cause health problems early on in life.[55] The Moon for Sagittarius Ascendant is lord of the eighth house of death and placed in the difficult twelfth house of loss, which is also not good for longevity either, and as a psychological indicator shows a troubled emotional nature. Scorpio as the Moon sign type shows the dark, dramatic and often reckless side to his mind, including the inappropriate use of drugs that killed him.

Belushi achieved great fame during his Mercury period, which rules his tenth house of career, but Mercury is also a difficult planet for Sagittarius Ascendant and an enemy of Jupiter and so does not help the longevity. He passed away under the subperiod of Saturn, a maraka (death-dealing) planet as lord of the second house of Capricorn, a maraka house in which Mercury, the dasha lord, is also located, making Mercury a maraka as well.

Belushi's strong second house, with an exalted Mars, gave him dramatic powers of expression. The Sun-Mars-Mercury conjunction located there gave him some Pitta traits, particularly in his speech, which could be cleverly abrasive. But these planets in a maraka place harmed his longevity as well. Rahu in the fifth house of discrimination aspected by fiery Mars gave a reckless side to his judgment as well that also proved harmful.

3. Sonny Bono, Vata

Birth Chart

VE SA ME SU			MO KE
RA			
		JU MA	ASC

Navamsha

RA		ASC VE	JU
SA MO	SU ME	MA	KE

Feb. 16, 1935, 09 21 PM, Detroit MI, 83W03, 42N20

Ascendant – 13° 33' Virgo	Sun – 04° 32' Aquarius
Moon – 19° 43' Cancer	Mars – 01° 01' Libra
Mercury – 04° 54' Aqua. Rx	Jupiter – 29° 39' Libra
Venus – 25° 58' Aqua.	Saturn – 07° 20' Aqua.
Rahu – 06° 48' Capricorn	Ketu – 06° 48' Cancer

Planetary Periods

Birth – Mercury/Venus	Ketu – March 23, 1948
Venus – March 23, 1955	Sun – March 23, 1975
Moon – March 23, 1981	Mars – March 23, 1991
Death – Mars/Moon	

Sonny Bono's chart is dominated by a close Sun, Mercury, Saturn conjunction in the sixth house of health and vitality, in Aquarius, a sign of Saturn. Venus is also not far away in the same sign. The Ascendant is expressive Virgo, ruled by Mercury, a Vata sign. Saturn, a Vata planet, dominates the Sun and the Ascendant lord, with the Ascendant itself another Vata sign. There are no aspects to the Ascendant. Sun-Saturn conjunctions tend towards Vata, more so since Mercury, another Vata planet, and ruler of the Ascendant is also involved.

Sonny Bono was a typically Vata person in build, temperament and psychology – thin, nervous and eccentric. His Jupiter-Mars (Libra) combination in the second house of speech aided him in his singing career. Jupiter is also the seventh lord, showing the role of his wife Cher in promoting that expression.

Bono's chart is a case not of disease but of accident, also ruled by the sixth house. He was killed in a skiing accident during his Mars/Moon period. Mars is a disease and accident causing planet for Virgo Ascendant and the ruler of the eighth house of death. It is located in the second house, a maraka or death-dealing house with Jupiter, a maraka or death-dealing planet as the seventh lord. Vata types with afflicted sixth houses tend toward accidents because they easily become careless and absent-minded.

Often it is difficult to tell if such planetary afflictions will result in disease or accident. In any case Bono's chart is not strong for longevity. In addition, these sixth house Aquarius planets are located in the eighth house or house of death from the Moon, and show similar problems in the Moon chart as well. However, the same planetary combinations, including some political (Raja Yoga) planets in the sixth house in socially-minded Aquarius, also brought him into politics.

4. Marlon Brando, Kapha

Birth Chart

SU MO	ME	VE	
KE			
			RA
MA	JU ASC	SA	

Navamsha

JU		ME	RA
VE			
SU MO			
SA KE	MA	ASC	

April 3, 1924, 11 00 PM, Omaha NE, 95W56, 41N16

Ascendant – 10° 56' Scor.	Sun – 21° 21' Pisces
Moon – 20° 16' Pisces	Mars – 24° 54' Sagittarius
Mercury – 04 °26' Aries	Jupiter – 27° 05' Scorpio
Venus – 06° 03' Taurus	Saturn – 07° 21' Libra Rx
Rahu – 07° 13' Leo	Ketu – 07° 13' Aquarius

Planetary Periods

Birth – Mercury/Venus	Ketu – Aug. 25, 1936
Venus – Aug. 25, 1943	Sun – Aug. 25, 1963
Moon – Aug. 25, 1969	Mars – Aug. 25, 1979
Rahu – Aug. 25, 1986	Death – Rahu/Mars

Jupiter is located in the Ascendant Scorpio, a watery sign. It exchanges houses with Mars, the Ascendant lord, which is located in Jupiter-ruled Sagittarius, bringing a Jupiter/ Kapha influence on both the Ascendant and its lord. Jupiter aspects both the Sun and the Moon, which are both located in the fifth house in Pisces, a sign ruled by Jupiter, extending Jupiter's dominance over the Sun and Moon as well. Such a strong Jupiter brings a good deal of Kapha into the person, but of a Jupiterian or active and expressive type.

Besides Jupiter, Brando has a powerful Venus, with a Mahapurusha Yoga of Venus in the seventh, an angular house. This affords him a great deal of charisma and attraction to the opposite sex. It brings additional Kapha into his constitution, and is good for his acting career, though not favorable for marriage or lasting relationships. Jupiter and Venus afford him a great deal of Kapha even though he was born at the time of the new Moon, when the Moon, the main Kapha luminary, is weak.

Brando has some secondary Pitta from Mars ruling Scorpio and influencing the sign through its exchange with Jupiter. Mars aspects both the Sun and the Moon, impacting the body and mind as well. Mars in the second house of speech gives Brando a powerful, explosive and sometimes violent expression. His Scorpionic nature was most obvious in his Godfather roles but extended through much of his career and its obsession with the dark and dramatic side of human life and death.

Kapha-Pitta creates a strong constitution and a good build and strong endurance but a tendency towards overweight, which Brando struggled with, particularly in his later years. Colored by a Scorpio Ascendant, it provides drama, darkness, turbulence and even aggression. The new Moon in mutable Pisces aids in his acting ability, giving him the ability to express various and changing emotions with precision. Brando's Venus period early in life raised him up in his acting career and brought him a great deal of adulation.

5. George Bush Jr., Pitta

Birth Chart

		RA	SU
			ASC SA, ME VE
			MA
	KE		JU MO

Navamsha

VE	SU		
			MO, JU SA, MA RA
ME	ASC		

July 6, 1946, 07 26 AM, New Haven, 72W56, 41N18

Ascendant – 14° 00' Can.	Sun – 20° 40' Gemini
Moon – 23° 36' Virgo	Mars – 16° 12' Leo
Mercury – 16° 43' Cancer	Jupiter – 25° 02' Virgo
Venus – 28° 23' Cancer	Saturn – 03° 23' Cancer
Rahu – 26° 29' Scorpio	Ketu – 26° 29' Taurus

Planetary Periods

Birth – Mars/Mars	Rahu – May 16, 1953
Jupiter – May 16, 1971	Saturn – May 16, 1987
Mercury – May 16, 2006	Ketu – May 16, 2023

George W. Bush has Cancer Ascendant but under the influence of conservative Saturn, reflecting more the public and political side of the sign. A quick look at this chart would appear to indicate a Vata or airy constitution. Saturn, a Vata planet, is located in the Ascendant and aspects the Ascendant lord, the Moon. Mercury, another Vata planet, is also in the Ascendant. The Sun and Moon are both located in signs (Gemini and Virgo) ruled by Mercury.

However, this is an unusual chart in which the more obvious indications in the birth chart are outweighed by other factors. First, the Ascendant has fiery planets, Sun and Mars, on either side, bringing in a Pitta influence indirectly. Such hemming in of the Ascendant affects the constitution. Any house that is hemmed in by planetary influences of a certain type will reflect these strongly, even though they have no direct aspect upon it.

This Pitta energy is reinforced by powerful influences from the Navamsha. Mars has much more strength than is apparent at first from its position in the second house. Mars is vargottama, located in the same sign in the basic birth chart and in the Navamsha, in this case Leo, which increases its strength in the birth chart and its ability to impact the personality type. Mars dominates the tenth house of the Navamsha, in the fiery sign Leo, along with Saturn, Jupiter and the Moon, and also aspects the Navamsha Ascendant, its own sign of Scorpio. The Navamsha is very strongly Pitta and in this case serves to outweigh the influences in the basic birth (Rashi) chart.

In addition, Bush was born under a Mars/Mars period, bringing yet further Mars influences into his nature. So he is a Pitta type with secondary Vata characteristics. His planetary type is Martian, of a political bent. Most of us have observed the fiery, often aggressive and combative nature of George Bush Jr., though he does have a Cancerian friendliness at an outward level. His second house Mars brings that fire power into the realm of speech. By aspect Mars also impacts the fifth house of intellect and judgment, which in his case is very martial. His body type is also Pitta, moderate in build, ruddy in complexion. This chart shows us the importance of the Navamsha chart in determining constitution.

In addition, the chart shows all the planets located between Rahu and Ketu, the lunar nodes, a combination called Kalasarpa Yoga, meaning the serpent of time. Those with such a combination have unusual, unpredictable and sometimes catastrophic events occur in their lives, which are not always owing to their actions.

Saturn is often a powerful planet for giving political gains for Cancer Ascendants when strongly placed in the chart. Bush also has very strong positions from the Moon, with Saturn, Mercury and Venus creating a powerful Raja Yoga (combination for political power) from it. His Jupiter is strongly placed along with the Moon (a Gajakesari Yoga). It brings the benefits of the father as Jupiter is the ninth lord. However, in Bush's case, Saturn by its aspects on the Ascendant and the Moon outweighs Jupiter, directing its good karma to more circumscribed ends.

6. George Bush Sr., Pitta

Birth Chart

		SU ME	VE
KE MA			ASC RA
	JU	SA	MO

Navamsha

		RE VA	
ME			
JU			MO
	KE	SA MA	ASC SU

June 12, 1924, 11 45 AM, Milton MA, 71W05, 42N15

Ascendant – 18° 22' Leo	Sun – 28° 33' Taurus
Moon – 25° 07' Virgo	Mars – 02° 40' Aquarius
Mercury – 06° 36' Taurus	Jupiter – 21° 23' Scorpio Rx
Venus – 24° 38' Gem. Rx	Saturn – 03° 02' Libra Rx
Rahu – 03° 32' Leo	Ketu – 03° 32' Aquarius

Planetary Periods

Birth – Mars/Rahu	Rahu – July 3, 1930
Jupiter – July 3, 1948	Saturn – July 3, 1964
Mercury – July 3, 1983	Ketu – July 3, 2000
Venus – July 3, 2007	

George Bush Sr. has a chart that is easier to understand astrologically than his son's and is more obviously Pitta or fiery in nature. Leo, a fire sign marks the Ascendant. Mars is the dominant planet, aspecting both the Ascendant and the Sun, with no other major aspects on the Ascendant. The strong tenth house Sun also brings more fire into the chart. These positions make Bush Sr. a Pitta type of Mars and the Sun planetary influence. His solar kingly style alienated voters, however, in this more democratic age.

Mars dominates the Moon and the psychology, aspecting both the Moon in Virgo and its ruler (Mercury). The Moon is surrounded by Rahu and Saturn, making his mind a bit paranoid, as well as contentious. Rahu also marks the Ascendant and inflates the personality. Yet the Virgo Moon also gave him discipline, diplomacy and a good grasp of information. The exalted Saturn in the third afforded him strength, effort and persistence. His fourth house Jupiter in Scorpio, a sign of Mars, resulted in a political bent of mind. His tenth house Mercury raised him to the presidency during its period, but is not terribly strong and he was unable to get reelected.

7. Cher, Vata

Birth Chart

	ME	RA SU	SA VE ASC
			MA
MO	KE		JU

Navamsha

KE			SA
ASC SU			
MA			JU
	MO ME	VE	RA

May 20, 1946, 07 25 AM, El Centro CA 115W34, 32N48

Ascendant – 15° 30' Gem.	Sun – 05° 53' Taurus
Moon – 25° 11' Sagittarius	Mars – 20° 14' Cancer
Mercury – 23° 22' Aries	Jupiter – 25° 17' Virgo Rx
Venus – 02° 39' Gemini	Saturn – 28° 01' Gemini
Rahu – 28° 58' Taurus	Ketu – 28° 58' Scorpio

Planetary Periods

Birth – Venus/Mercury	Sun – Aug. 5, 1948
Moon – Aug. 5, 1954	Mars – Aug. 5, 1964
Rahu – Aug. 5, 1971	Jupiter – Aug. 5, 1989
Saturn – Aug. 5, 2005	Mercury – Aug. 5, 2024

Venus, a Kapha planet, rises in Gemini, an expressive air sign, a little more than a degree from the Ascendant. But its influence is tempered by Saturn, also located in Gemini. Saturn is in a close opposition to an expansive Sagittarius Moon, marking its influence on both the rising sign and the Moon sign, on both the physiology and the psychology. Saturn is in Vargottama, in the same sign in the basic birth chart and the navamsha, and also rules the navamsha ascendant which is Aquarius.

This strength of Saturn, a Vata planet, brings out the Vata side of Venus as well. It makes Cher a Vata type, though Venus remains her dominant planet in terms of her appearance and expression. Saturn in Vedic astrology often creates artists and rebels, particularly when conjoined with Venus or Mercury or in air signs. Saturn with Venus creates a kind of dark beauty that Cher was famous for.

Venus is within five degrees of Rahu, giving her a Venus-Rahu conjunction, though across signs. Venus-Rahu also creates mystery and illusion. Venus moreover carries a Rahu influence, from Rahu being located in Venus-ruled Taurus.

Cher has some Pitta qualities as well with Mercury, her Ascendant lord, located in Aries, a fire sign. Her debilitated Mars in the second house in Cancer gives energy to her voice but can make her contentious as well. The seventh and tenth lord Jupiter in the fourth house, not only conjoins marriage (seventh house) and career (tenth house) but also colors her basic emotional nature. The seventh house Moon in expansive Sagittarius is good for expression and charisma, though it does not bring marital happiness. Many female artists and entertainers have seventh house Moons, which is good for their public adulation but not for the personal life, which they often do not have.

8. Bob Dylan, Vata-Pitta

Birth Chart

KE	MO SA	VE SU JU	ME
MA			
	<u>ASC</u>		RA

Navamsha

<u>ASC</u>	SU		VE
RA JU			
MA			KE
SA MO		ME	

May 24, 1941, 09 05 PM, Duluth, MN, 92W06, 46N47

Ascendant – 27° 16' Scor.	Sun – 10° 28' Taurus
Moon – 28° 28' Aries	Mars – 12° 56' Aquarius
Mercury – 00° 00' Gemini	Jupiter – 06° 37' Taurus
Venus – 19° 56' Taurus	Saturn – 27° 02' Aries
Rahu – 05° 30' Virgo	Ketu – 05° 30' Pisces

Planetary Periods

Birth – Sun/Mars	Moon – Aug. 1, 1946
Mars – Aug. 1, 1956	Rahu – Aug. 1, 1963
Jupiter – Aug. 1, 1981	Saturn – Aug. 1, 1997
Mercury – Aug. 1, 2016	

Bob Dylan has a profound and troubled Mars-ruled Scorpio as his Ascendant type. His Moon sign is headstrong Aries, also ruled by Mars, bringing a double Mars influence on his nature. However, Mars is located in Aquarius, an air sign ruled by Saturn, and exchanges signs with Saturn, which is located in Aries ruled by Mars. This Mars-Saturn exchange is the dominant factor in his constitution, as Vata with Pitta.

Dylan is an artist, writer, musician and rebel, reflecting the innovative but volatile temperament usually associated with Vata. But he also exhibits a critical, if not angry bent of mind, showing a good deal of Pitta as well. The seventh house, dominated by the Sun and its aspect on the Ascendant, brings in yet more Pitta. The combust Jupiter is not able to bring in much Kapha, but Venus in its own sign and not severely combust does soften his energy and give him recognition and charisma.

The Aries Moon in the sixth house gives him a psychology of conflict, assertion and rebellion. Saturn is in a close conjunction with the Moon, and debilitated in Aries, coloring the psychology, adding a degree of alienation to the mind and giving mood swings and a tendency to depression or the use of drugs. Saturn is strongly placed in the Navamsha, aspecting Jupiter, the lord of the Navamsha Ascendant, affording it more strength. Mercury at the very beginning of Gemini still aspects the Ascendant, which is at the end of Taurus, also strengthening Vata.

The Mars-Saturn exchange through the fourth and sixth houses is a common factor in vehicular accidents. Dylan was almost killed in a motorcycle accident, which occurred during his Rahu period. Some degree of recklessness in the psychology probably contributed to it. His angular Venus and Jupiter, however, protected his life.

9. DIANE FEINSTEIN, Pitta

Birth Chart

<u>ASC</u>		MO	VE SU
RA			ME
SA			MA JU KE

Navamsha

		VE	KE
			SA ME
<u>ASC</u>			
SU MA RA		JU	MO

June 22, 1933, San Francisco CA, 122W25, 37N47

Ascendant – 21° 11' Pisces	Sun – 07° 31' Gemini
Moon – 29° 57' Taurus	Mars – 29° 31' Leo
Mercury – 00° 48' Cancer	Jupiter – 22° 58' Leo
Venus – 23° 59' Gemini	Saturn – 22° 54' Cap. Rx
Rahu – 08° 50' Aquarius	Ketu – 08° 50' Leo

Planetary Periods

Birth – Mars/Saturn	Rahu – Dec. 29, 1936
Jupiter – Dec. 29, 1954	Saturn – Dec. 29, 1970
Mercury – Dec. 29, 1989	Ketu – Dec. 29, 2006
Venus – Dec. 29, 2013	

The combination of Jupiter and Mars (Guru-Mangala Yoga) brings together a person's power of action (Mars) with higher principles (Jupiter or Guru). This is a good combination for lawyers, politicians and social reformers of an ethical nature, particularly when the combination occurs in friendly signs like Leo where these two planets normally do well.

In Feinstein's chart this Mars-Jupiter combination is the predominant influence, driving her into her political career that led her to the US Senate. Jupiter is the ruler of the Ascendant, Pisces. Mars is not only located with Jupiter, it aspects the Ascendant with its special eighth sign aspect, impacting both the Ascendant and its lord. Both planets are located in Leo, a fire sign, in the sixth house of health, giving strength to the constitution as well. They are located with Ketu, which is both like Mars in energy and like Jupiter in giving a spiritual motivation, further strengthening the combination. This Mars-Ketu influence gives Feinstein a fiery or Pitta constitution but as harmonized by a principled Jupiter. Mars-Jupiter or a higher Mars energy would be her planetary type as well.

Her Taurus Moon in the third house gives vitality and motivation, as well as endurance in her work. The Sun and Venus in Gemini in the fourth house of the mind provides good communication skills, as does Mercury in the fifth house of creative intelligence.

10. Michael J. Fox, Vata

Birth Chart

	MO VE	SU	ME
KE			MA
ASC JU SA			RA

Navamsha

		JU	RA MO VE
ME SA MA			
			ASC SU
KE			

June 9, 1961, 12 15 AM, Edmonton CAN, 113W28, 53N33

Ascendant – 25° 17' Cap.	Sun – 24° 53' Taurus
Moon – 08° 08' Aries	Mars – 25°17' Cancer
Mercury – 16° 01' Gemini	Jupiter – 13° 30' Cap. Rx.
Venus – 09° 38' Aries	Saturn – 05° 48' Cap. Rx.
Rahu – 07° 35' Leo	Ketu – 06° 35' Aquarius

Planetary Periods

Birth – Ketu/Jupiter	Venus – March 1, 1964
Sun – March 1, 1984	Moon – March 1, 1990
Mars – March 1, 2000	Rahu – March 1, 2007

Fox is an actor in mainly comic roles who came down with Parkinson's disease at a young age. Relative to the Ayurvedic constitution, Capricorn is rising along with its ruler Saturn. This creates more Vata in the constitution. Fox is short in stature, with a nervous/expressive temperament and other very Vata characteristics and a youthful Mercurial appearance.

However, there are notable health afflictions in his chart relative to both the first and sixth houses. The first house of the body is influenced by two debilitated planets that are both temporal malefics for the Ascendant. Jupiter is debilitated and retrograde in Capricorn itself, with Mars in Cancer near its maximum degree of debility which occurs at 28 Cancer aspecting the Ascendant. Saturn as the Ascendant lord is retrograde, which also tends to weaken the health. Saturn and Mars both afflict the Ascendant and Jupiter in the birth chart. In the navamsha, they afflict both Mercury and the Ascendant.

In addition, Rahu, which makes one susceptible to nervous system disorders, is in its poorest house location in the eighth house of death and severe illness. It afflicts the Moon in the navamsha as well. While Mercury, the sixth lord and significator of the nervous system, is located in the sixth house in its own sign of Gemini, it is hemmed in between malefics with the Sun on one side and Mars on the other, weakening it considerably.

The disease first manifested with minor and controllable symptoms in 1991, near the beginning of Fox's Moon major period, becoming more pronounced in 1998 in the Moon-Venus period. As the Moon exchanges signs with Mars, it brings that planet's negative influence into play. As Mars' major period followed the Moon in 2000 and Rahu's major period commences after Mars in 2007, a progression of the disease is indicated, increasing under Rahu. Benefics in angles, with Jupiter in the first house and Moon and Venus in the fourth house, give him some help, relief and good treatment, but cannot arrest the disease entirely.

A gemstone for Saturn, the Ascendant lord, would be an important consideration to help deal with the disease. A gemstone for Rahu or hessonite garnet would also be good. Other spiritual remedial measures are worthy of consideration as well.

11. Al Gore, Kapha

Birth Chart

SU	RA	VE	
ME			MA SA ASC
MO JU		KE	

Navamsha

	KE	ME JU	
MA			MO
SA VE			
SU		ASC RA	

March 31, 1948, 12 53 PM, Washington DC, 77W02, 38N54

Ascendant – 11° 05' Can.	Sun – 17° 47' Pisces
Moon – 10° 05' Sagittarius	Mars – 25° 00' Cancer
Mercury – 23° 45' Aqua.	Jupiter – 05° 28' Sagittarius
Venus – 02° 53' Taurus	Saturn – 22° 52' Cancer Rx
Rahu – 22° 52' Aries	Ketu – 22° 52' Libra

Planetary Periods

Birth – Ketu/Saturn	Venus – Dec. 11, 1949
Sun – Dec. 11, 1969	Moon – Dec. 11, 1975
Mars – Dec. 11, 1985	Rahu – Dec. 11, 1992
Jupiter – Dec. 11, 2010	Saturn – Dec. 11, 2026

Al Gore, like George W. Bush who he ran against in the 2000 American presidential election, has a Cancer ascendant dominated by Saturn, bringing out its political side. Gore has a typical tall and large Kapha frame and Kapha facial features, indicating that as his primary Ayurvedic type. He also has a certain Kapha type slowness and a premeditation about his movement and expression along with a goodhearted, compassionate Kapha nature.

Gore's sometimes stiff and contentious appearance is caused by his Mars and Saturn, two harsh malefics, rising in Cancer, but his underlying disposition is caring and supportive. This is owing to his Moon-Jupiter conjunction in Sagittarius ruled by Jupiter, as well as the Sun located in Pisces, another sign of Jupiter. These factors provide for an overriding Jupiterian influence on the chart, making Gore a Jupiterian Kapha and planetary type. The Moon in its own sign in the tenth house of the Navamsha is another Kapha-increasing factor. Pitta is a secondary factor owing to the Mars rising and Moon-Jupiter conjunction occurring in Sagittarius, a fiery sign. Though the Moon is in the sixth house, which is a house of disease, it is so favorably placed with Jupiter that the combination gives him good health and stamina.

Gore's strong Sagittarius Moon also marks his psychological type. This makes him into a crusader and concerned with ethical issues like the environment. Rahu in the tenth house, its strongest position, brought him into the Vice-presidency during its period. But the afflictions to the first house, which involve the debility of Mars, the tenth house ruler, prevented him from achieving the highest office.

12. Steffi Graf, Pitta

Birth Chart

RA	VE SA	SU MO ME	ASC
	MA		JU KE

Navamsha

	ME	ME JU	
JU			MO SA RA
KE			VE
		ASC MA	SU

June 14, 1969, 04 40 AM, Mannheim GER, 08E29, 49N29

Ascendant – 03° 03' Gem.	Sun – 29° 28' Taurus
Moon – 20° 32' Taurus	Mars – 12° 07' Scorpio Rx
Mercury – 10° 27' Taurus	Jupiter – 03° 22' Virgo
Venus – 13° 48' Aries	Saturn – 11° 48' Aries
Rahu – 02° 29' Pisces	Ketu – 02° 29' Virgo

Planetary Periods

Birth – Moon/Venus	Mars – July 17, 1971
Rahu – July 17, 1978	Jupiter – July 17, 1996
Saturn – July 17, 2012	Mercury – July 17, 2031

An important principle of Vedic astrology is that natural malefic planets (Sun, Mars, Saturn, Rahu, Ketu) do well when located in upachaya houses – houses of increasing energy (3, 6, 11) – generally serving to improve the health of a person. They give a strong immune system, athletic interests, and a competitive urge. Naturally this serves to color the constitution and psychology of a person.

Tennis players in general tend towards Pitta constitution. Their sport is a competitive one-to-one interaction that requires both strength and speed. The chart of Steffi Graf demonstrates a quick Gemini ascendant, along with a steady Taurus Moon and Sun. But the dominant factor in the chart is Mars. A retrograde Mars in the sixth house of competition in its own sign Scorpio aspects the Ascendant and its lord Mercury. It also aspects both the Sun and the Moon in Taurus, covering all the main factors in the chart. From the Moon, Mars in Scorpio forms a Mahapurusha Yoga as well, giving further strength to the planet. In addition, Mars is located in the Ascendant of the Navamsha chart.

These Martian factors turn Graf into an athlete and grant her a strong capacity for self-discipline and endurance. The Sun, though in Taurus, is within a few degrees of the Ascendant and so brings its fire to bear upon it as well. Saturn, the other main malefic, occupies the eleventh, another upachaya house, the house of victories, and another sign of Mars, along with benefic Venus. This shows her many wins in her field. The influence of Saturn, which aspects the Ascendant, along with the airy nature of the Ascendant, give her quickness and speed and secondary Vata characteristics. The planetary type is Mars but of an athletic bent.

13. George Harrison, Vata

Birth Chart

VE		SA	JU
SU KE			
ME			RA
MA		MO ASC	

Navamsha

	RA SA JU		ME
SU			VE
MO MA	ASC	KE	

Feb. 24, 1943, 11 42 PM, Liverpool GB, 02W55, 53N25

Ascendant – 05° 23' Libra	Sun – 12° 23' Aquarius
Moon – 07° 05' Libra	Mars – 28° 19' Sag.
Mercury – 16° 48' Cap.	Jupiter – 22° 29' Gemini Rx
Venus – 06° 15' Pisces	Saturn – 12° 51' Taurus
Rahu – 01° 32' Leo	Ketu – 01° 32' Aquarius

Planetary Periods

Birth – Rahu/Rahu	Jupiter – July 28, 1960
Saturn – July 28, 1976	Mercury – July 28, 1995
Death – Mercury/Sun	

Harrison is a double Libra, with the Moon rising in Libra. As Libra is an air sign this brings a good deal of Vata into his physical and psychological makeup. The Sun is also located in Aquarius, another air sign, strengthening this indication. Harrison was an idealistic, spiritual and revolutionary Libra type, with his main expression in music, in the arts.

Jupiter's aspects on the Sun, Moon and Ascendant bring in some Kapha, but from an air sign itself is not enough to dominate the constitution. Yet his Jupiter period did give him great fame as well as contact with spiritual teachers, this from its location in the ninth house of the guru and good fortune.

Harrison, however, did not have good longevity. He died of lung cancer in his Mercury major period at about the age of sixty. In this regard, Mercury is located in a sign of malefic Saturn in the fourth house and hemmed in by two malefics, Mars and Sun, in the third and fifth houses. In the Navamsha Mercury is located in the eighth house of death, as the eighth lord, aspected by both Mars and Saturn, the two major malefics. Mercury as the twelfth lord can bring health problems to Libra Ascendants, even though it also rules the very auspicious ninth house.[56] Harrison died of lung cancer, with the lungs an organ that relate to Mercury.

Saturn itself is located in the eighth house of death in the birth chart, which can be good for longevity, but is debilitated in the sixth house of disease in the Navamsha, which gave it a disease-causing influence. Though the Ascendant lord Venus is exalted in the sixth house of health, it is the eighth lord as well and brought in some health weakness, particularly as it is afflicted by Mars. A gemstone for Mercury would have aided his longevity. One for Saturn could also be considered.

14. Audrey Hepburn, Vata

Birth Chart

VE	RA SU JU	ME	
ASC MO			MA
SA		KE	

Navamsha

ME VE			KE SA
MO			MA
JU RA	ASC	SU	

May 4, 1929, 03 00 AM, Ixelles BE, 04E22, 50N50

Ascendant – 05° 45 Aqua.	Sun – 20° 15 Aries
Moon – 13° 35' Aqua.	Mars – 02° 17' Cancer
Mercury – 07° 27' Taurus	Jupiter – 27° 53' Aries
Venus – 29° 55' Pisces Rx	Saturn – 07° 10' Sag. Rx
Rahu – 28° 52' Aries	Ketu – 28° 52' Libra

Planetary Periods

Birth – Rahu/Mercury	Jupiter – Dec. 30, 1937
Saturn – Dec. 30, 1953	Mercury – Dec. 30, 1972
Ketu – Dec. 30, 1989	Death – Ketu/Rahu

Audrey Hepburn is another typical Vata constitution actress – thin, expressive, sensitive, creative and enthusiastic. Aquarius, an air sign ruled by Saturn rises, along with the Moon. Saturn aspects both the Ascendant and the Moon. The Moon under such Saturn influences, waning and not far from the Sun does not bring much Kapha into the chart, making Vata dosha her Ayurvedic type.

However, Hepburn has an exalted Venus in the second house of the face and of speech, giving her both facial beauty and acting ability. Venus is the strongest planet in the chart for her expression but cannot counter Saturn's influence on her physical body.

The Moon as the lord of the sixth house of disease weakens the health by its placement in the first house. Both Mars and Saturn, the two prime malefics, aspect the first house and the Moon with no benefic aspects to counter them. The result of this is that her chart reflects some weakness in her health, and Hepburn came down with colon cancer and died in her early sixties. Saturn's rulership over the excretory organs and its role in causing degenerative diseases like cancer is reflected in her chart.

Mars is located in the sixth house of disease. While such placement of malefic planets in the sixth house is normally good for health (under the rule that malefics generally do well in upachaya houses, which include the sixth), Mars does aspect both the sixth house and its lord (the Moon) and is debilitated, bringing a negative side to its effects. This makes its influence disease-causing and reducing of longevity.

Hepburn died in her Ketu period. Ketu's period in general can cause disease and death. Ketu acts like the lord of the house it is positioned in, here acting as Venus, a maraka (death-dealing) planet. In the ninth house, it can bring misfortune into the life. For her type of chart, I would probably recommend an emerald, the gemstone of Mercury, which is the only angular benefic placed in the chart.

15. Katherine Hepburn, Pitta

Birth Chart

VE SA	SU ME	MO	JU
			RA
KE			
MA		ASC	

Navamsha

ASC JU, VE MO, KE			SA
			ME RA
SU		MA	

May 12, 1907, 05 47 PM, Hartford CT, 72W41, 41N46

Ascendant – 15° 23' Libra	Sun – 28° 28' Aries
Moon – 04° 57' Taurus	Mars – 23° 14' Sagittarius
Mercury – 15° 32' Aries	Jupiter – 16° 27' Gemini
Venus – 25° 50' Pisces	Saturn – 02° 14' Pisces
Rahu – 04° 15' Cancer	Ketu – 04° 15' Capricorn

Planetary Periods

Birth – Sun/Saturn	Moon – Aug. 18, 1909
Mars – Aug. 18, 1919	Rahu – Aug. 18, 1926
Jupiter – Aug. 18, 1944	Saturn – Aug. 18, 1960
Mercury – Aug. 18, 1979	Ketu – Aug. 19, 1996

Katherine Hepburn had a very strong chart with exalted planets in the sixth (Venus), seventh (Sun), and eighth (Moon) houses. This combination fortifies the Ascendant by its influence and gives both good health and great success in life.

The exalted Sun in the seventh house, however, is the main planet that aspects the Ascendant and brings Pitta as the dominant force into her nature. The planetary type is the Sun, which gives healthy Pitta and good longevity. It also dominates her personality and gave her the strong character that she was noted for in the roles that she played.

Jupiter aspects the Ascendant, but from an air sign, in which its Kapha influence is low. The Ascendant lord Venus is exalted in the sixth house but with Saturn, a Vata planet. Saturn also aspects the Moon. So secondary Vata characteristics are there. Rahu in her tenth house gave her the fame that started early in life during its period, beginning in 1926.

This strong Saturn, as a Raja Yoga Karaka and the general ruler of longevity in the chart, aided in her long life. As a malefic in the sixth house, an upachaya house, it gives a strong immune system. Venus exalted as the ruler of the first and eighth houses, the two main houses of longevity, is another factor for long life. Her exalted and steady Taurus Moon in the eighth house of longevity is yet another. Sun types in general are often gifted with long life because they carry the healthier side of the fire element that can ward of disease.

16. Michael Jordan, Pitta

Birth Chart

	<u>ASC</u>		
JU SU			MA RA
SA ME KE			
VE	MO		

Navamsha

ME		JU	
KE			SA
			RA
<u>ASC</u>	MO MA SU		VE

Feb. 17, 1963, 10 20 AM, Brooklyn NY, 73W56, 40N38

Ascendant – 28° 26' Aries	Sun – 04° 54' Aquarius
Moon – 14° 58' Scorpio	Mars – 16° 39' Cancer Rx
Mercury – 09° 09' Cap.	Jupiter – 25° 43' Aquarius
Venus – 19° 41' Sag.	Saturn – 22° 10' Capricorn
Rahu – 04° 49' Cancer	Ketu – 04° 49' Capricorn

Planetary Periods

Birth – Saturn/Jupiter	Mercury – July 20, 1965
Ketu – July 20, 1982	Venus – July 20, 1989
Sun – July 20, 2009	Moon – July 20, 2015

Michael Jordan is an extremely competitive, high achieving Pitta (fiery) personality, with secondary Vata (air) characteristics. The Ascendant is Aries, an aggressive and assertive, headstrong fiery sign. Mars, the Ascendant lord, exchanges signs with the Moon, being in Cancer ruled by the Moon, while the Moon is in Scorpio, ruled by Mars, bringing a strong Mars influence to the Moon. Mars also aspects the Sun and is with both the Sun and the Moon in a Martian sign in the Navamsha. Such an influential Mars becomes the dominant planetary type.

The strong Saturn in the tenth house in its own sign of Capricorn not only gives great career success and financial gains but adds a Vata influence to the chart. The Sun and Jupiter in Aquarius, an air sign, contribute to this, as does airy Rahu being located with Mars. His basketball career involved much time for him 'in the air'.

Jordan's chart shows how debilitated planets can drive people to great achievements. The debilitated Mars in Cancer gives Jordan an extraordinary need to win and to achieve. The debilitated Moon in Scorpio, another Mars sign, contributes to this. The exchange of these mutually debilitated planets has the effect of increasing the person's drive to succeed. While this can be a psychological problem and an obsession, it can stimulate a person to great efforts.

17. John Kennedy, Vata

Birth Chart

	ME MA	VE SU JU	KE
			SA
			MO
RA			<u>ASC</u>

Navamsha

KE		SU	
JU			SA VE
ME	MA MO		RA <u>ASC</u>

May 29, 1917, 03 00 PM, Brookline MA, 71W07, 42N20

Ascendant – 27° 17' Virgo	Sun – 15° 08' Taurus
Moon – 24° 30' Leo	Mars – 25° 43' Aries
Mercury – 27° 53' Aries	Jupiter – 00° 20' Taurus
Venus – 24° 02' Taurus	Saturn – 04° 27' Cancer
Rahu – 19° 46' Sagittarius	Ketu – 19° 46' Gemini

Planetary Periods

Birth – Venus/Mercury	Sun – Aug. 27, 1920
Moon – Aug. 27, 1926	Mars – Aug. 27, 1936
Rahu – Aug. 27, 1943	Jupiter – Aug. 27, 1961
Death – Jupiter/Saturn	

What is most interesting about Kennedy's chart from the standpoint of Ayurvedic astrology are his significant health imbalances, mainly of a Vata nature, with severe back pain and Addison's disease. Saturn, a Vata planet, aspects both the Ascendant Virgo, a Vata sign with a tendency to chronic diseases, and the lord of the Ascendant Mercury. Virgo marks the Navamsha Ascendant as well, where it has the influence of Rahu, another Vata planet.

Mercury, the Ascendant lord, meanwhile is in the eighth house of disease, along with another malefic Mars. Kennedy's chart is one of congenitally poor health, a weak constitution from birth. Kennedy took many medications to deal with his many health problems. His more stocky, almost Kapha appearance in his later life came from his use of steroids. His natural physique when he was younger was thin and wiry.

The amazing thing was that with such a physique Kennedy could succeed both in the army and in politics. This occurred mainly because of his strong ninth house, with Jupiter and the Sun and Venus in its own sign. It was his father's (ninth house in Vedic astrology) help and the considerable political and financial support that came with it, which allowed Jack Kennedy to compensate for his physical weakness and succeed.

Kennedy himself had some strength of character to go along with that. His dramatic Leo Moon gave him some Pitta psychological characteristics, including the charisma and warmth of personality that he was famous for. His Moon chart is stronger than the basic birth chart, boosting him up politically in life. The Sun is also strong in the ninth house of fortune and is Vargottama (in the same sign of the Rashi and Navamsha), giving it additional power. Kennedy's Vata qualities gave him success working with the media, speaking and appearing on television.

The sign Virgo in Vedic thought is Kanya, meaning a young girl. In Vedic thought Virgo is usually a highly sexual sign, not one of chastity! Kennedy demonstrated that with his many affairs. His Mercury-Mars conjunction in a sign of Mars in the eighth house of sexuality contributed to that.

Jupiter not only raised him to power by aspecting the Ascendant, it is a maraka or death-dealing planet for Virgo, governing the seventh house. Its period both raised him to the office of the Presidency and killed him as well. Kennedy would have greatly benefited from an emerald, a gemstone for Mercury, with such a highly afflicted Ascendant lord.

18. J. Krishnamurthi, Vata

Birth Chart

	SU	ME	MA JU VE
RA			
ASC			KE
MO		SA	

Navamsha

MA	MO	RA	
ME			
SA JU			ASC
SU	KE VE		

May 12, 1895, 12 23 AM LMT, Mandanapalle, India, 13N33, 78E30

Ascendant – 26° 29' Cap.	Sun – 28° 24' Aries
Moon – 02° 53 Sag.	Mars – 19° 24' Gemini
Mercury – 06° 28' Taurus	Jupiter – 12° 47' Gemini
Venus – 06° 02' Gemini	Saturn – 10° 15' Libra Rx
Rahu – 26° 31' Aquarius	Ketu – 26° 31' Leo

Planetary Periods

Birth – Ketu/Venus	Venus – Nov. 3, 1900
Sun – Nov. 4, 1920	Moon – Nov. 3, 1926
Mars – Nov. 3, 1936	Rahu – Nov. 3, 1943
Jupiter – Nov. 3, 1961	Saturn – Nov. 3, 1977
Death – Saturn/Venus	

This extraordinary chart is dominated by a powerful idealistic Saturn. Saturn, the lord of the Capricorn Ascendant, is located in its sign of exaltation in Libra in the tenth house of career and recognition. It fully aspects the Moon by its third aspect and the Sun, which is also exalted, by its seventh aspect. Such a prominent Saturn, influencing the main factors of the Ascendant, Sun and Moon, affords the person a predominant Vata constitution as well as making him a Saturn type, of a spiritual disposition.

J. Krishnamurthi had a typical thin Vata build with angular features. He had a very sensitive body, mind and digestive system, with tremors of his hands and feet. He was also a Saturnian character, a loner, an austere and aloof spiritual teacher. The exalted Saturn as second lord also gave him great powers of speech for the many talks he was known for.

Pitta was the secondary dosha with his exalted Sun in Aries and his Moon in Sagittarius, both fiery signs, endowing him also with qualities of leadership and a critical intelligence.

The afflicted Moon in the twelfth house aspected by Mars and Saturn afforded him a weak constitution as a child. Venus and Jupiter, poorly placed in the sixth house of disease in Gemini, caused him to suffer from asthma. However, the overall strength of Saturn, the Ascendant Lord, and the Sun, the lord of the eighth house of longevity, gave him a long life in spite of this. Saturn's aspect on the seventh house Cancer and its lord the Moon made him a lifelong bachelor. Such a Saturn afforded great detachment and control of the mind as well.

This same exalted Saturn caused Krishnamurthi to renounce his career and status at an early age. In his Moon period, with the Moon in the reclusive twelfth house, he gave up his public role as the projected world teacher for the Theosophical Society and went on his own as a solitary teacher working outside of all organizations. The afflictions of the Moon, by Mars and more so by Saturn, create such renunciation.

19. Michael Landon, Kapha

Birth Chart

		MO	KE
SA			MA
ASC JU RA	VE	SU ME	

Navamsha

	JU SA	RA	
SU MO			
ASC MA VE	ME KE		

October 31, 1936, 12 12 PM, Jamaica NY, 73W48, 40N41

Ascendant – 29° 20' Sag.	Sun – 15° 07' Libra
Moon – 06° 00' Taurus	Mars – 26° 38' Leo
Mercury – 04° 08' Libra	Jupiter – 00° 24' Sag.
Venus – 17° 26' Scorpio	Saturn – 23° 06' Aqua. Rx.
Rahu – 03° 48' Sag.	Ketu – 03° 48' Gemini

Planetary Periods

Birth – Sun/Mercury	Moon – Aug. 19, 1938
Mars – Aug. 19, 1948	Rahu – Aug. 19, 1955
Jupiter – Aug. 19, 1973	Saturn – Aug. 19, 1989
Death – Saturn/Saturn	

Michael Landon was a successful television actor who died of liver cancer at a relatively young age of fifty-four. Jupiter and Rahu are together in a Sagittarius Ascendant ruled by Jupiter. The Ascendant receives no other aspects. Jupiter both rules and aspects the Navamsha ascendant, which is also Sagittarius. This strong Jupiter brings Kapha into the physical body. The Moon meanwhile is exalted in Taurus, an earth sign, strong in brightness and aspected only by Venus, another Kapha planet, bringing Kapha into the psychology as well.

However, the chart shows health weaknesses and not a good longevity. Rahu afflicts the Ascendant lord Jupiter, particularly with bad health habits and a self-indulgent tendency. Most of his adult life, the period from ages nineteen to fifty-three was spent in Rahu and Jupiter major periods. Landon suffered from alcoholism and possible other drug abuse. The Moon, the lord of the eighth house of longevity, is poorly placed in the sixth house of disease and aspected by the sixth lord Venus. The Moon being exalted does not help its longevity indications. It only gives more strength to the house of disease because it is also the eighth lord. Venus itself is weak in the twelfth house aspected by both Mars and Saturn.

Landon's death occurred not long into Saturn's period. Saturn is a malefic and maraka (death-dealing) planet for Sagittarius Ascendant, ruling the second house. It is debilitated in the navamsha along with Jupiter, which rules both the basic birth chart (rashi) and navamsha. Jupiter as related to the liver also indicates the site of the problem. Saturn additionally aspects Mars, the sixth lord, and the sixth house Aries, further impacting the health. His chart shows how Kapha planets can cause disease, when poorly placed.

20. Bruce Lee, Pitta

Birth Chart

KE	SA JU		
	ASC SU	ME, MO VA, VE	RA

Navamsha

MO	ME	RA	
MA			SA JU
VE	KE	ASC SU	

Nov. 27, 1940, 07 12 AM, San Francisco CA, 112W25, 37N47

Ascendant – 13° 10' Scor.	Sun – 12° 12' Scorpio
Moon – 18° 22' Libra	Mars – 11° 31' Libra
Mercury – 22° 14' Libra	Jupiter – 14° 30' Aries Rx
Venus – 08° 19' Libra	Saturn – 16° 27' Aries Rx
Rahu – 14° 57' Virgo	Ketu – 14° 57' Pisces

Planetary Periods

Birth – Rahu/Moon	Jupiter – Feb. 10, 1943
Saturn – Feb. 10, 1959	Death – Saturn/Rahu

Bruce Lee was a famous martial artist and actor, one of the first and prototypal of that genre, who died suddenly and mysteriously in his early thirties. His occupation and life-style, centered around fighting and even involvement with the criminal underworld, was quite Pitta. Not surprisingly, Scorpio, the secretive sign of Mars marks the Ascendant, with the Sun, a Pitta planet and powerful tenth lord located there. This Sun in Scorpio marks his strong personality and his physical type.

However, the chart reveals a secretive and troubled psychology. Mars, along with a waning Moon, Venus and Mercury are located in the twelfth house of loss. Opposite is a debilitated and retrograde Saturn, about three degrees from its maximum point of debility at twenty degrees Aries, along with a retrograde Jupiter. The sixth-house/twelfth house axis of health and disease is highly activated and dominated by the two malefics Mars and Saturn. His apparently strong and outgoing Sun in the first house is limited by these hidden influences. Saturn aspects both the sixth house and its lord (Mars) and the eighth house and its lord (Mercury), the two main factors of longevity.

There is some doubt whether Lee died of a brain disease or was somehow murdered. Of course in astrology the sixth is both the house of disease and the house of enemies, making this question not an easy factor to determine. For Scorpio Ascendant, Mars also rules both the first house of the self and the sixth house of enemies. But the many sixth and twelfth house planets could easily indicate some mysterious and sudden disease. In any case, with a twelfth house dominated chart (Venus as the twelfth lord is also the final dispositor); such a life was unlikely to last long or maintain its visibility. The strong first house is easily eclipsed by a stronger twelfth house.

21. Marilyn Monroe, Kapha-Vata

Birth Chart

	VE	SU ME	RA
MA JU			<u>ASC</u>
MO			
KE		SA	

Navamsha

		RA VE ME	SU MA SA
<u>ASC</u>			MO
	KE JU		

March 1, 1926, 09 30 AM, Los Angeles CA, 118W15, 34N03

Ascendant 20°15' Cancer	Sun 17°37' Taurus
Moon 26°16' Capricorn	Mars 27°54' Aquarius
Mercury 13°57' Taurus	Jupiter 04°00' Aquarius
Venus 05°55' Aries	Saturn 28°37' Libra Rx
Rahu 25°26' Gemini	Ketu 25°26' Sagittarius

Planetary Periods

Birth – Mars/Jupiter	Rahu – Nov. 15, 1931
Jupiter – Nov. 14, 1949	Death – Jupiter/Mars

Marilyn Monroe was well known for her curvy feminine features, which are typically Kapha according to Ayurveda. We can see this in the chart with a strong Moon aspecting its own watery (Kapha) Cancer Ascendant. The prominent Venus in the tenth house also helps promote Kapha and by its elevation to the tenth house, the highest position in her chart, marks her career and planetary type.

Saturn's aspect on the Ascendant gives her Vata characteristics and, in the fourth house of the mind, a troubled psychology. As an exalted seventh lord it gives her older and powerful husbands. Yet Saturn casts its shadow over the chart and her psychology as both a natural and temporal malefic aspecting the fourth house and its lord. Venus, as the lord of the fourth house of emotions, is aspected by Saturn, which itself occupies the fourth house, denying emotional contentment and happiness in the home life. Its exaltation in this case, though giving material benefits, only gives Saturn more strength to cause emotional distress.

The Moon is often troubled when it is located in the seventh house, particularly for women. It grants the general attraction of many men but is not good for marital stability or personal happiness. It often reflects childhood trauma and vulnerability. In Monroe's case the Moon is also in a sign of Saturn. It is placed in the difficult eighth house in the Navamsha and aspected only by Saturn.

Jupiter and Mars together form a Raja Yoga or combination for fame, as rulers of the ninth and tenth houses. This occurs in the eighth house, a house of sexuality. Yet the eighth is also a house of death and weakens her psychological stability and her longevity by this poor placement. Involving the fifth lord and Jupiter, the significator for children, they deny children as well. Although she was pregnant many times, she never carried a pregnancy to term.

The eighth house also relates to drugs and poisons. Her drug-induced death occurred in the Jupiter major, Mars minor period when her eighth house of death was fully activated. While regarded as a suicide, some have considered that foul play was involved. While there are psychological afflictions in the chart, they do not seem severe enough to cause suicide, so there may be some point to this charge. Jupiter and Mars are also located in the second house, a maraka or death-causing house from the Moon. Marilyn could have benefited from a number of gemstones, including those for Moon, Jupiter and Mars.

22. JOE MONTANA, Pitta

Birth Chart

		SU KE ME	VE
MA			MO
			JU
	RA SA		ASC

Navamsha

ME			
VE			
MA			ASC SA
	RA		SU MO

June 11, 1956, 03 25 PM, New Eagle PA, 79W57, 40N12

Ascendant – 23° 47' Virgo	Sun – 27° 33' Taurus
Moon – 08° 24' Cancer	Mars – 11° 21' Aquarius
Mercury – 07° 43' Taurus	Jupiter – 02° 29' Leo
Venus – 13° 21' Gem. Rx	Saturn – 04° 40' Scorpio Rx
Rahu – 14° 13' Scorpio	Ketu – 14° 13' Taurus

Planetary Periods

Birth – Saturn/Venus	Mercury – March 22, 1968
Ketu – March 22, 1985	Venus – March 22, 1992
Sun – March 22, 2012	Moon – March 22, 2018

Virgo Ascendant is commonly found in the case of people with numerous health disorders, but it is also a common Ascendant for athletes, actors, artists and even politicians. The reason is that as a mutable earth sign, Virgo endows its natives not only with physical vulnerability but also with skills and adaptability for success within the material world. Joe Montana, the most famous football quarterback of recent decades, is a good example of a Virgo rising athlete, but several other such charts could be shown.

Montana's chart also demonstrates the power of malefic planets in upachaya or increasing houses (3, 6, and 11) to give good health and competitive edge. Like several other charts we have shown, it shows a powerful Mars in the sixth house, giving competitive energy and skill. Mars is the only planet to aspect both the Virgo ascendant and its lord Mercury. This affords him the agility of the Virgo ascendant with the fire power and drive to win of Mars. Mars is exalted in the sixth house of the Navamsha chart as well.

In addition, Mars in Aquarius exchanges signs with Saturn in Scorpio in the third house. Saturn in the third house adds to his sports interests and competitive drive. Saturn also aspects Mercury and brings some secondary Vata into the constitution, as does the Mercury influence of the Ascendant. Mercury (Taurus) and Venus (Gemini) exchange signs as ninth and tenth lords, the best Raja Yoga combination for fame and recognition.

Yet such malefics in upachaya houses, though generally good for health, can cause health problems from accidents or from overexertion. Montana had a back injury shortly after the start of his Ketu period that he did quickly recover from, but which almost ended his career. Like many such athletes, the effects of these injuries increase with age.

23. JACQUELINE ONASSIS (KENNEDY), Vata

Birth Chart

	RA MO	VE JU	
			SU ME
			MA
SA		<u>ASC</u> KE	

Navamsha

	SA MO	<u>ASC</u> KE	JU
	RA	SU MA	ME VE

July 28, 1929, 02 30 PM, Southampton NY, 72W2, 40N53

Ascendant – 25° 06' Libra	Sun – 12° 17' Cancer
Moon – 02° 44' Aries	Mars – 21° 57' Leo
Mercury – 09° 31' Cancer	Jupiter – 16° 42' Taurus
Venus – 28° 53' Taurus	Saturn – 01° 56' Sag. Rx
Rahu – 24° 20' Aries	Ketu –24° 20' Pisces

Planetary Periods

Birth – Ketu/Venus	Venus – Feb. 20, 1935
Sun – Feb. 20, 1955	Moon – Feb. 20, 1961
Mars – Feb. 20, 1971	Rahu – Feb. 20, 1978
Death – Rahu/Moon	

Jacqueline Kennedy's chart is a good example of the power of mysterious Rahu. Rahu is the main influence behind her Vata or airy constitution and her unusual life, which was marked by unexpected events and a great fame that was more of a curse than a blessing to her personally. Jackie was thin, hypersensitive and not very physically strong, with the Rahu-Ketu axis on her Ascendant and Moon, bringing various complications and extreme ups and downs into her life.

Rahu is located within a degree of a direct opposition to her airy Libra Ascendant and in the same sign as the Moon. It is similarly located in the seventh house of her Navamsha. Meanwhile a debilitated Saturn dominates her Navamsha Moon, bringing more Vata in at that level as well. The Moon is also poorly placed in its Nakshatra position, in a sensitive (Gandanta) position at the beginning of Ashvini.

Rahu with the Moon is a factor of eclipses. The Moon is also her tenth lord and gives prominence and recognition. She certainly experienced an eclipse (assassination) of her husband (seventh house), who was the most powerful man in the world. This tragedy marked her character.

Jackie contracted cancer, which is often a Vata disease, and passed away quite coincidentally, under her Rahu major Moon minor period! Her Ascendant lord Venus is in the eighth house of death with Jupiter, the sixth lord of diseases. Venus is also debilitated in the Navamsha. Such a Jupiter-Venus combination did not help her longevity, though the two planets in the eighth house of inherited wealth did give her affluence. In her case, the use of a diamond would have aided in her longevity as it would protect both the Ascendant and Venus.

24. Luciano Pavarotti, Kapha

Birth Chart

MO			KE
SA			ASC
			VE
RA	MA JU	ME	SU

Navamsha

ASC		KE	
MA			JU
SA MO			SU VE
ME	RA		

Oct. 12, 1935, 01 40 AM, Modena, Italy, 10E55, 44N40

Ascendant – 29° 32' Can.	Sun – 24° 47' Virgo
Moon – 22° 26' Pisces	Mars – 24° 48' Scorpio
Mercury – 07° 37' Pis. Rx	Jupiter – 01° 07' Scorpio
Venus – 16° 22' Leo	Saturn – 11° 09' Aqua. Rx
Rahu – 24° 14' Sag.	Ketu – 24° 14' Gemini

Planetary Periods

Birth – Mercury/Moon	Ketu – May 30, 1945
Venus – May 30, 1952	Sun – May 30, 1972
Moon – May 30, 1978	Mars – May 30, 1988
Rahu – May 30, 1995	Jupiter – May 30, 2013

Opera singers often have a large Kapha constitution with strong lungs and a tendency towards overweight. Luciano Pavarotti, perhaps the most famous tenor of our times, is typically of this nature and body type. His chart clearly reveals the same factors.

The Ascendant is Cancer, a water sign. The Moon, the ruler of the Ascendant, is located in Pisces, another watery sign. It is also full and at its maximum of its brightness. Only one planet aspects both the Ascendant and its ruler. That is Kapha Jupiter, itself located in Scorpio, another watery sign. So Kapha factors strongly dominate the Ascendant and its ruler, which are also Kapha in nature. Meanwhile, the Navamsha Ascendant is Pisces, another watery sign. Its only aspect is that of its exalted ruler Jupiter in Cancer, another watery sign.

Pavarotti is a Jupiter-Moon type, which expresses itself through his song and artistry. In this regard, Jupiter is often a musical planet and can give good singing ability. Venus located in the second house of speech, in dramatic Leo, also aids in giving him a good and artistic voice. The Sun in health sensitive Virgo opposite the Moon in emotionally sensitive Pisces is a combination that tends to overweight and to health problems like diabetes. Yet in the third house of talent it contributes to artistic expression.

25. Bhagwan Shree Rajneesh (Osho), Pitta

Birth Chart

RA		<u>ASC</u>	
			JU
SA, MO VE, ME MA	SU		KE

Navamsha

JU KE			MA
SU			<u>ASC</u>
			ME
SA		MO	VE RA

Dec. 11, 1931, 05 13 PM, Kutchwada, India, 77E23, 23N15

Ascendant – 21° 03' Tau.	Sun – 25° 34' Scorpio
Moon – 22° 19' Sag.	Mars – 08° 07' Sag.
Mercury – 13° 28' Sag.	Jupiter – 29° 43' Can. Rx
Venus – 19° 15' Sag.	Saturn – 28° 33' Sag.
Rahu – 08° 27' Pisces	Ketu – 08° 27' Virgo

Planetary Periods

Birth – Venus/Saturn	Sun – June 12, 1938
Moon – June 12, 1944	Mars – June 12, 1954
Rahu – June 12, 1961	Jupiter – June 12, 1979
Death – Jup./Sun	

Rajneesh, perhaps the most brilliant, independent and controversial of all modern gurus, has an unusual chart which shows both the powers and the dangers of the eighth house. The eighth is one of the main houses of disease, death, misfortune and disgrace. It shows catastrophic or terminal illnesses, accidents or assaults on a person. Yet it is also a house of longevity and healing. Spiritually it can give deep wisdom, occult powers or Kundalini energy.

Rajneesh's extraordinary eighth house Sagittarius Moon has the influence of all five planets. It is located with Mars, Mercury, Venus and Saturn while exchanging signs or mutual reception with a retrograde Jupiter in Cancer, the sign of the Moon. Jupiter meanwhile is located in the eighth house from the Moon, emphasizing the eighth house connection from the Moon sign as well. The Sun is in Scorpio is in the eighth sign, further adding its energy to the situation.

Rajneesh had the charismatic, spiritual, artistic and intellectual power that the eighth house can bring. He also had the controversy, opposition, imprisonment and short life. He had a typical eighth house psychology with his involvement in higher states of consciousness, sex and even politics, which are all connected to this house of mystery and danger. The benefic planets in the eighth are hemmed in by Mars and Saturn, which contributed to his relatively early death at the age of 59.

One could argue with such a combination of planets that Rajneesh had all three doshas in his nature. But Pitta predominates because Mars aspects both the Moon and its lord Jupiter and so is the strongest of the eighth house planets. Rajneesh also has a Taurus Ascendant aspected by a powerfully placed Sun in Scorpio. The Pitta or fiery influence of the Sun outweighs the Kapha influence of the Ascendant. In terms of planets he had a dual Mars and Jupiter energy.

Yet in his case he was more of a house type than a planetary type person. Rajneesh can be best understood as an eighth house person. This is another kind of astrological classification that can explain a lot that the general planetary type delineation can gloss over. Sixth, eighth and twelfth house people, those whose charts are dominated by these houses and their lords, for example, tend to have weak health and poor longevity regardless of the actual planets, signs and doshas involved. I have not taken the time in this book to delineate all such 'house types' but it is a worthy examination and has its place in Vedic astrological typologies.

The Ascendant lord Venus is particularly weak in the eighth house. It is also debilitated, with Rahu and under both Mars and Saturn aspects in the Navamsha. Rajneesh passed away in his Jupiter (eighth lord) and Moon (in the eighth house) period. The eighth is also a house of mysterious diseases or poisons. Rajneesh's followers claimed he was poisoned with slow acting poisons by the US government when he was imprisoned in the USA. His chart suggests something sinister like that, though another theory is that his own followers poisoned him.

26. Ronald Reagan, Pitta

Birth Chart

	RA SA		
VE SU			
ME			
MA ASC		JU KE	MO

Navamsha

	MO, JU ME, KE	VE	SA
			ASC
	SU	RA	MA

Feb. 16, 1911, 04 16 AM, Tampico IL, 89W47, 41N38

Ascendant – 13° 49' Sag.	Sun – 04° 01' Aquarius
Moon – 11° 06' Virgo	Mars – 18° 37' Sag.
Mercury – 11° 51' Cap.	Jupiter – 21° 40' Libra
Venus – 28° 30' Aquarius	Saturn – 08° 51' Aries
Rahu – 21° 22' Aries	Ketu – 21° 22' Libra

Planetary Periods

Birth – Moon/Moon	Mars – April 18, 1920
Rahu – April 18, 1927	Jupiter – April 18, 1945
Saturn – April 18, 1961	Mercury – April 18, 1980
Ketu – April 18, 1997	Venus – April 18, 2004

Ronald Reagan's chart features a strong Mars rising in a fiery Sagittarius. This makes him aggressive, self-righteous and a reformer. It also creates his Pitta nature and makes Mars his dominant planet. A liberal in his youth, Reagan became a conservative politician under Saturn's major period later in life.

Jupiter, the lord of the Ascendant, meanwhile is aspected by Saturn. The Sun is in Aquarius, an airy sign, ruled by Saturn. Such factors make Vata his secondary dosha and of some prominence as well. A prominent and self-disciplined Moon in Virgo, a Mercury ruled sign, in the tenth house of career gave him his acting ability as well as a strong love of the public. This strong Moon gave Reagan his charisma, which allowed people to ignore his often destructive actions as president. Venus in its own sign in the tenth house of the Navamsha also helped.

Reagan became president at the start of his Mercury major period in 1980, with Mercury as the tenth lord and lord of the Moon. His debilitated Saturn in the fifth house of the intellect, along with Rahu, contributed to his poor memory and eventual Alzheimer's disease. Saturn's aspect on Mercury brought out that affliction during Mercury's period, after the subperiod of Mercury-Rahu.

27. Robert Redford, Pitta-Kapha

Birth Chart

<u>ASC</u>			KE
SA			MA
			MO, ME VE, SU
RA	JU		

Navamsha

	SU		SA RA
JU			<u>ASC</u>
KE	MO ME	MA	VE

August 18, 1936, 08 02 PM, Santa Monica CA 118W29, 34N01

Ascendant – 05° 59' Pisces	Sun – 03° 00' Leo
Moon – 26° 15' Leo	Mars – 12° 40' Cancer
Mercury – 25° 25' Leo	Jupiter – 21° 41' Scorpio
Venus – 16° 59' Leo	Saturn – 27° 53' Aqua. Rx
Rahu – 07° 42' Sagittarius	Ketu – 07° 42' Gemini

Planetary Periods

Birth – Venus/Ketu	Sun – March 29, 1937
Moon – March 29, 1943	Mars – March 29, 1953
Rahu – March 29, 1960	Jupiter – March 29, 1978
Saturn – March 29, 1994	Mercury – March 29, 2013

Robert Redford's chart at first glance appears to show a fair amount of Kapha, with Kapha Jupiter aspecting a Kapha Pisces Ascendant. While there is some Kapha in his nature, and the compassion of the Pisces Ascendant, if we look more closely, we see that it is outweighed by his four planets in Leo, including both the Moon and the Sun, the ruler of Leo. Leo also marks the sixth house so that planets here impact the health as well, in this case with the strong Sun giving him a strong immune system and a love of work.

Redford's Leo Sun and Moon type is the dominant factor in his constitution. The Sun is also exalted in the Navamsha as the ruler of the Navamsha Ascendant Leo. So his Ayurvedic type is Pitta-Kapha. His planetary type is that of the Sun, with an artistic charisma.

His Rahu in the tenth house of career gave him a great deal of fame, particularly as its lord Jupiter is in the ninth house, a Raja Yoga combination. His ninth house Jupiter gives an ethical nature as well. His career started early under such a favorable Rahu followed by a favorable Jupiter. His Saturn in the twelfth house has made him more reclusive since its period began but also promotes the political and charitable side of his nature.

28. John Ritter, Vata

Birth Chart

	RA		
MO			VE
			SA
	JU	MA KE	ME ASC SU

Navamsha

JU	MO		ASC SA
MA KE			
SU			ME RA
	VE		

Sept. 17, 1948, 07 59 AM, Burbank CA 118W28, 34N11

Ascendant – 17° 42' Virgo	Sun – 01° 28' Virgo
Moon – 22° 56' Aquarius	Mars – 16° 14' Libra
Mercury – 26° 25' Virgo	Jupiter – 27° 33' Scorpio
Venus – 16° 10' Cancer	Saturn – 06° 40' Leo
Rahu – 13° 52' Aries	Ketu – 13° 52' Libra

Planetary Periods

Birth – Jupiter/Saturn	Saturn – March 4, 1961
Mercury – March 4, 1980	Ketu – March 4, 1997
Death – Ketu/Mercury	

John Ritter has a strongly Vata chart according to Ayurveda. Virgo, a Vata sign rises, along with the Sun and Mercury, the ruler of Virgo. The Moon is located in the sixth house of disease in Aquarius, an air sign ruled by Saturn, and under a Saturn aspect as its sole planetary aspect. Saturn dominates the Navamsha Ascendant Gemini, which is another air sign ruled by Mercury. Ritter's planetary type is Mercury as the exalted Mercury dominates both the Ascendant and the Sun, giving good communication skills. It is also the final dispositor in the chart. This powerful Mercury as first and tenth house ruler gives him great success in a Mercury-based acting career.

However, Ritter's sixth house Moon is weak in terms of long-term health and longevity. Saturn in the twelfth is considered to be good for Virgo Ascendant in terms of career, particularly in arts and in acting, but its position is also not good for health. The Ascendant is hemmed in between two malefics with Saturn in the twelfth and Mars in the second, weakening it further. Meanwhile Rahu is in the eighth house of death, where it is weak and can cause sudden or catastrophic diseases.

His unexpected and early death occurred during his Ketu-Mercury period. Ketu is located in the second house, a maraka or death-dealing house. As the overall chart is weak in terms of health, Ketu's destructive powers have the capacity to manifest during the midlife period. Ketu is with Mars, the eighth lord, and the worst malefic for Virgo Ascendant. The Mercury subperiod brought Ketu's influence to the physical body.

29. Franklin D. Roosevelt, Vata-Pitta

Birth Chart

	SA JU	KE	MO MA
ME			
SU VE			<u>ASC</u>
	RA		

Navamsha

		VE KE	SU
MO			
			SA
<u>ASC</u>	MA RA ME, JU		

Jan. 30, 1882, 08 30 PM, Hyde Park NY, 73W56, 41N48[57]

Ascendant – 28° 06' Leo	Sun – 18° 54' Capricorn
Moon – 13° 54' Gemini	Mars – 04° 47' Gemini Rx
Mercury – 04° 57' Aqua.	Jupiter – 24° 43' Aries
Venus – 13° 49' Capricorn	Saturn – 13° 52' Aries
Rahu – 13° 28' Scorpio	Ketu – 13° 28' Taurus

Planetary Periods

Birth – Rahu/Mercury	Jupiter – April 23, 1890
Saturn – April 23, 1906	Mercury – April 23, 1925
Ketu – April 23, 1942	Death – Ketu/Rahu

Franklin D. Roosevelt suffered from polio and was paralyzed from the waist down from his late thirties. Nevertheless, he was able to rise up and become the president of the United States. Polio is a Vata, an air or windy disease, as are most paralytic conditions. Yet though physically under a Vata influence, Roosevelt had a strong will and character. He was able to maintain important psychological Pitta traits from his Leo Sun and his Mars aspects to both the Sun and the Moon.

Relative to his polio, the Sun as the Ascendant lord is located in the sixth house of disease, along with Venus, an inimical planet for Leo Ascendant. The Sun is aspected by Saturn, the sixth lord, which is debilitated in the ninth house and brings misfortune in the form of disease. Yet the Sun in the sixth in an upachaya house gave him a strong will to fight the disease. The Sun is strongly placed in the seventh house of the Navamsha aspecting Sagittarius, another Pitta sign, as the Navamsha Ascendant.

There are notable health weaknesses from the Moon, which is located in airy Gemini and aspected by both Mars and Saturn, with the Sun located in the eighth house from the Moon. The Moon in the Navamsha has the same weak condition of being aspected by both Mars and Saturn. The Moon is located in Ardra, a difficult Nakshatra, ruled by Rahu. The sixth house and sixth lord in the Navamsha, Venus in Taurus, is also highly afflicted by Ketu, Mars and Rahu.

The chart is notable for strong communication abilities with Mercury in the seventh house and a Gemini Moon (though this position of Mercury, a maraka planet for Leo, is not good for health). Many wealth-giving combinations can be found as well (Mercury as second and eleventh lord in the seventh and Mars, the Yoga karaka, fourth and ninth lord in the eleventh). Roosevelt had much inherited wealth from his family.

Roosevelt came down with polio under Saturn-Rahu in August of 1921. Saturn and Rahu influences are common in mysterious, degenerative and nervous system disorders. He was able to stabilize his condition under Mercury's period, but not through that of Ketu, which started in 1942.

30. Martha Stewart, Pitta

Birth Chart

MA KE		JU SA	
			SU ME
			VE
MO		ASC	RA

Navamsha

ASC	MO		
SA			KE ME JU
MA RA			VE
SU			

August 3, 1941, 01 33 PM, Jersey City NJ 74W05, 40N44

Ascendant – 17° 12' Libra	Sun – 17° 55' Cancer
Moon – 02° 22' Sagittarius	Mars – 23° 15' Pisces
Mercury – 02° 22' Cancer	Jupiter – 21° 46' Taurus
Venus – 16° 06' Leo	Saturn – 04° 15' Taurus
Rahu – 01° 45' Virgo	Ketu – 01° 45' Pisces

Planetary Periods

Birth – Ketu/Venus	Venus – May 6, 1947
Sun – May 6, 1967	Moon – May 6, 1973
Mars – May 6, 1983	Rahu – May 6, 1990
Jupiter – May 6, 2006	Saturn – May 6, 2022

In Martha Stewart's chart, Libra rises, a balance-seeking Venus ruled Ascendant, good for public relations and business. The only major aspect is that of fiery Mars from the sixth house of work and health. This creates a strong constitution and aggressive personality for dealing with the public. Venus, the Ascendant lord, is located in Leo, another fire sign, in the eleventh house of ambition. The Moon is located in Sagittarius, another fire sign, in the third house of personal efforts and desires. The Sun in the tenth house is strong and gives leadership power and teaching ability along with Mercury.

Putting these factors together, we see that fiery or Pitta influences prevail in her constitution. Her sharp Mars is heightened in its power by being exalted in the Navamsha. The Sun is strongly placed in the tenth house of career in Cancer, reflecting her domestic interests turned into a major business. The chart as a whole is highly disciplined and almost military in its power. Jupiter and Saturn in the eighth house give not only power over other peoples finances and institutions, but also a danger of scandal.

Rahu raised Martha up during its major period but led to her fall in its later period of Rahu-Moon, about the time Rahu was transiting her seventh house cusp or descendant. Rahu in the twelfth often raises people up in life but brings them down before its period is over. The Moon at the beginning of Sagittarius is also in a place of karmic retribution in Vedic astrology.

31. Barbara Walters, Vata

Birth Chart

	RA	JU	MO
			VE
SA		KE ME	MA SU ASC

Navamsha

SU	ASC SA KE		VE
			JU
		MO ME RA	MA

Sept. 25, 1929, 06 50 AM, Boston MA, 71N04, 42N22

Ascendant – 11° 11' Virgo	Sun – 09° 00' Virgo
Moon – 00° 38' Gemini	Mars – 29° 40' Virgo
Mercury – 00° 29' Libra	Jupiter – 23° 22' Taurus
Venus – 06° 51' Leo	Saturn – 01° 37' Sagittarius
Rahu – 21° 13' Aries	Ketu – 21° 13' Libra

Planetary Periods

Birth – Mars/Mercury	Rahu – Nov. 22, 1932
Jupiter – Nov. 22, 1950	Saturn – Nov. 22, 1966
Mercury – Nov. 22, 1985	Ketu – Nov. 22, 2002
Venus – Nov. 22, 2009	

Barbara Walters owes her greatest fame to her interviews as a part of a long career as a news reporter and television personality. These are mainly Mercury-based skills. Her chart shows the Ascendant, Sun and Moon all located in signs ruled by Mercury. The Sun is close to the Ascendant in Virgo. The Moon dominates the tenth house of career in Gemini. Strengthening this airy, Vata and Mercury energy is the aspect of Saturn from the fourth house, aspecting the Ascendant and both the Sun and the Moon – the only planet to do this in the chart. Two benefics, Mercury and Venus, in the signs adjacent to the Ascendant, strengthen it yet further. This makes her a Mercury Vata type with great powers of expression and dealing with the public.

The Sun and Mars in the first house bring in some secondary Pitta. Walters has been hard-hitting and aggressive in her interviews as well. Walters is a Vata-Pitta type, dominated mainly by Mercury energy, as tempered by the influences of Saturn and Mars. Saturn, however, dominates her psychology. Located in the fourth house of the home and also aspecting the Moon, it makes her into a career woman. The aspect of Mars on the fourth house strengthens her driven personality. Her auspicious Mercury period, (Mercury as lord of the first and tenth houses) has kept her in the public prominence for many years and also maintained her younger looking appearance.

32. Sigourney Weaver, Pitta

Birth Chart

RA	MO ASC		
			MA
			SA
JU	VE		KE SU ME

Navamsha

MA RA			ASC SU MO
			VE KE
JU		SA	

Oct. 8, 1949, 06 15 PM, Manhattan NY, 73N59, 40N46

Ascendant – 13° 17' Aries	Sun – 22° 10' Virgo
Moon – 12° 09' Aries	Mars – 26° 19' Cancer
Mercury – 12° 07' Vir. Rx	Jupiter – 29° 50' Sag.
Venus – 05° 09' Scorpio	Saturn – 20° 53' Leo
Rahu – 23° 24' Pisces	Ketu –23° 24' Virgo

Planetary Periods

Birth – Ketu/Mercury	Venus – May 20, 1950
Sun – May 20, 1970	Moon – May 20, 1976
Mars – May 20, 1986	Rahu – May 20, 1993
Jupiter – May 20, 2011	Saturn – May 20, 2027

Sigourney Weaver is a strong actress noted for aggressive roles, like her battle with aliens in several movies of that name. Her chart is dominated by a powerful Moon-Mars exchange. The Moon is rising in Aries Ascendant and also exchanges signs with Mars (Cancer), the Ascendant ruler. This exchange covers the main factors of both the Ascendant and the Moon, the body and the psychology (including the fourth house). Weaver is both a Mars Ascendant or body type and a Mars psychological type which agrees with her career roles. This makes her a strong Pitta in terms of Ayurveda. She reflects a moderate Pitta build and physique as well.

The Sun-Mercury-Ketu combination in Virgo in the sixth house of work endows her with self-discipline and is good for acting, though it can cause some digestive problems. Jupiter's aspect on the Ascendant raises her up in terms of education and family. The eighth house Venus in Scorpio gives sex appeal. Saturn in the fifth house denies children. Yet it is the influence of Mars that colors the chart as a whole.

33. Oprah Winfrey, Kapha

Birth Chart

		JU	
			KE
ME, SU VE, RA			
ASC	MO MA	SA	

Navamsha

		ASC VE SU	
SA			MA KE
RA			ME JU
		MO	

Jan. 29, 1954, 04 30 AM, Koscuisko MS, 89W35, 33N03

Ascendant – 06° 27' Sag.	Sun – 15° 46' Capricorn
Moon – 11° 18' Scor.	Mars – 00° 21' Scorpio
Mercury – 25° 56' Cap.	Jupiter – 23° 26' Taurus Rx
Venus – 15° 38' Cap.	Saturn – 15° 49' Libra
Rahu – 00° 01' Cap.	Ketu – 00° 01' Cancer

Planetary Periods

Birth – Saturn/Moon	Mercury – Sept. 15, 1961
Ketu – Sept. 15, 1977	Venus – Sept. 15, 1985
Sun – Sept. 15, 2005	Moon – Sept. 15, 2011

The dominant planet in Oprah Winfrey's chart, not surprisingly, is expansive Jupiter. Jupiter marks her planetary type and her Kapha constitution. Jupiter is the lord of the Ascendant, Sagittarius, and is located in a Kapha and earthy sign Taurus. It aspects both the Sun and the Moon and all the other planets except Saturn. Located in the sixth house of health and digestion, it also impacts the body and immune system, aspecting the sixth lord Venus as well. This gives her an interest in health and healing as well, making her into something of a care-giver through the media.

Venus in its own sign in the Navamsha Ascendant of Taurus contributes to the Kapha in her nature. Her emotional nature is colored by her Scorpio Moon located in the twelfth house, adding spirituality to her nature, and providing an interest in psychology as well.

This chart has many combinations for wealth (dhana yogas), notably an exchange between Venus and Saturn as the eleventh and second lords, the two main houses of income, with Saturn itself exalted. Venus is with Mercury, the tenth lord and the Sun, the ninth lord, which together form a Raja Yoga or royal combination in the second house of wealth. Yet the Moon and Mars in the twelfth house of loss as well as the Jupiterian disposition make for a great deal of generosity. Note that she achieved great success under her Venus major period.

PART FOUR

Appendices

The Vedic Rishis

1

VEDIC knowledge was transmitted by various great teachers called rishis or seers because of their direct perception of universal truth. Vedic astrology, Ayurveda and Yoga derive from the same ancient Vedic teachers and tradition.

Vedic astrology as it developed historically goes back mainly to the great sage Vasishta, the seer of the seventh book of the Rig Veda, and his grandson Parashara. Vasishta is probably the most famous rishi of the Rig Veda and has the largest number of hymns attributed to him.[58] Parashara also has several very important and esoteric hymns to Agni in the Rig Veda.[59]

The astrological text attributed to Parashara, the Brihat Parashara Hora Shastra remains the most important text in Vedic astrology today and the Parashara school and system remains the most dominant, particularly in north India.[60] While there were many Parasharas, and the Parashara of Vedic astrology was probably a much later figure than the first Parashara of the Rig Veda, his school preserves much of the astrological knowledge attributed to the Vasishta family.[61]

The Vasishta family or gotra also pioneered the main tradition of compiling the Vedas. The last Vyasa or compiler of the Vedas, Krishna Dwaipayana (often simply called Vyasa, though he was the twenty-eighth, not the first in the line) to whom the existent compilation of the Vedas is attributed, was in the gotra of Parashara.

Meanwhile, the main Yoga traditions in India follow the same line as Vedic astrology, going back to Parashara and Vasishta, with Patanjali, the compiler of the Yoga Sutras, himself being in the Vasishta line.

Vasishta himself was well known as a great yogi.[62]

Ayurveda as it developed historically goes back mainly to the rishi Bharadvaja of the Angirasa order of Rishis, the son of Brihaspati, and seer of the sixth book of the Rig Veda. Ayurvedic knowledge was transmitted through his descendants like Dhanvantari, king of Kashi (Benaras).

However, Ayurveda and Vedic astrology are closely connected to all the three main Vedic seer families – the Angirasas, Bhrigus and Kashyapas, which themselves are related to the stars and planets. The Angirasa order, the main Vedic seer family, born of the coals of Agni or the sacred fire, is led by Brihaspati or the planet Jupiter.[63] The Atharva Rishis, in whose Atharva Veda we find the oldest Vedic descriptions of countering both health problems (the roots of Ayurvedic treatment) and stellar afflictions (the roots of Vedic astrological remedial measures), are a special branch of the Angirasas.

The Bhrigu order, the second main Vedic seer family, born of the bright light of the sacred fire,[64] is led by Shukra or the planet Venus. The Bhrigus were great teachers of the Ayurvedic science of rejuvenation (Rasayana) as well as of Tantra, Yoga and Vedic astrology, including the famous Bhrigu Samhita, a key Vedic astrology teaching that contains the karmic life records of numerous people both born and yet to be born! The oldest line of Vedic astrology, that of the text Surya Siddhanta, is attributed to the sage Asura Maya, who is generally regarded as a teacher in the Bhrigu line.[65] The Vasishtas, we should note, combined both Angirasa and Bhrigu lines.[66] The Vasishtas themselves were offshoots of the Agastya line, which is still strong in South India, and like it was both an Angirasa and Bhrigu line.

The Kashyapa order, the third main Vedic seer line, relates to the sage Kashyapa which is a name for the Sun as the perceiver of all and relates to the form of the Sun God called Pushan. It had many great yogis, astrologers and doctors in its family as well. The Buddha was placed in this line as well, with Kashyapa as the name of the Buddha that existed five thousand years before the present Shakyamuni Buddha.

Following Vedic inner-outer connections, the Vedic Rishis relate to specific stars, which parallel certain parts of the body. For example, the seven primary Vedic Rishis are identified both with the seven stars of the Big Dipper and the seven sensory openings in the head (the two eyes, two ears, two nostrils and mouth). The Vedic lunar constellations or Nakshatras are also said to be the domains of certain Rishis.

Glossary

Agni – Fire as a cosmic and biological principle

Angaraka – Mars

Angirasas – Rishi line born of Agni

Angular Houses (Kendras) – Houses 1, 4, 7 and 10

Antardasha – Secondary planetary period

Ascendant – Rising Sign

Aspect – Influences of planets cast onto the zodiac from their position

Atman – Higher Self

Avataras – Divine incarnations

Ayanamsha – Difference between sidereal and tropical zodiac

Ayur or Ayus – Longevity

Ayurveda – Vedic science of medicine

Bhava – House in Vedic astrology

Bhrigus – Rishi line born of Varuna

Bhukti – Secondary planetary period

Bija mantra – Single syllable mantras

Brahma – Cosmic creator

Brihaspati – Jupiter, Rishi

Budha – Mercury

Chandra – Moon

Dasha – Planetary period

Debilitation – Worst sign location for a planet

Devata – Deity

Dhana Yoga – Planetary combination for wealth

Divisional Charts – Secondary charts like the Drekkana that divide the signs into various smaller sections

Drishti – Aspect in Vedic astrology

Duhsthanas (Difficult Houses) – Houses 6, 8 and 12

Exaltation – Best sign location for a planet

Gandanta – End portion of water signs and first portion of fire signs, said to cause difficulties

Ganesha – Elephant-headed God, governs time, karma and wisdom

Gayatri – Special verse to the Sun God as Savitar

Gochara – Transit

Graha – Planet

Harmonic Charts – Another name for divisional charts

Homas – Vedic fire rituals

House (astrological) – Domain of life defined from the Ascendant or rising sign

Ishta Devata – Deity of ones choice, ones personal deity.

Ishvara – God as the creator, preserver and destroyer of the universe

Kala – Time

Kapha – Biological water humor

Karma – Results of past actions

Ketu – South node of the moon

Kuja – Mars

Lagna – Ascendant

Lakshmi – Goddess of prosperity, wife of Vishnu, the cosmic preserver

Mahapurusha Yoga – Planetary position that creates a great person of a certain planetary type

Maraka houses – death-dealing houses, 2 and 7; these houses and their rulers become inimical for health when the chart is weak.

Nakshatras – 27 lunar constellations, asterisms or mansions of the Moon

Navagraha – Nine planets

Navamsha – Ninth divisional chart

Natural Status – basic nature of a planet as benefic or malefic

Ojas – Higher energy of Kapha dosha

Parashara – Main rishi or seer behind the main school of Vedic astrology

Pitta – Biological fire humor

Purusha – Higher Self, Cosmic Person

Prana – Life-force, higher energy of Vata dosha

Puja – Hindu rituals generally involving the offering of flowers

Rahu – North node of the moon

Raja Yoga – Planetary combination for power and influence

Rashi – Sign of the zodiac

Rashi Chakra or Rashi Chart – Basic birth chart with planets placed in signs

Ratna – Gemstone

Rishis – Vedic seers and sages

Sarasvati – Goddess of learning, wife of Brahma, the cosmic creator

Shani, Shanischarya – Saturn

Sharira, Karana – Causal body

Sharira, Sthula – Gross or physical body

Sharira, Sukshma – Subtle or astral body

Shiva – Cosmic destructive and transformative consciousness

Shukra – Venus, Rishi

Surya – Sun

Tejas – Higher energy of Pitta dosha

Temporal Status – nature of a planet relative to the houses it rules from the Ascendant

Transit – Current planetary positions relative to positions in the birth chart

Trine Houses (Konas) – Houses 1, 5, 9

Upachaya houses – Houses of initial difficulty but increasing strength, 3, 6 and 11, sometimes also 10; malefics generally do well in these.

Upaya – Vedic astrological remedial measure

Varga – Another name for a divisional chart

Vargottama – Planet in the same sign of the Rashi or basic birth chart and Navamsha or divisional ninth.

Varshaphal – Solar return or annual chart

Vastu – Vedic directional science

Vata – Biological Air Humor

Vedas – Main mantric source books of Vedic knowledge

Vimshottari Dasha – 120 dasha or planetary period cycle, most common used

Vishnu – Cosmic preserver

Yaga – Another name for Vedic rituals or yajnas

Yajnas – Vedic rituals, generally using the sacred fire

Yantras – Geometrical meditation devices

Yoga (in astrology) – Special combination of planetary influences

Yoga karaka – Planet that gives Raja Yoga or power and affluence for the chart.

Sanskrit Pronunciation Key

16 Vowels (some have 2 forms)

अ		a	another
आ	ा	ā	father (2 beats)
इ	ि	i	pin
ई	ी	ī	need (2 beats)
उ	ु	u	flute
ऊ	ू	ū	mood (2 beats)
ऋ	ृ	ṛ	macabre
ॠ	ॄ	ṝ	trill for 2 beats
ऌ		ḷṛ	table
ए	े	e	etude (2 beats)
ऐ	ै	ai	aisle (2 beats)
ओ	ो	o	yoke (2 beats)
औ	ौ	au	flautist (2 beats)
अ’		aṃ	hum
अ”		aḥ	out-breath

Eight Intermediate Sounds

य	ya	employable
र	ra	abra cadabra
ल	la	hula

व	va	variety
श	śa	shut
ष	ṣa	shnapps
स	sa	Lisa
ह	ha	honey

25 Consonants

क	ka	paprika
ख	kha	thick honey
ग	ga	saga
घ	gha	big honey
ङ	ṅa	ink
च	ca	chutney
छ	cha	much honey
ज	ja	Japan
झ	jha	raj honey
ञ	ña	inch
ट	ṭa	borscht again
ठ	ṭha	borscht honey
ड	ḍa	shdum
ढ	ḍha	shd hum
ण	ṇa	shnum
त	ta	pasta
थ	tha	eat honey
द	da	soda
ध	dha	good honey
न	na	banana
प	pa	paternal
फ	pha	scoop honey
ब	ba	scuba
भ	bha	rub honey
म	ma	aroma

Bibliography

Beckman, Howard. Vibrational Healing With Gems. Pecos, New Mexico: Balaji Publisher, 2000.

Brihat Parashara Hora Shastra.

Charak, KS. Essentials of Medical Astrology. New Delhi, India: Institute of Vedic Astrology, 1996.

Charak, KS. Subtleties of Medical Astrology. New Delhi, India: Institute of Vedic Astrology, 1996.

Frawley, David. Astrology of the Seers: A Guide to Vedic/Hindu Astrology. Twin Lakes, WI: Lotus Press, 1991, 2000.

Frawley, David. Ayurvedic Healing: A Comprehensive Guide. Twin Lakes, WI: Lotus Press, 1989, 2001.

Frawley, David. Yoga and Ayurveda: Self-healing and Self-realization. Twin Lakes, WI: Lotus Press, 1999.

Garuda Purana.

Harness, Dennis. The Nakshatras. Twin Lakes, WI: Lotus Press, 1999.

Mantra Pushpam.

Mihira, Varaha. Brihat Jataka.

Mihira, Varaha. Brihat Samhita.

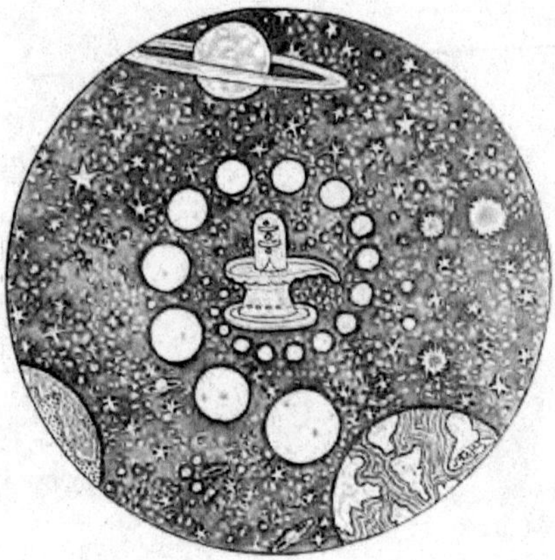

Endnotes

5

[1] Jyotirmaya Purusha in Sanskrit or Hiranmaya Purusha, the Purusha made of golden light.

[2] The six Vedangas are Shiksha (pronunciation), Chhandas (meter), Vyakarana (grammar), Nirukta (etymology), Kalpa (ritual) and Jyotish (astrology).

[3] The four Upavedas are Ayurveda (medicine), Dhanurveda (martial arts), Sthapatya Veda or Vastu (architecture), and Gandharva Veda (music and dance).

[4] Note Underworld: Flooded Kingdoms of the Ice Age by Graham Hancock.

[5] That is why the Vedas are said to be impersonal or apaurusheya. They have no human author but reflect the cosmic mind.

[6] Note the Brihadaranyaka Upanishad II.5.

[7] Maitrayani Upanishad VI.1.

[8] This complicated process is explained in the Vasishta Samhita, an important ancient Yoga text, chapter 5.

[9] In Sanskrit the sthula, sukshma and karana shariras or the gross, subtle and causal bodies.

[10] In Vedic thought Prana and Vayu are often identified with the causal body and the state of deep sleep. But in other texts Prana and the Sun have this role, which would more connect to Pitta.

[11] The general rule is that for any domain of life, Vedic astrology will examine a certain house, its ruler, its significator, the same houses from the Moon and in the Navamsha (ninth divisional chart), and the relevant divisional charts. For example, for children one would consider the fifth house, its ruler, Jupiter as its significator, the fifth house from the Moon and the fifth house in the navamsha, and the saptamsha or seventh divisional chart that relates to children..

[12] This follows the definition of Yoga in the Yoga Sutras, the main classical text on Yoga, as chitta vritti nirodhah or the calming of the movements of the heart or chitta, which in Yogic thought often relates to the causal body.

[13] My main astrology teacher, Dr. B.V. Raman of Bangalore, perhaps modern India's greatest astrologer, spoke of the centrality of karma relative to the birth chart.

[14] Note Ayurvedic books like the author's Tantric Yoga and the Wisdom Goddesses for a study of Prana, Tejas and Ojas.

[15] Note that Vedic thought relates the Moon to the manas principle which is often translated as 'mind', but more specifically refers to our feeling nature and general field of conditioned consciousness. It does not relate to the intellect, which comes under the term buddhi in Vedic thought.

[16] There is a sidereal branch of western astrology but it has never become very popular.

[17] Note books on Vedic astrology for a fuller explanation of this difference, as in the author's Astrology of the Seers.

[18] Original astrology was based upon observing the fixed stars. A tropical model, which is abstract, probably came later.

[19] These qualities have other usages in medical astrology. Fixed signs show more structural issues with the body, moveable issues with energy, and dual issues with the mind.

[20] In divisional charts each sign is divided up according to certain numbers and the positions of the planets within them are reorganized according to the new sign positions created by the division. For example, with the Drekkana or third divisional chart, each sign is divided into three parts with the first third relating to the sign itself, the second to the next sign of the same element and the third to the third sign of the same element.

[21] Pandit Nanak Chand Sharma of Delhi, one of modern India's greatest Ayurvedic doctors, mentioned this to me.

[22] There is some difference of opinion about this but generally if the Moon is in the same or adjacent signs to the Sun it is weak and malefic. It is also more benefic when waxing and more malefic when waning.

[23] Yet Mercury with the Sun is not considered malefic, as Mercury is never far from it.

[24] Note the book Varshaphal by Dr. K.S. Charak.

[25] The main source for this material is the Brihat Samhita of Varaha Mihira.

[26] Gandanta positions in Vedic astrology.

[27] Another Gandanta position in Vedic astrology.

[28] Astrology of the Seers pgs. 94-103.

[29] The psychological level of interpretation is called Adhyatmic in Sanskrit, relating to the self. It is discriminated from the material level interpretation called Adhibhutic or relating to the material elements. Each planet and house has both dimensions. A good astrologer knows how to read both the psychological and material impacts of each factor in Astrology.

[30] An earlier version of this chapter first occurred in the original edition of Astrology of the Seers. I removed it from the second edition and am placing it in this book, where it is more relevant.

[31] The Maitrayani Upanishad explains this division relative to the Nakshatras.

[32] Chandogya Upanishad III.10.3.

[33] Note Yoga and Ayurveda, Chapter 10.

[34] Note Yoga of Herbs for an in depth discussion of the energetics of herbs.

[35] The American Institute of Vedic Studies (www.vedanet.com) offers advanced training for students who want to focus in this direction.

[36] Note Howard Beckman at www.vedicworld.org for such devices.

[37] We can extend this rule a little further for those more knowledge-

able of Vedic astrology. Gems can be worn on the fingers of planets with which they have a friendly relationship (composite natural and temporal) in the birth chart.

[38] Note Ayurveda and Marma Therapy (Frawley, Ranade, and Lele) for more information on this subject.

[39] Such general tables reflect mainly the relationship between planets and the Ascendant ruler that indicates the self of the person. Yet we should remember that each planet is always good for the affairs of that houses that it rules.

[40] Such tables of benefic and malefic temporal rulers will vary slightly according to different Vedic astrologers because of these complexities and different considerations.

[41] We might also want to consider shadbala and other means of determining planetary strengths and weaknesses.

[42] This is the kind of information that is part of our distance learning program and advanced astrological trainings.

[43] Rig Veda II.24.1.

[44] Astrology of the Seers pgs. 227-233.

[45] Mahat Tattva in Yogic thought.

[46] Chandogya Upanishad I.5.

[47] Astrology of the Seers pgs. 119-225.

[48] These go back to ancient astrological classics like the Brihat Samhita of Varaha Mihira.

[49] Astrology of the Seers pgs. 229-232, 265-268.

[50] Particularly Gandanta (transitional Nakshatras) like portions of Jyeshtha, Mula, Magha and Aslesha, and sometimes Ashvini, Revati, Krittika and Ardra.

[51] Note James Kelleher, a Vedic astrologer who sells these tapes, at www.jameskeller.com.

[52] The main problem with the Navamsha is that it rests upon a very accurate birth time. The Navamsha ascendant changes in less than fifteen minutes. We cannot be certain of this accuracy for many charts. Often Vedic astrologers will rectify the chart to find the Navamsha ascendant that best suits the person.

[53] Notably the Shadbala system, the strength of planets in divisional charts like the Vimshopak system and the Nakshatra positions of planets.

[54] I have not brought in Uranus, Neptune and Pluto into the examination of these charts, but their positions can be of some value as well.

[55] The Moon afflicted in sixth, eighth or twelfth houses often reduces the longevity and can threaten the life of a child. In modern charts, it more commonly reduces the life span of a person. It can also show a troubled psychology. It is one of the first factors we look at in the Vedic chart for seeing the well-being of a person on all levels and shows how much importance the Moon has in the chart.

[56] Mercury is located in the eighth house in both the Drekkana and Dwadashamsha charts as well. These are the two other main divisional charts for health.

[57] I have taken his birth time as 8 30 PM as opposed to 8 45 PM which would give him an early Virgo Ascendant.

[58] The seventh book of the Rig Veda has the largest number of hymns of any of the family books (II-VIII) and most of these are attributed to Vasishta. This shows the Vedic roots of the rishis behind Vedic astrology. Vasishta was also connected to the southern rishi Agastya. Old Vedic astrology traditions like that of Surya Siddhanta had their connections to the south as well, with Lanka being used as a prime meridian point.

[59] These occur in the first book or mandala of the Rig Veda I. 65-73. They are among the most beautiful, mystical and cryptic of the Vedic mantras, though they are not specifically astrological in nature.

[60] In South India, Varaha Mihira's Brihat Jataka is generally more important.

[61] The Parashara of Vedic astrology appears to have lived a few generations before the Mahabharata War or the time of Sri Krishna. The Parashara of the Rig Veda lived at the time of the great King Sudas, whose era was well before the time of the entire Kuru dynasty, of which about the thirtieth king was on the throne at the time of the war.

[62] Another important ancient Yoga text of the Vasishta family is the Vasishta Samhita.

[63] Aitareya Brahmana III.34.

[64] Aitareya Brahmana III.34.

[65] The Bhrigus and Venus are regarded as the gurus of the Asuras or anti-Gods. The Asuras represent the pranas or vital impulses and the more worldly part of our nature. Yet on a higher level they represent occult powers.

[66] Vasishta himself was said to have been born of the Gods Mitra and Varuna. Varuna is the progenitor of the Bhrigus, while Mitra, another name for Agni, relates to the Angirasas.

Index

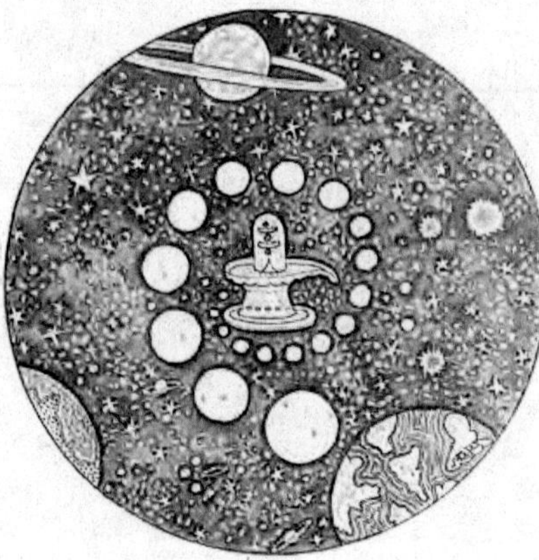

Resources

American College of Vedic Astrology (ACVA)
P.O. Box 2149, Sedona AZ 86339
Ph: 928-282-6595: Fax 928-282-6097
www.vedicastrology.org
The American College of Vedic Astrology is a non-profit educational organization dedicated to teaching the art and science of Vedic Astrology or Jyotish. ACVA's purpose is to provide the highest quality of education and training in Vedic Astrology to students and professional astrologers worldwide; emphasizing ethics and professionalism in the mastery of the principles and practice of Vedic Astrology. The primary objective of the American College of Vedic Astrology is to advance the study of Vedic Sciences by providing a certification program which utilizes symposia, research and online education.

American Institute of Vedic Studies
Dr. David Frawley (Pandit Vamadeva Shastri), Director
Training in Ayurvedic medicine, Vedic astrology, Yoga and Vedic Studies.
PO Box 8357, Santa Fe NM 87504
Ph: 505-983-9385, www.vedanet.com: info@vedanet.com

Auroma International
Dept. AYAS
P. O. Box 1008
Silver Lake, WI 53170
Ph: 262-889-8569
Fax: 262-889 8591
E-mail: auroma@lotuspress.com
Website: www.auroma.net
Importer and master distributor of Auroshikha Incense, Chandrika Ayurvedic Soap and Herbal Vedic Ayurvedic products.

The Astrological Magazine
Started Dr. B.V. Raman, oldest magazine on Vedic astrology.
Raman Publications, Sri Rajeswari, Bangalore 560020, India,
Ph: 91-80-3348646/ 369229, Fax: 91-80-3313260
www.astrologicalmagazine.com: info@astrologicalmagazine.com

BAVA, British Association of Vedic Astrology
www.bava.org
Main Vedic astrology organization for Great Britain associated with the American College of Vedic Astrology and the Council of Vedic Astrology.

Balaji Natural Gems
www.planetaryjewels.com
Howard and Jennifer Beckman, directors. Clinical Ayurvedic and Jyotish gem therapy, products and courses. Leading suppliers of natural precious gemstones for Jyotish and Ayurvedic prescription.

California College of Ayurveda
Classroom and clinical instruction in Ayurveda, with classes on Vedic astrology.
1117A East Main St., Grass Valley CA 95945
Ph: 866-541-6699 (toll free)
www.ayurvedacollege.com: info@ayurvedacollege.com

Council of Vedic Astrology (CVA)
www.councilvedicastrology.org
The Council of Vedic Astrology (CVA), founded in 1993, is a

non-profit trade organization dedicated to promoting the art and practice of Vedic Astrology. CVA is the largest international Vedic Astrology Organization in the West with members in over 12 countries. The CVA is modeled and allied with the Indian Council of Astrological Sciences (ICAS) founded by the late Dr. BV Raman, the largest and oldest astrological body in India.

Dancing Shiva, Yoga and Ayurveda
Instruction in Yoga, Ayurveda and Vedic Astrology
Offers Dr. Frawley's Yoga and Ayurveda Program
Mas Vidal, Director
7466 Beverly Blvd. 2nd Floor, Los Angeles CA 90036
Ph: 323-934-8332, www.dancingshiva.com

European Institute of Vedic Studies/Editions Turiya
Atreya Smith, Director
Represents Dr. Frawley's Ayurvedic and Vedic astrology work in Europe, with French version of Astrology of the Seers course and book.
I.E.E.V sarl, B.P. 4 , 30170 Monoblet, France
Ph: (33) 466 85 04 11, Fax: (33) 466 85 0542
www.atreya.com: www.ayurvedicnutrition.com

Florida Vedic Institute/Universal Yoga
Instruction and consultations in Yoga, Ayurveda and
Vedic Astrology
Baba Hari Nam Prem, Director
420 East S.R. 434 Suite D., Longwood FL 32750
www.floridavedicinstitute.com, universalyoga@netzero.com

Institute for Wholistic Education
Dept. AYAS
3425 Patzke Lane
Racine, WI 53405
262 619 1798
Email: institute@infobuddhism.com
Website: www.wholisticinstitute.org
Information and distance learning courses on Ayurveda and information on Vedic Astrology

Internatural
Dept. AYAS
P. O. Box 489
Twin Lakes, WI 53181 USA
800-643 4221 (toll free order line)
262-889 8581 (office phone)
262-889 8591 (fax)
E-mail: internatural@lotuspress.com
Website: www.internatural.com
Retail mail order and internet reseller of Ayurvedic products, essential oils, herbs, spices, supplements, herbal remedies, incense, books, yoga mats, supplies and videos.

Journal of Vedic Astrology/
Institute of Vedic Astrology Publications
Source of Vedic Astrology, bimonthly journal edited by K.S. Charak, covers medical issues.
72 Gagan Vihar, Delhi 110051, India: Ph: 91-11-224 3563
www.vedicastro.com: vedicastro@vsnl.com

James Kelleher
Navagraha chanting tapes, astrological consultations, publications and classes.
www.jameskelleher.com

Lotus Brands, Inc.
Dept. AYAS
P. O. Box 325
Twin Lakes, WI 53181 USA
Ph: 262-889-8561
Fax: 262-889-8591
E-mail: lotusbrands@lotuspress.com
Website: www.lotusbrands.com
Manufacturer and distributor of natural personal care and herbal products, massage oils, essential oils, incense, aromatherapy items, dietary supplements and herbs.

Lotus Light Enterprises
Dept. AYAS
P. O. Box 1008

Silver Lake, WI 53170 USA
800-548 3824 (toll free order line)
262-889 8501 (office phone)
262-889 8591 (fax)
E-mail: lotuslight@lotuspress.com
Website: www.lotuslight.com
Wholesale distributor of essential oils, herbs, spices, supplements, herbal remedies, incense, books and other supplies. Must supply resale certificate number or practitioner license to obtain catalog of more than 10,000 items.

Lotus Press
Dept. AYAS
P. O. Box 325
Twin Lakes, WI 53181 USA
Ph: 262-889-8561
Fax: 262-889-2461
E-mail: lotuspress@lotuspress.com
Website: www.lotuspress.com
Publisher of books on Ayurveda, Reiki, aromatherapy, energetic healing, herbalism, alternative health and U.S. editions of Sri Aurobindo's writings.

Sanskrit Sounds - Nicolai Bachman
Offers Vedic astrology terminology and mantra CD
PO Box 4352, Santa Fe, NM 87502
www.SanskritSounds.com, Shabda@comcast.net

Dr. Dinesh Sharma
Dr. Sharma is a doctor of Ayurveda, a medical doctor, Vedic astrologer and Vastu expert. He offers consultations and training programs worldwide.
Email: dr.dineshsharma@gmail.com

Chakrapani Ullal
Vedic astrology consultations and classes, regular internet newsletter with important information on Vedic astrology.
www.chakrapani.com

Vedic Cultural Fellowship (VCF)
HC70 Box 620, Pecos NM 87552 USA
Ph: 505-757-6194, www.vedicworld.org
The Vedic Cultural Fellowship's mission is to bring the finest teachers of the varied branches of Vedic knowledge together with seekers from around the globe. First incorporated as a charity in the UK in 1993, in 1998 the Vedic Cultural Fellowship received status from the US Federal government as a Hindu church. The main directors are Howard Beckman, Jennifer Beckman, Dr. David Frawley and Prince Malik. Workshops, intensives and retreats will be offered at New Rishikesh ashram and center nestled in the foothills of the Rocky Mountains in near Santa Fe, New Mexico.

Offers special residential and correspondence course (distance learning program) on 'Vedic Gem Therapy' with credit through the American Institute of Vedic Studies. The course first covers the background of Ayurveda, then goes on to expansive lessons on clinical Ayurvedic gem therapy, as well as in-depth instruction for recommending gems from the Jyotish horoscope.

About the Author

Biographical Information

Dr. David Frawley is one of the leading western exponents of both Ayurvedic medicine and Vedic astrology. He has authored a number of important books on both subjects and various training manuals that have served to instruct thousands of students worldwide over the past twenty years. He is a former president of the Council of Vedic Astrology, the largest Vedic astrology association outside of India.

His interests extend to other Vedic fields, including Yoga, Vedanta, Tantra and Vedic Studies. Notably, Dr. Frawley's work has received a rare recognition in India, where he has been honored as one of the most important Vedic teachers today. He the director of the American Institute of Vedic Studies in Santa Fe, New Mexico.

American Institute of Vedic Studies

PO Box 8357, Santa Fe NM 87504-8357, Ph: 505-983-9385
Dr. David Frawley (Pandit Vamadeva Shastri), Director
Web: www.vedanet.com, Email: info@vedanet.com

The American Institute of Vedic Studies is an educational center, directed by Dr. David Frawley, devoted to the greater systems of Vedic and Yogic knowledge. It teaches related aspects of Vedic Science including Ayurveda, Vedic Astrology, Yoga and Vedanta with a special reference to their background in the Vedas. It offers articles, books, courses and training programs and is also engaged in several research projects including:

- Ayurvedic Astrology: The Vedic astrology of healing for body and mind, including the use of gems and mantras.
- Yoga and Ayurveda: The interface of all eight limbs of classical Yoga with Ayurvedic medicine for body and mind.
- Vedic Yoga: Restoring the ancient Vedic Yoga that is the foundation for the Yoga tradition.
- Translations and interpretations of the Vedas, particularly the Rig Veda.
- Vedic History: The history of India and of the world from a Vedic perspective, reflecting the latest archaeological work in India.

ASTROLOGY OF THE SEERS

Distance Learning Program in Vedic Astrology and Ayurveda

This comprehensive training program, authored by Dr. David Frawley, explains Vedic astrology in clear and modern terms, providing practical insights how to use and adapt the system for the contemporary student. For those who have difficulty approaching Vedic astrology, the course provides many keys for unlocking its language and its methodology, both in terms of chart interpretation and for the practical application of remedial measures.

The course is unique in that it teaches Vedic astrology with a special reference to Ayurvedic medicine. This distinguishes it from other introductory courses on Vedic astrology in which the Ayurvedic component is small or non-existent. The course is of special interest to Ayurvedic students and to those looking to specialize in medical astrology.

The goal of the course is to provide the foundation to enable one to become a professional Vedic astrologer. Its orientation is threefold:

- To teach the fundamentals of Vedic astrology and chart interpretation through the planets, signs, houses, aspects, yogas, divisional charts and dashas.
- To set forth the Vedic 'Astrology of Healing' (Ayurvedic Astrology), including an in-depth analysis of gem therapy, as well as the use of mantras and deities.

- To introduce the Nakshatras, Muhurta, Ashtakavarga and Vedic methods of timing, including the Vedic calendar.

The course can be taken as part of a longer tutorial program in Vedic astrology through the American College of Vedic Astrology (ACVA). It starts at a beginning level, but goes into depth into its subject. Since 1986 over three thousand people from all over the world have taken the course.

Ayurvedic Healing

Distance Learning Program in Ayurvedic Medicine

This comprehensive program covers all the main aspects of Ayurvedic theory, diagnosis and practice. It is not just an introduction to Ayurveda but an extensive training program on Ayurveda in all of its branches. The course has a special emphasis on herbal medicine, using western as well as Indian herbs, providing an accessible model for treatment in the West. It explains diet and food in great detail as well. It adds to these an integral mind-body approach that includes spiritual and psychological treatment methods, with colors, aromas, gems, mantra and meditation.

The goal of the course is to provide students a foundation for becoming Ayurvedic practitioners, providing them certification as an 'Ayurvedic Health Educator'. It is an inexpensive alternative for those who cannot afford or do not have the time for expensive classroom or clinical instruction.

The course is authored by Dr. David Frawley (Pandit Vamadeva Shastri), uses his books on Ayurveda and represents his approach to Ayurveda, adapting Ayurveda to the modern world without losing its spiritual integrity. Since 1988 over five thousand people worldwide have taken the course, which has also been used as textbook material for two year Ayurveda colleges in the West.

Advanced Yoga and Ayurveda Course

Distance Learning Program in Yoga and Ayurveda

This new course by Dr. David Frawley, just introduced in 2005, teaches the healing and transformational approaches of both Yoga and Ayurveda. It is not simply an asana course but a complete study of Yoga and Ayurveda relative to the full system of classical or Raja Yoga.

It aims at providing the student with the foundation for an integrated Yoga-Ayurveda therapy on physical, psychological and spiritual levels. It certifies the graduate as a 'Yoga and Ayurveda Health Educator'.

The course shows the therapeutic application of all the eight limbs of Yoga from the life-style principles and practices of the Yamas and Niyamas to the Ayurvedic and healing usage of Asana, Pranayama, Pratyahara, Dharana, Dhyana and Samadhi. It contains a complete study of the Yoga Sutras from a Vedic angle. It introduces Ayurvedic Yoga and its Vedic Yoga basis. It also brings in the perspective of Tantra relative to understanding the energetics of the subtle body and for meditation techniques.